"E '

THE UNSTABLE ECONOMY

THE
UNSTABLE
ECONOMY

Booms and Recessions in the

United States since 1945

by **Victor Perlo**

INTERNATIONAL PUBLISHERS
New York

CHARTS BY ELLEN PERLO

ACKNOWLEDGMENT
*The manuscript was read and valuable suggestions made
by Hyman Lumer, Matthew Hallinan, and James S. Allen.
Exceptionally important assistance was provided by
Thomas A. Curtis in preparing the manuscript for publi-
cation. The index was prepared by Barry Cohen.*

Library of Congress Catalog Card Number: 72-94393
ISBN: (cloth 0-7178-0379-1; (paperback) 0-7178-0380-5
Printed in the United States of America

Contents

I.

Introduction

IN 1970 a serious recession and financial crisis hit the United States—the worst since the 1930s. The National Bureau of Economic Research measured 30 business cycles between 1834 and 1961. The four cycles since World War II, however, were relatively mild and of shorter duration on the down side. For example, the average contraction over the whole period studied lasted 19 months, while the average postwar contraction lasted ten months.[1] And none of the postwar declines compared in severity with the Great Crisis of 1929–32—the worst in history.

In this country, and in most other major capitalist countries, the government engaged in far-reaching attempts to smooth out the business cycle, to reduce its amplitude, or even to end it altogether. Theories abounded on how to accomplish this. By the 1960s, the optimistic view was disseminated that it had been accomplished, for all practical purposes. There might be moderate recessions, but no "depressions" or "panics" were anticipated. Whiie business-cycle courses had been prominent in university economics departments, by the mid-1960s they had almost vanished from the curricula.

The optimism was reinforced by the period of expansion that began in February 1961. By mid-1969 it had exceeded 100 months, as measured by the standards of the National Bureau of Economic Research. The previous record expansion, during World War II, lasted 80 months, and the record before that was only 50 months.

The downturn which began in the summer of 1969 was scarcely noticed, at first, by Establishment economists. But it turned out to be considerably more serious than its immediate predecessors. While the decline in production was not especially deep, it was stubborn. In three of the previous cyclical downturns after World War II, the former peak industrial production was surpassed in 21 months. In the fourth, it was surpassed in 24 months. But in this fifth cycle, the previous peak was

7

not surpassed for more than 30 months. The persistence of depressed production brought with it corresponding hardships in the form of unemployment and reduced income for millions of people.

Also, for the first time since World War II, there was a real financial panic, featuring the crash of stock and bond prices and the bankruptcy of prominent brokerage houses. The world's largest privately owned transportation company, the Penn Central Railroad, went bankrupt. The largest specialist munitions manufacturer, Lockheed, was kept afloat only with massive government subsidies. Finally, the dollar had to be devalued, as at the bottom of the Great Depression in 1933.

Every major economic crisis in history has had its peculiar features—but this one was perhaps the most peculiar yet. It was the first real economic decline in wartime not caused by the physical damages of war. It was the first real crisis accompanied for over a year by a continuous, *rapid increase* in prices. And for most of its duration it was limited to the United States.

Interest in the business cycle is bound to revive. All of the old questions will be asked: Why do depressions occur? What can be done to cure them? Can they be prevented, and, if so, how?

Big businessmen are concerned because economic crises weaken their position in world economics and politics, seriously undermining the social stability of their rule. Smaller businessmen are concerned because every downturn in the economy threatens their existence, indeed wipes out a substantial proportion of them.

Students and professional people are concerned. After decades in which the demand for professional workers ran ahead of the steadily increasing supply, suddenly the tables were turned. Tens of thousands of engineers, chemists, physicists, writers, and management specialists are laid off. Hundreds of thousands of graduating professionals pouring out of today's degree factories compete for a dwindling number of jobs.

Workers are concerned most of all. They are the ones who suffer evictions, loss of belongings, hunger, the premature curtailment of their children's education and—by the millions—the indignity of enforced idleness, of being rejected by the system, of having o useful way to spend their time.

And, among the workers, the worst hardships are inflicted on the Black, Chicano, Puerto Rican, and Indian peoples. Last to be hired during booms—with masses of youth never getting jobs—they are first to be fired during depressions. Never beyond the fringes of poverty, entire ghetto communities are immediately subjected to acute privation along with the ever present burdens of segregation, discrimination, and police repression, which become more severe in hard times.

Prior to World War I, economic crises were looked upon by capitalist economists as unfortunate accidents. But by the 1920s, it was recognized that this subject could no longer be dismissed so cavalierly. In the crisis of 1920–21, masses of workers became unemployed during the period of global social upheaval and spreading anticapitalist views following the Russian revolution. A presidential committee called for a study of the business cycle and unemployment. Wesley Mitchell, of the National Bureau of Economic Research, wrote in the committee's report:

> The great mass of the unemployed . . . are workers who have been "laid off" because of business depression. The reason why millions of men lose their jobs at such times is that employers are losing money. Hence it is best to begin a study of methods of stabilizing employment by looking into the processes which every few years throw business into confusion.
>
> Fifteen times within the past one hundred and ten years, American business has passed through a "crisis" . . . no two crises have been precisely alike.
>
> . . . Longer experience . . . and better statistical data have gradually discredited the view that crises are "abnormal" events, each due to a special cause. The modern view is that crises are but one feature of recurrent "business cycles." Instead of a "normal" state of business interrupted by occasional cycles, men look for a continually changing state of business—continually changing in a fairly regular way. A crisis is expected to be followed by a depression, the depression by a revival, the revival by prosperity, and prosperity by a new crisis.[2]

Mitchell *describes* many of the phenomena characteristic of various phases of the cycle without explaining why these occur. Explanations for the business cycle are numerous. The most common mode of analysis is strictly empirical. The National Bureau of Economic Research, for example, examines the data of each cycle without attempting to generalize causes. The most typical approach among Establishment economists is to find specific "errors" committed by businessmen as the causes of each cycle; the remedies offered are similarly specious.

The most widely used economics textbook in the United States is Paul Samuelson's *Economics*; its author, a Nobel prize-winner, is regarded as one of the most able and sophisticated Establishment economists. He lists six "better-known" theories of the business cycle: monetary, psychological, innovative, underconsumption, overinvestment, and the sunspot-weather-crop theory. He observes that all economists agree that wide fluctuations in the production of capital investment rather than in personal consumption are the dynamic factors in the business cycle, and he proposes to examine the causes for these wide fluctuations. He ends up with a composite of most of the six theories (he does, however, reject the sunspot theory!) and then adds a seventh, "the acceleration principle."

But when one sums it up, he emerges with an eclectic mush, a *description* that fails to get at the underlying roots of the subject. And he himself falls into the kind of fallacy he ascribes to others. He merely adds another to the list of theories "which just appear to be conveying an explanation when really they are not saying anything at all."[3]

James S. Duesenberry's *Business Cycles and Economic Growth* is a standard specialized text on the subject. His analysis is much more muddled than Samuelson's. It includes the following theses: capital investment is governed by a series of parameters—he lists ten. When one or more of these parameters changes, it can destroy equilibrium and set off a cycle. Major depressions can be generated in any one of a half-dozen ways. They occur at more or less regular intervals because (a) it takes time to recover from one depression and reach the stage where another can occur; and (b), to quote him: "There are enough ways for a depression to start, once a period of prosperity has continued for a few years, that if one does not work another will."[4]

Lack of a stable theory of the business cycle leads to the narrowest kind of pragmatism in capitalist economic analysis. Typically, the Establishment economist expects that what is happening before his eyes will simply go on happening. In bad times, he is gloomy, sees no end in sight; in good times, he is euphoric, sees no storm cloud on the horizon.

Capitalist economists did not even "discover" the business cycle as a regular phenomenon until well into the 20th century. By the late 1920s, after a few years of boom and extravagant stock-market speculation, they proclaimed a "new era" of permanent prosperity. Forty years later, the same mistake was repeated.

The 1969 Annual Report of the Council of Economic Advisors,

representing the views of the highest ranking Establishment economists, said:

> The vigorous and unbroken expansion of the last eight years is in dramatic contrast to the 30-month average duration of previous expansions. No longer is the performance of the American economy generally interpreted in terms of stages of the business cycle. . . . The forces making for economic fluctuations have been contained through the active use of monetary and fiscal policies. . . . [5]

In the first instance, the supposed permanent success was attributed to the self-regulating virtues of capitalism—the "unseen hand" of interacting personal interests that were supposed to provide everybody with a fair share in this best of all possible worlds. In the second instance, the expected miracle was credited to government economic regulation. But events soon showed that neither the automatic laws of capitalist economy nor their modification by government led to permanent prosperity.

When President Nixon took office at the start of 1969, the main objective of the capitalists he represents was to raise the rate of profit by holding down wages, while slowing the ominous rate of price increase. They hoped through "just a little" slowdown in the growth rate to cause sufficient competition and fear of unemployment among workers to achieve that result. So Nixon pressed for, and got, a "tight" money policy. He slashed new government contracts. These policies helped to precipitate the economic downturn, which went far beyond the mere slowdown aimed at, without accomplishing the objectives of quelling labor or slowing inflation.

During the long decline, Nixon offered no new remedies. He proved quite ineffective in attempts to turn the economy around, but this didn't keep him from asserting in December 1970, at the very bottom of the cycle: "I believe that we will build a new prosperity that will last; not a period of good times between periods of hard times, but a steady prosperity that people can count on and plan for."[6]

The president's super-optimism, however, is far from unanimous. Benjamin Strong, President of U.S. Trust Co. of New York, put it sharply enough: "In my opinion, we have come no nearer to solving the economic cycle than we have to controlling the amount of distribution of the fall of rain."[7]

J. Roger Wallace of the New York *Journal of Commerce* expresses a similar view in somewhat milder terms. And economist Eliot Janeway stresses the interacting political and economic crises afflicting modern capitalism.

Undoubtedly the present crisis will continue to bring about fresh explanations and attempted cures. The efforts of capitalist economists to arrive at a coherent and consistent explanation of these cycles, let alone to find the magic key to their elimination, are most unlikely to succeed.

Nonetheless, there has been one *consistent* explanation of the business cycle. Developed over a century ago, it has been considerably refined and expanded since. It is the one explanation that has held up throughout and that has been able to predict the coming of crises— sometimes with remarkable accuracy. That is, of course, the Marxist theory of cycles. To be exact, we should call it the Marxist-Leninist theory because it has been expanded to take into account the features of capitalism in this century, the century of imperialism.

For example, Stalin, speaking for Soviet economists, predicted the great crisis of 1929–32 shortly before it broke out—at a time when the spokesmen of capitalism were lulling themselves with the theory of a "new era" of permanent prosperity.

The internationally famous Marxist economist Eugene Varga predicted the crisis of 1957–58 almost to the month. Of course, Marxist economists have sometimes been mistaken. For example, most of them thought that the crisis of 1949–50 would last much longer and go much deeper than it actually did. Such errors show that all social theories have to be continually developed, modified, improved in the light of changes in social forces, in the means of production, and in the shifting interactions of political and economic life.

Marxism-Leninism shows the way to end cycles and has proved that its method works. The answer is simple—it involves carrying out a socialist revolution and building a socialist society in place of capitalism.

There are no reasons for the business cycle to exist in the planned economy of socialism, which does away with the exploitation of labor and its inherent contradictions.

Marxist theory arrived at these conclusions, and the experience of socialist practice has substantiated them. The Soviet Union, the first socialist state, has been in existence well over 50 years now, and there has never been a downturn in production—with one temporary exception—the period when its major industrial areas were invaded by the Hitlerite armies in World War II.

The essential difference between socialism and capitalism in this respect was first dramatically demonstrated in the desperate years of 1930–32. Those years of terrible decline and suffering throughout the capitalist world were years of accelerated growth in the USSR—the years of the first Five-Year Plan.

In trying to regulate their economies, the rulers of capitalism have freely borrowed from socialism. They have adopted national "plans," as in France and Japan; and corporate "plans," as in the United States. These attempts to apply socialist techniques to capitalism are instructive—and rarely mentioned—evidences of the superiority of socialism. And they do have some effect on economic situations under capitalism. But they *do not* eliminate the contradictions that are rooted in capitalism—contradictions which arise out of the private ownership of a productive apparatus that is, in the main, socially operated by the cooperative labor of tens and hundreds of thousands of people working for a single corporate employer.

In this book we will examine these contradictions, in principle and in practical detail, as they apply to the United States. We will examine the attempts to avert their consequences through government regulation, and explain the partial, temporary successes and long-run fundamental failures of these attempts.

The capitalists and their ideologists cannot permit themselves to understand the mass suffering caused by crises. Some minimize it; others attribute it to the laziness and vices of the hungry and unemployed; still others dismiss it with calls for patience.

W. Clement Stone, centimillionaire chairman of the Combined Life Insurance Company of America and a big Republican Party campaign contributor, responded to an interviewer on the economic crisis in late 1970, as follows:

There is what I call a wholesome recession. . . . My company is doing exceedingly well. . . . A lot of people haven't realized you have to work for your money. . . . As for employees, with a fear of losing jobs they're really putting their heart into their work. . . . Anyone who wants a job can find a job.[8]

And this at a time when five million were unemployed, according to very incomplete official figures, and approximately 25 million souls were existing on welfare payments or unemployment benefits!

But the people who remain callous so long as the unemployed keep quiet are very much concerned with the potential of revolt on the part of those who suffer the hardships that come with the business cycle. Thus, President Truman, in a speech shortly after World War II, said:

In 1932, the private enterprise system was close to collapse. There was real danger that the American people might turn to some other system. If we are to win the struggle between freedom and communism, we must be sure that we never let such a depression happen again.[9]

Samuelson wrote in 1955:

To democratic nations, the business cycle presents a challenge—almost an ultimatum. Either we learn to control depressions and inflationary booms better than we did before World War II, or the political structure of our society will hang in jeopardy. . . . If, as before the war, America marks time for another decade, the collectivized nations of the world, who need have no fear of the business cycle as we know it, will forge that much nearer or beyond us. Worse than that, peace-loving people who do not pretend to know very much advanced economics will begin to wonder why it is that during two World Wars individuals were freed for the first time from the insecurity of losing their jobs and livelihoods.[10]

There may never again be a crisis as deep or prolonged as that of 1932. But the would-be saviors of capitalism are confronted with problems and conflicts within American society resulting from the inherent inequities of capitalism, which become ever more complicated and more acute. Working people will not tolerate the levels of oppression and suffering they once endured; the flashpoints of the people's wrath are lowered. Crises of overproduction, even though milder than in the pre-war period, can more profoundly rock the stability of capitalism, and the contradictions of the system are expressed more sharply in crises other than those of overproduction.

The first section of this book examines the economic contradictions involved in crises and business cycles as they have developed in the United States in the past quarter of a century. The interweaving of class conflict with economic developments is stressed and demonstrated.

The next section examines the modern capitalist theory of the cycle and how to combat it, and studies government contracyclical regulation of the economy in the United States, along with its political objectives, social bias, and limitations. New features, the development of the related economic goal of spurring economic growth, and the special role of chronic militarism are investigated.

A third section relates domestic economic cycles to the foreign economic relations of the United States. Major features of government regulation in other capitalist countries that differ significantly from those in the United States are summarized.

A final chapter sketches the direction of a people's program for controlling the cycle and spurring the kinds of growth that are beneficial to the majority, along with a survey of the political context of the struggle over economic policy and a projection of its ultimate outcome.

II.

Why Cycles?

CYCLES ARE phenomena of modern industrial capitalism. They first appeared early in the 19th century, in the wake of the Industrial Revolution, and they will disappear along with capitalism. That's not a mere forecast; it has been proven by a half-century of cycle-free development in the USSR, and by shorter periods in other socialist countries.

Capitalism is a system based on private ownership of the means of production, and wage labor. Profits, the object of capitalist enterprise, derive from the difference between the values produced by labor and the wages paid to labor. Typically, the daily wages are less than half the values created. Marx called the difference "surplus value" and the process of its creation the exploitation of labor. This term is often used in the United States to signify payment of substandard wages. However, here we use the term "exploitation" in the Marxist sense, applying to all wage and salary earners, including most of those who are relatively well paid.

Surplus value is divided into various kinds of property income, some disguised: dividends, interest, rent, undivided corporate profits, profits of unincorporated enterprises, inflated salaries, bonuses and expense accounts for corporate officials and executives; excessive depreciation and other "cash flow" items; fees paid to bankers, lawyers, and other "insiders." Part of surplus value also goes to pay taxes. The "net income" publicly reported by most large corporations covers only a minor fraction of the total surplus value extracted from their workers' labor.

In contrast to the private nature of ownership, the process of production is social. In many instances, thousands and thousands of workers are employed by a single corporate entity, and the products of their labor are marketed throughout the capitalist world. This represents a decisive difference from earlier systems of exploitation—feudalism and slavery—in which production was largely individual and products were consumed locally.

The capitalist's production objective is the expansion of his capital. As Marx put it, "It will never do, therefore, to represent capitalist production as something which it is not, namely, as production whose immediate purpose is enjoyment or the manufacture of the means of enjoyment for the capitalist."[1]

Certainly, the capitalists do not stint on their living standards. But their main aim is to "save" their profits and reinvest them so that they can become still bigger capitalists. The psychological (and subjective) motivation is the greed of the capitalists. A man has to be greedy to succeed as a capitalist—and even to survive. For throughout the history of this system the smaller capitalist has been swallowed up by the larger, and this has never been more true than today. Either he is "greedy" and clever enough at it to exploit his workers massively, reinvesting his profits so that he can exploit still more workers, or he will soon stop being a capitalist and himself become an exploited worker. In present-day American terms, either he will conglomerate or be conglomerated.

It is especially important to bear this in mind today when there has developed so much propaganda about U. S. capitalism as a "consumer society," about the "consumer being king," etc. Anybody who has had any practical dealings with top executives of major corporations knows that this is utter nonsense—that the object of business is to make a profit and to use that profit to make more profit. Period.

We have said that the object of production is surplus value and that this is created in the process of production. The finished goods that emerge from the factory door contain the quantity of surplus value represented by the amount of exploitation of the workers in that factory.

Capital, [says Marx] has absorbed so and so much unpaid labor. . . . Now, comes the second act of the process. The entire mass of commodities . . . must be sold. If this is not done, or done only in part, or only at prices below the prices of production, the labourer has been indeed exploited, but his exploitation is not realised as such for the capitalist. . . . The conditions of direct exploitation and those of realising it are not identical. They diverge not only in place and time, but also logically.[2]

Marx uses the term "realisation" to signify the process of selling and collecting the money for the product.

Every practical man knows this simple truth. Indeed, companies making whole lines of products, from computers to pharmaceuticals, spend much more money trying to sell the goods than they do to produce them.

But the modern capitalist economists, beginning with Keynes, and more especially his postwar followers, systematically ignore it. They draw up economic models in which the amount of income saved equals the amount invested, etc. This false harmony in the accounts makes it impossible to understand the causes of crisis and impossible to estimate accurately the effects of government policies designed to influence the course of economic development.

Marx goes on to expand on his statement of the "divergence" of the amount of goods produced and the amount sold. The amounts produced "are only limited by the productive power of society," the amounts sold "by the proportional relation of the various branches of production and *the consumer power of society.*"[3] (Italics added)

Now if everybody spent every cent of his share of the values produced, production would balance. But consuming* power

is not determined either by the absolute productive power, or by the absolute consumer power, but by the consumer power based on antagonistic conditions of distribution, which reduce the consumption of the bulk of the society to a minimum varying within more or less narrow limits.[4]

To make maximum profits, the employers seek to hold wages down as much as possible and to increase the intensity of labor, that is, to get more product out of each hour of labor. But that tends to reduce the share of workers in the revenues produced, to prevent their consuming power from increasing as fast as the value of goods produced. The capitalists, for their part, do not increase personal consumption in line with their increasing share of production because of their "greed for an expansion of capital."

This contradiction between the tendencies of production and consumption prevents the full potential of production and of employment from being realized over a prolonged period.

*Many contemporary Marxist writers use the term "consuming power" in the same sense as capitalist economists use the term "purchasing power." Marx applies it to the power to buy capital goods or means of production as well as the power to buy consumers goods. In *Capital*, the translator has used the terms "consuming power" and "consumer power" interchangeably.

It is no contradiction at all on this self-contradictory basis that there should be an excess of capital simultaneously with a growing surplus of population. For while a combination of these two would, indeed, increase the mass of produced surplus-value, it would at the same time intensify the contradiction between the conditions under which this surplus-value is produced and those under which it is realised.[5]

This is recognized by modern capitalist economists who disdain Marx and who do *not* recognize the relations of exploitation which give rise to the contradiction. For example, Keynes defines *effective* demand as equaling the aggregate income that capitalists expect to receive and pay out to their workers—based on the number of workers they intend to hire. This number does not correspond to their full capacity, but "to the level of employment which maximizes the entrepreneur's expectation of profit."[6]

Similarly, Washington economists strive to regulate the economy so as to achieve the "ideal" rate of unemployment—four or five per cent—depending on the time period and the economist, as being most suited to economic stability and maximum profits.

Interaction of the Rate of Profit and Overproduction

During the boom phase of the cycle, overproduction of capital and of commodities generally creeps up in disguise, so to speak. On the surface, demand is brisk; there are even shortages of particular labor skills. Yet disturbing things happen. "Air-holes" appear in the economy and on the stock market. More and more companies complain of a "profit squeeze." And this hits from several directions.

During the whole period of revival and boom, attempts to cut costs and increase _ or productivity and the scale of production led to the introduction o new, more expensive, labor-saving equipment, huge power installations, and other capital-intensive "infrastructures." But the expansion of the market has not been sufficient to yield the same rate of profit on all this new fixed capital as has been obtained on the older, less expensive machinery and equipment. This is a crude example of the operation of the law of the declining tendency of the rate of profit. This law—fundamental to the cyclical process as well as to longer-range problems of capitalism—is explained in Chapter V.

By the time the recovery has reached boom level, unemployment is at a comparatively low level. Workers are unafraid to strike, while employers fear the loss of profitable business opportunities. Organized workers win substantial wage increases. In many cases employers voluntarily raise wages of unorganized workers to ensure an adequate supply of labor, especially in the skilled trades. The higher wages increase the demand for consumers goods—but not enough to take up all the flood of goods that can be turned out in the new, expanded and improved industrial plants.

Shortages of particular raw materials cause their prices to soar, and this cannot be fully offset at the processing level. In the modern corporate economy, all of the partly parasitic "overhead" expenses—from advertising to executive expense-account living—get out of line. Attempted price increases do not stick, or, in a chronically inflationary situation such as that of present-day United States, the increases cannot keep up with the rise in costs.

Gradually, profit declines hit more and more companies, and even whole industries. In modern capitalist analytic language, the "diffusion index" for profits declines, that is, a larger percentage of corporations show a declining trend of profits even before the total profits of all corporations turn downward.

At a certain point in this development, the lack of adequate markets becomes apparent, at least in key industries. The "profit squeeze " and slackening markets reinforce one another. The difficulties become sufficiently general to cause many capitalists to hesitate to make new investments since they doubt the possibility of obtaining an adequate rate of profit on them. The total level of new capital investment declines; this is the decisive signal of a crisis situation.

All of these interacting phenomena are varying reflections of the contradictions built into the capitalist system of production—a system where the object of production is the profits obtained through exploitation of wage labor; a system where the profits exist *potentially* in commodities produced by the workers but have to be converted into money, the "real" symbol of profit, through sale on a market, but the market cannot be coordinated in its pattern or absolute size with the scale of production; furthermore, a crucial part of the market reflects in a reverse mirror the rate of exploitation of labor. The more the latter expands, increasing the *potential profit*, the more the former contracts in relative size, preventing the full *realization* of that profit and its full conversion into money.

Sooner or later these contradictions are temporarily resolved in a crisis. This leads to the destruction of the value of part of the capital through bankruptcy, distress sale, or price markdowns. And a considerable amount of capital is physically destroyed as plants are shut down permanently and the surplus stocks of some commodities are destroyed by government agencies or cartels of producers. With the total capital reduced by more, relatively, than the total profit, at some point the rate of profit is restored, production stabilizes, and conditions are created for the next upward phases of the business cycle.

A mere "adjustment" isn't enough; the crisis has to be sharp enough to result in bankruptcies and the destruction of capital values. Otherwise the rate of profit cannot be restored on the remaining capital.

Marx called them crises of *overproduction* because they appear as an overproduction of capital, as overcapacity, overstocking of goods, etc. Not overproduction in any absolute sense, but *overproduction for the objective of capitalist production—maximum profit.*

And here are some eloquent words that express the theoretical essence of Marx's analysis and, at the same time, the social significance of the capitalist cycle:

There are not too many necessities of life produced, in proportion to the existing population. Quite the reverse. Too little is produced to decently and humanely satisfy the wants of the great mass.

There are not too many means of production produced to employ the able-bodied portion of the population. Quite the reverse. . . .

On the other hand, too many means of labour and necessities of life are produced at times to permit of their serving as means for the exploitation of labourers at a certain rate of profit . . . too many to permit the consummation of this process without constantly recurring explosions.

Not too much wealth is produced. But at times too much wealth is produced in its capitalistic, self-contradictory forms.[7]

Talk of absolute surpluses of foodstuffs in the wealthy United States seems callous when we are confronted by the evidence of mass malnutrition and even hunger among tens of millions of people. And talk of overproduction of machinery falls flat when we are confronted with the mass unemployment of millions of ghetto youth, of millions more in Appalachia and other depressed areas of the country, even in "good times."

And yet, "crisis of overproduction", is the correct phrase if we keep in mind that we are dealing with the concept "overproduction from the viewpoint of capitalism, from the viewpoint of making profits."

A summation of the very essence of the question is here given by Marx:

> The ultimate reason for all real crises always remains the poverty and restricted consumption of the masses as opposed to the drive of capitalist production to develop the productive forces as though only the absolute consuming power of society constituted their limit.[8]

Under-consumptionists and Trickle-Downers

Well, say some economists, the solution is simple. Increase wages and other mass incomes, and all the goods can be sold at a reasonable profit. These economists, called under-consumptionists, consider only one side of the question. Quite aside from the invariable resistance of the capitalists, who do not care about their arguments, the increase in mass purchasing power is a two-sided weapon. The purchasing power of workers is a cost of production to the capitalists. An increase in that purchasing power means a cut in his rate of exploitation of labor. At the peak of the boom, writes Marx, "The working class actively reinforced by its entire reserve army, also enjoys momentarily articles of luxury ordinarily out of its reach, articles which at other times constitute for the greater part 'necessities' only for the capitalist class. . . ."

He directly takes up the argument of the under-consumptionists, who say that the crises result because "the working class receives too small a portion of their own product and the evil would be remedied as soon as it receives a larger share of it and its wages increase in consequence." To them, he says:

> One could only remark that crises are always prepared by precisely a period in which wages rise generally and the working class actually gets a larger share of that part of the annual product which is intended for consumption. From the point of view of these advocates of sound and "simple" (!) common sense, such a period should rather remove the crisis. It appears, then, that capitalist production comprises conditions independent of good or bad will, conditions which permit the working-class to enjoy that relative prosperity only momentarily, and at that always only as a harbinger of a coming crisis.[9]

Nowadays, in fact, the capitalists blame crises on rising wages, but the blame is in the system that causes crises, be wages high or low, rising or falling. The most reactionary economists, those who are direct spokesmen for big capital, say the solution to crises is simple. Hold down wages, and do everything to give more "incentive" to capital. Then there will be a constantly rising flow of investment, well-being will trickle down from those on top to those below, increasing jobs and everybody's prosperity. This Simple-Simon argument, self-serving to the capitalists' interests, collapses when applied. Because then the rapidly rising production capacity comes into the most glaring contradiction with the consuming power of the masses, deliberately kept stagnant in order to increase the rate of profit.

The "New Era" of the 1920s in the United States gave that argument its test. Labor productivity soared; profits soared. Everything boomed except wages, which stayed virtually unchanged. And the ensuing crash was the worst in history.

The fact is there is no combination of industrial and labor practices and policies which can avert the cumulation of contradictions that lead to cyclical development. Government policies, as we shall see, can influence the timing and course of the cycle, but cannot exorcise it.

Phases of the Cycle

Marxists describe four phases of the economic cycle: crisis, depression, recovery, and boom. Capitalist economists describe pretty much the same phases, but in different language. Samuelson uses the terms contraction, revival, expansion, peak.[10]*

The Marxist terminology is more vivid and more precisely reflects the character of cyclical development. Marx saw each crisis as the start of a new cycle. It is a violent cathartic—a temporary cure for the contradictions of the economy. By an enforced economic retreat it creates a new balance, from which economic activity can again expand:

*The National Bureau of Economic Research, the official authority on the business cycle, uses the same terms, except for the last-named phrase. The National Bureau uses "recession" instead of "peak." But it means pretty much the same thing—the "upper turning point" of the cycle. Today, the term "recession" is commonly used in the same sense that the National Bureau originally used the term "contraction," so the National Bureau's original terminology would be confusing.[11]

This phase of a cycle is characterized by overproduction of commodities which cannot find outlets, by a sharp fall in prices, by an acute shortage of means of payment and by stock exchange crashes which bring in their train mass bankruptcy, a sharp curtailment of production, a growth in unemployment, and a fall in wages. The fall in the prices of commodities, unemployment, direct destruction of machinery, equipment, and entire works—all this means a tremendous destruction of society's productive forces. Through the ruin and collapse of a large number of concerns and the destruction of part of the productive forces, the crisis forcibly adapts, and that within a very short time, the magnitude of production to the magnitude of effective demand.[12]

Not all of these things happen in every crisis, but most of them do. In the most recent crisis in the United States, for example, the fall in the prices of commodities was limited to raw materials and only real wages fell, not money wages.

During the depression phase, industrial production stagnates, trade is sluggish, there is an abundance of spare money capital. Excess inventories are partly destroyed and partly sold off at reduced prices. Capitalists try to cut costs in every way, especially by increasing the exploitation of labor. They push workers harder, using the threat of unemployment. Sometimes they are able to enforce wage cuts. They institute technical improvements and labor-saving equipment to increase labor productivity and restore profits even with prices below their peaks.

This renewal of machinery stirs up production in the machinery and metal industries. Workers in these areas increase the demand for consumers goods. So do the gradually increasing number of government workers and those in service industries. Thus conditions are created for a transition to economic recovery.

During the recovery phase, production passes its previous peak and gradually gathers momentum. Inventories are rebuilt; capitalists begin to expand again; new plants are constructed; new foreign markets penetrated. Prices start upward and credit begins to expand. The pace of recovery quickens.

In the boom period there is a surface appearance of all-around prosperity. Predictions of permanent good times abound; the stock market soars dizzily. But, beneath the surface, conditions for the next crisis are fast ripening. There are fewer and fewer really new opportunities for investment. More and more individual enterprises run into trouble. Capitalists, squeezed out of production, turn more and more to speculation—wild real-estate ventures and the purchase of stocks at prices that "discount not only the future, but the hereafter."

More and more things are going on credit. Capitalists borrow to stock up raw materials before prices go still higher. Speculators borrow to play the market. Workers borrow to buy goods promising a modicum of comfort. Money becomes "tight," interest rates soar. So do prices. Capacity again has gotten far ahead of effective demand. The contradictions are temporarily hidden by the stretching of credit to the last notch, by the last big expansions of investment, by the new peaks on the stock market, by rising production that goes into inventories—but not to final buyers. But sooner or later the "bubble bursts." A new crisis breaks out, and the cycle starts all over again.

This is a rough sketch. Every cycle has its individual features. All cycles of the past several decades have been influenced by government economic regulation—and increasingly so. But the fundamental contradictions remain in force; the cycle retains its historic general shape, as described so graphically by Engels nearly 100 years ago:

As a matter of fact, since 1825, when the first general crisis broke out, the whole industrial and commercial world, production and exchange . . . are thrown out of joint about once every ten years. Commerce is at a standstill, the markets are glutted, products accumulate, as multitudinous as they are unsaleable, hard cash disappears, credit vanishes, factories are closed, the mass of the workers are in want of the means of subsistence because they have produced too much of the means of subsistence; bankruptcy follows upon bankruptcy, execution upon execution. The stagnation lasts for years; productive forces and production are wasted and destroyed wholesale, until the accumulated mass of commodities finally filters off, more or less depreciated in value, until production and exchange gradually begin to move again. Little by little the pace quickens. It becomes a trot. The industrial trot breaks into a canter, the canter, in turn, grows into the headlong gallop of a perfect steeplechase of industry, commercial credit, and speculation which, finally, after breakneck leaps, ends where it began—in the ditch of a crisis. And so over and over again. We have now, since the year 1825, gone through this five times, and at the present moment (1877) we are going through it for the sixth time. And the character of these crises is so clearly defined that Fourier hit all of them off when he described it first as "*crise pléthorique,*" a crisis from plethora.[13]

III.

The Main Contradiction

THE CONTRADICTION that exists in capitalist societies between
production and consumption is rooted in the dynamics of the exploitation of labor. To understand this, let us suppose a worker's wage is
equivalent to the value he produces in four hours, while his total
workday extends for eight hours. Then he is producing four hours of
surplus value, and the rate of surplus value is 100%, that is, the capitalist's share is equal to that of the worker's. Suppose now that two
hours is added to the working day while wages are left unchanged or,
even if overtime is paid, increased prices and taxes leave the worker
with the same consuming power as before. Now the worker's share is
still equal to the product of four hours labor, while the capitalist's share
is increased to six hours. The rate of surplus value, or exploitation, is
$\dfrac{100 \times 6}{4}$ or 150%. The capitalist gets one and one-half times as
much as the worker.

If the rate of exploitation were constant and the surplus value
extracted were invested and consumed by the capitalists in fixed
proportions such as would preserve a balanced structure in the overall
economy, production would develop more or less smoothly, without
cycles. But these conditions are never fully met and are approached for
only comparatively brief moments. The most important single element
of instability is therefore rooted in the existence and characteristics of
surplus value.

The Census of Manufactures for 1967 shows wages of production
workers equal to $81.0 billion, or 31.2% of the $259.3 billion of value
added by manufactures. The difference between these two figures
($178.3 billion) is a first approximation of the amount of surplus value
produced. It is more than two times the amount of wages paid and
indicates a rate of surplus value of 221%.

But that figure is not wholly accurate. To arrive at the values created
by the workers in a given year, the value added should be reduced by

the amount of depreciation of machinery and buildings. To the wages of production workers should be added that part of the salaries of employees who are also really contributing to the production process —engineers, designers, and so forth. On the other hand, to express the full value created by the factory workers, the value added should be increased by the distributive mark-up. For example, in the automobile industry, the distributive markup added to the factory price is more per car produced than the wages paid at the factory.

The ratio of wages to value added has been declining rather steadily since World War II, with a corresponding increase in the rate of surplus value. In 1947, wages were 40.7% of value added; in 1957, 35.6%; and in 1969, 30.7%. The rates of surplus value increased from 146% in 1947 to 181% in 1957, and to 226% in 1969.

If, at the other extreme of calculation we include all salaries paid in operating manufacturing establishments, the indicated rise in the rate of surplus value slows down but is still present. The statistics are shown in Table 1. They cover the census years 1947, 1953, and 1967, and the years 1957, 1960 and 1969—the peak years of business cycles, for which statistics of the Annual Survey of Manufactures are used.

The calculations relating solely to wages come closer to representing the actual state of affairs than those including salaries as well. But, either way, the data show a rise in the rate of exploitation of labor—the

TABLE III-1. TRENDS IN RATE OF SURPLUS VALUE IN MANUFACTURING*
1947–1969

	Percent Wages of Value Added	Corresponding Rate of Surplus Value	Percent Wages & Salaries of Value Added	Corresponding Rate of Surplus Value
1947	40.7	146	52.4	87
1953	40.3	148	54.7	83
1957	35.6	181	51.6	94
1960	33.9	195	51.0	96
1963	32.6	207	48.9	104
1967	31.2	221	47.5	111
1969	30.7	226	46.7	114

*Excludes salaries paid at central administrative and auxiliary units of manufacturing companies.
Sources: U.S. Census of Manufactures; 1947, 1953, 1963 and 1967. Annual Survey of Manufacturers; 1957, 1960 and 1969.

fastest rise ever over a period of two decades. However, there was one previous decade in which the rate of surplus value increased at a comparable pace—the decade of the 1920s. It did not reach the high point of 1969, but the rapid increase contributed in a fundamental way to the crisis of 1929-32.

While the main point is the trend, the high absolute rate of surplus value shown by this calculation—more than 200%—is also significant. It indicates a narrow *primary* mass market base for consumers goods. It shows that the American economy *has to* have relatively huge secondary sectors in order to achieve any kind of balance.

Marx discussed the secondary sectors—services, government, finance—in other connections but not in relation to the cycle. They were not so large nor so important in the cycle in the 19th century. But their influence on cyclical movements has to be examined very carefully now.

The high rate of surplus value is obscured in U.S. government statistics, which lump together wages and salaries and include the salaries of corporation officials in both the primary and secondary sectors of the economy. Simultaneously, these statistics understate the amount of property income. Thus they give the misleading picture that the "compensation of employees" comprises 73% of the national income.

The high rate of surplus value is something that all employers know, but they do not speak about it—except to one another. It is especially high in technically advanced, armament-stimulated, monopolized industries. Investment houses have analyzed the accounts of IBM, the giant of the computer-electronics industry. They find that factory costs, including labor and materials, come to only one-fourth or one-fifth of the selling price. Lesser electronics companies, according to published assertions of their own chief executives, sell their products at three times factory cost and aim for four times cost.[2]

If we assume that prime cost is evenly divided between labor and materials, then the rate of surplus value in the electronics industry is in the neighborhood of 500%.

Analysis of data contained in published annual reports of the "Big Three" auto companies indicates a rate of surplus value of close to 200%. However, a study by the organization of big employers, the National Industrial Conference Board, indicates a rate of surplus value of about 300%.[3]

In less centralized industries, the policy of manufacturers is to set a price equal to twice factory cost. This is not a documented figure; it is informally cited as the standard by manufacturers and others familiar with a wide range of businesses, from textiles to household appliances. Again, assuming an equal division between wages and materials, this would be equivalent to a rate of surplus value of around 300%.

In reality, of course, there are many times when manufacturers are forced to sell below their desired prices and when costs exceed expectations. But the examples only verify the general statistical indication of a high rate of surplus value, probably exceeding 200% on the average in American industry.

The exploitation of labor is effectuated at the place of work. A common error of liberal economists is to argue that exploitation of labor has been replaced by exploitation of consumers through monopoly prices. Robert Heilbroner, for example, is an advocate of this view.

This reasoning, however, overlooks the heterogeneous social composition of consumers. The capitalist, the corporate executive, profits much more from high prices than he loses from them. He has, moreover, the best opportunity of avoiding high prices by "getting it wholesale," charging items to company expense accounts, receiving quantity discounts, and so forth. The main victims of monopoly retail prices are the workers, especially the poorest, most oppressed workers, who are charged the most exorbitant prices. And, as usual, this is felt especially by the Black and other groups who are segregated into ghettos. The victims are the workers; the profiteers are the corporate monopolists, who exploit the workers at the place of production.

Monopoly does not change the place where exploitation occurs, but results in a larger share of surplus value being collected in the retail marketing of consumers goods, and a smaller share in wholesale trade among the capitalists. This should be taken into account in measuring the rate of surplus value as a whole.

Taxation has become another channel for the realization of surplus value. An increasing portion of taxes is taken from workers and spent for the benefit of capitalists. This becomes part of the overall profits of the capitalist class, by the amount redistributed through taxes to its advantage, just as if wages were reduced and profits increased in the first place.

To take account of the effects of monopoly pricing and promonopoly taxation, we calculate the trend in the exploitation of labor by comparing the physical volume of the worker's production with the volume of his consuming power, after allowing for changing retail prices and tax deductions from his pay. This is accomplished technically by comparing productivity per worker or per man-hour with real take-home pay per worker or per man-hour. Suppose that productivity per man-hour increases 20% in a given five-year period, while real take-home pay per man-hour (spendable earnings in dollars of constant purchasing power as calculated by the Labor Department) increases 10% in the same period. Then the rate of exploitation of labor increases 9.1% — $\left(\dfrac{120}{110} = 1.091 \right)$, and the worker's share in the value of his product decreases 8.3%, $\left(\dfrac{110}{120} = 0.917 \right)$.

This method is somewhat more accurate and complete than that involving the use of census figures. Also statistics become available more quickly and cover all years. This method of calculation does not yield an estimate of the rate of surplus value but only of its trend. We have made calculations of this type for the entire postwar period. The results are expressed as index numbers, on the standard base of 1957– 59 = 100.

Between 1946 and 1969 the index of productivity per man-hour in manufacturing increased from 60.8 to 145.5, an increase of 139%, or nearly 2^1/$_2$ times. Meanwhile, real take-home pay increased from 80.2 to 112.8, or by 40.6. This means that if the rate of surplus value, as defined by Marx, was 100% in 1946, it was 175% by 1969!

The index of real take-home pay per unit of production decreased from 131.9 to 77.5, or by 41%, that is, the worker's share in the values he produced declined by two-fifths!

Key trends are shown graphically in Chart I, where the figures are converted to a 1946 base, and extended to 1970. The top line of the chart shows the consumer price index nearly doubling between 1946 and 1970. It far outstrips the increase in labor costs per unit of production, which goes up barely one-fourth during these 24 years. Correspondingly, labor's share in production declines more than two-fifths.

The year-by-year figures are shown in Appendix Table I. They show that the rate of exploitation of labor has been increasing and labor's share in production decreasing almost continuously during this quarter

CHART I

Prices, Labor Costs and Workers' Share in Production
1946-1970 index numbers, 1946=100

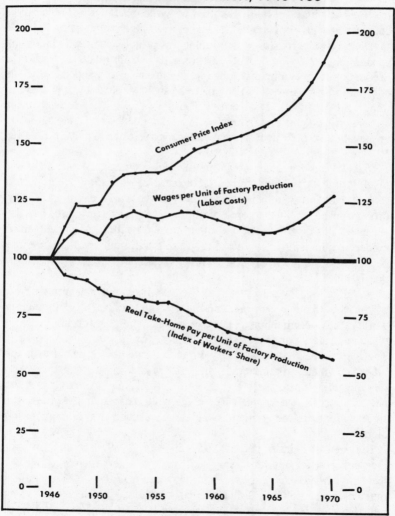

Consumer Price Index

Wages per Unit of Factory Production
(Labor Costs)

Real Take-Home Pay per Unit of Factory Production
(Index of Workers' Share)

of a century. In only two years, 1953 and 1956, were there slight interruptions to the trend.

The government publishes figures that seem to tell an opposite story. It uses an index of the ratio of prices to unit cost in manufacturing which shows little change over the entire postwar period. Its fall below 100 on the 1957–59 base in 1970 was used as evidence of the administration charge that workers were getting excessive wage increases.

Seemingly, this series is similar in principle to our index of production per dollar of real take-home pay. Both relate the worker's production to his compensation, one in current prices and the other in constant prices. How, then, can there be such a radical difference in the trends shown by the two series? The answer is that the government series is rigged and grossly misleading—designed to assist the antilabor propaganda of big business. This allegation is documented in Chapter VII.

Calculations for other areas of material production yield a similar result to that calculated for manufacturing. But what about the trade and service industries and the white-collar workers? True, an increasing proportion represent the corporate bureaucracy in advertising, overdeveloped sales departments, and other areas reflecting the parasitism of modern capitalism. While personally exploited, many workers in these occupations are paid out of real values created by workers in industry, that is, out of a part of the surplus value.

Nevertheless, for purposes of cyclical analysis, the consuming power of these workers is just as important as that of factory production workers. Government statistics permit calculations for all nonfarm wage and salary employees similar to those for manufacturing workers. There is much that is arbitrary in these statistics, especially in the official estimates of productivity in the trade and service industries. And the arbitrariness is of such a character as is designed to smooth out and hence conceal real trends. But even with these manipulations, the figures confirm the general conclusion reached for manufacturing alone.

Between the base period 1957–59 and 1969, productivity per man-hour for all non-farm wage and salary workers increased 34.8%. Real take-home pay per man-hour increased 17.4%, or just half as much.[4] Production per dollar of real take-home pay increased 15%, with a corresponding percentage increase in the rate of exploitation of labor. Similarly, real wages per unit of output, or the worker's share in production, declined 13%. These changes were about half as pronounced as those shown for factory production workers. But they were still sufficiently sharp to contribute significantly to the ripening of a crisis of overproduction.

During World War II there was a substantial *increase* in the ratio of wages to value added and a corresponding reduction in the rate of surplus value. The same applied, although in lesser degree, during the Korean War. Labor shortages and, in the case of World War II, an aggressive trade union movement, led to higher wages, despite wartime controls. Wartime price controls held down prices, and hence the value added by manufacture.

But during the Vietnam War, for the first time this century there has been a marked increase in the rate of exploitation of labor during a war. This was due to the inability of the trade unions to win adequate wage increases and to the absence of price controls. This partly explains the eruption of a crisis of overproduction, for the first time during a war.

The appended Table I shows the index of exploitation of labor (production per unit of real wages), increasing very sharply in 1969. The rise in the index from 124.5 in 1968 to 129.0 in 1969 was the sharpest for any year shown except 1947. Similarly, there was an unusually sharp year-to-year drop in labor's share in production. Thus, relative overproduction developed very rapidly.

The basic contradiction explained by Marx (as quoted in Chapter II), represented by the relative stagnation of mass consuming power, was rapidly aggravated. Hence it is understandable that the contradiction that had been growing for many years reached an acute stage in 1969. It is similarly understandable that the crisis of overproduction, which had been maturing for many years, actually began in 1969, although its most dramatic events did not occur until 1970.

IV.

Offsets to Increasing Exploitation

THERE WAS only one period when the rate of exploitation of labor increased as rapidly as it did after World War II—during the decade of the 1920s—which culminated in the great crisis of 1929–32. But although the present period of rapidly rising exploitation has lasted more than twice as long, the postwar crises have thus far been relatively mild and short-lived.

A major reason for the difference is the existence of factors that partly offset the economic effect of a rapidly increasing rate of exploitation, accompanied by a corresponding modification of its cyclical impact. The changed pattern of the cycle also resulted from other causes, which will be discussed in later chapters. This chapter is limited to those factors that tended to balance or offset the more rapid rise of production than of the consuming power of the masses of productive workers.

Opponents of Marxism often point to these offsetting factors as evidence that Marx was wrong. On the contrary, Marxists are fully aware of the complexities of capitalist economy. Marx did not deal with offsets precisely like those of today because they were not operative in his time. But he devoted a major chapter of *Capital* to "causes that counteracted" the law of the declining tendency of the rate of profit—another major ingredient in the cyclical mechanism of capitalism (see Chapter V).

In each case, Marx found that the particular counteracting cause initially stimulates economic activity and delays a crisis. But operating within the limitations of capitalist property relations, it winds up by turning into its opposite. Instead of moderating the contradictions, it aggravates them and contributes sooner or later to plunging the economy into a crisis. The same principle applies to the offsets discussed in the present chapter.

The main offsets have been shifts in the destination of the national product and the provision of additional consumption income to workers—other than wages for productive labor.

Shifts in the Destination of the National Product

There has been a major reduction in the share of consumption in the gross national product (GNP) and a corresponding increase in the combined share of investment and government expenditures. In terms of the "Departments of Production" defined by Marx, there was an increase in the share of Department I—means of production—and a decrease in the share of Department II—means of consumption.* Spending for commodities in Department I, aside from the replacement of consumed materials, is financed out of surplus value. Therefore an increase in the share of Department I in total production is consistent with an increase in the proportion of surplus value or in the rate of the exploitation of labor. So long as Department I continues to expand, relatively, at a sufficiently rapid rate, an increase in the rate of surplus value can be absorbed without the incidence of overproduction.

Private consumption amounted to just under three-fourths of the GNP in 1929 (74.9%), and to about the same share in the three years just before World War II. But in the first postwar cycle (1946–48), consumption was down to 68.6% of the GNP, and in the next cycle, which included the Korean War, it fell to 64.9%. It remained close to this percentage in the next two cycles but dropped to 62.9% in the long cycle 1961–69. Most of this last decline took place during the Vietnam War years. In 1968 consumption fell to 61.9% of GNP, the lowest ever, except for the years of World War II (see Table IV-1). Note that the decline in the share of consumption occurred mainly during wars and that losses in this sector were not recovered after these wars.

The cycle-to-cycle percentage changes may not seem very great, but consider the drop from 64.6% in 1960 to 62.0% in 1969. This means that personal consumption expenditures in 1969 were $24 billion less than they would have been had the same percentage been maintained. Actually, the relative decline in consumption was sharper than is indicated by the official figures. These add on to actual consumption

---

*In actual practice, the major increase in the United States was not as great in the share of producers' goods as in the shares of munitions and of government outlays. These latter items were not significant in Marx's time. Their role in the circulation of commodities, however, is somewhat analogous to that of producers' goods. Diagrams of capital and commodity flow under modern conditions, including these major sectors, are presented in the author's article "Marx's Commodity Circulation Scheme under State Monopoly Capitalism" (in German), in *Jahrbuch fur Wirtschaftsgeschichte*, 1969/111, Berlin.

expenditures imputed items that are assumed to increase much faster than cash outlays, and artificially slow down the statistical decline in the share of consumption. But, even as reported, the $24 billion drop in relative consumption accounts for most of the decline in labor's share in the values it created.*

There was also a decline in the share of consumption for residential construction. While technically classified as a part of investment, this is in many ways more akin to expenditures for consumers' durable goods. Residential construction declined from 5.5% of GNP in 1948–56 to 4.5% in 1957–64 and to under 3.5% in the Vietnam War years 1965–69.

TABLE IV-1. PERCENTAGE DISTRIBUTION OF GROSS NATIONAL
PRODUCT AVERAGES FOR BUSINESS CYCLE PERIODS—
1946–1969

	Consumer Expenditures	Plant and Equipment Expenditure	Government Spending for Goods and Services			All Other
			Total	Military	Civilian	
1946–48	68.6	9.6	12.0	5.0	7.0	5.8
1949–53	64.9	9.4	18.0	9.4	8.6	7.7
1954–57	64.0	9.9	19.3	10.1	9.2	6.8
1958–60	64.6	9.4	20.3	9.6	10.7	5.7
1961–69	62.9	10.0	21.4	8.6	12.8	5.7

Source: Economic Report of the President, 1970, Table C-1, *Survey of Current Business,* July 1970, p. 177. Cyclical average percentages are averages of percentages for separate years and not percentages of totals for the entire cyclical period.

"All other" includes residential structures, net exports of goods and services, and change in business inventories. The decline in "all other" areas between 1946–48 and 1949–53 consists mainly of a decline of net exports. This results largely from the termination of big government foreign aid exports in the immediate postwar years, which might just as well be classified as government expenditures. If that were done, the increase in government spending in the second cycle would not be so pronounced.

The decline in "all other" after 1949–53 consists mainly of a reduction in residential construction.

*The dollar equivalent of the decline in the share earned by factory wage earners between 1960 and 1969, as shown in Appendix Table III-1, comes to about $16 billion or only two-thirds of the dollar equivalent of the decline in the share of consumption. But the remaining third is more than accounted for by the increased exploitation of workers in other spheres of production and distribution.

Part of the decline in the share of consumer expenditures was accounted for by an increase in the share of investment in plant and equipment. During the first two decades after World War II, this averaged about 9.5% of the GNP, considerably more than during the decade immediately prior to World War II. During the Vietnam War years 1965–69, this increased to a record high of 10.5%.

The rise in the share of plant and equipment did more to stimulate growth than seems apparent from the relatively small numerical increase in its percentage share. In GNP statistics, fixed capital—plant and equipment—is measured in wholesale prices, while consumer expenditures are measured in retail prices. Hence, the relative weight of plant and equipment, in terms of actual productive activity, is considerably more than that indicated by GNP figures.

Production of equipment and plant, concentrated in the basic durable goods industries and construction, largely determines the course of this crucial sector of the economy. Since it is also the most variable sector, a fast increase in fixed capital outlays tends to spur a boom, while the rate of its decline significantly influences the depth of a depression.

During this quarter of a century, fixed capital spending has increased rather steadily, while declines have been relatively mild and short. This has much to do with the comparative shallowness and brief duration of economic downturns.

Thus plant and equipment outlays proved a powerful offset to the decline in the relative share of workers in production. At the same time, the long-term effect has been to deepen the basic contradiction in the economy and increase its vulnerability to serious crises.

The unprecedented and prolonged surge in fixed capital spending expressed the tendency of production to expand without any limit other than that permitted by the physical possibilities, without regard to the restricted increase in personal consumption. This contradiction has been elaborated by Marx and is explained in Chapter II.

Actually, the rise in capital spending resulted in an exceptionally fast increase in industrial capacity, considerably exceeding the pace of increase in total fixed capital outlays. Normally, more than half of all plant and equipment expenditure consists of replacement of worn-out or obsolete units. Only the expenditure that remains—usually less than half the total—expands capacity. But needed replacements do not increase very rapidly. Therefore, in periods of rapidly rising fixed capital investment, such as the Vietnam War years, there is a more than proportional rise in capacity.

In fact, industrial capacity increased 33.5% in the five years 1965–69, compared with 19.6% in the previous five years, 25.9% in the 1955–59 period, and 27.4% in the five years 1949–54.[2] The high rate of increase in the earliest of these periods included the necessity for "catching up" from World War II shortages and investments stimulated by the Korean War boom. The fact that expansion during the Vietnam War has been so much faster emphasizes the unusual scale of the buildup. It signifies the creation of relative overproduction, of temporarily excess capacity.

This is confirmed by government indexes of capacity utilization. In the second quarter of 1966, manufacturing industry operated at 92.3% of capacity, but by the third quarter of 1969, the peak quarter of the cycle, production was down to 86.9% of capacity, and for the depression year 1971, production fell to 74.4% of capacity, lower than for any earlier year since before World War II.[3]

Government Additions to Mass Consuming Power

The most rapidly expanding sector of the economy in recent decades was the government, whose outlays jumped from 12.0% of GNP in the 1946–48 cycle to 21.4% in the 1961–69 cycle. Most of that increase occurred during the Korean War, but it continued at a slower pace thereafter. The military spending share of the GNP actually reached its peak during the Korean War, but civilian government spending increased steadily after that war. Also, after 1953, there was a very rapid increase in government "transfer payments"—excluded from GNP statistics but taken into account in this chapter.

Changes in government spending have various effects, depending on the objectives of the spending, who gets the money, and who supplies it through taxes or loans. Special effects of changes in military spending are examined in Chapter XI. Here a particular question is examined: To what extent does the increased government share in the economy offset labor's declining relative share in the private sector by providing additions to mass consuming power?

Analysis shows that this effect has been significant but diminishing. Government expenditures go to workers as direct wage and salary payments to government employees; wage and salary payments by government contractors; and pensions, welfare payments and other "transfer payments." The combined total comes to about three-fourths of all government expenditures. But a significant part goes to capitalists, who serve as officials of government agencies and contractors, or as "transfer payments" through business subsidies and subsidies to capitalist farmers. The remaining total, actually going to workers, comes to about two-thirds of government expenditures. This share has remained fairly constant during the past quarter of a century. But the share of these expenditures ultimately paid for by workers has increased, from about one-half to more than two-thirds, over the same interval.

In essence, the working class as a whole, including government workers, is contributing through direct and indirect taxes all of the wages and salaries earned by government employees and workers for government contractors, as well as "transfer payments" received by workers.

Another way of looking at this is to say that the entire working class is contributing, so to speak, the labor of over 20 million employees of government agencies and contractors through extra surplus value extracted from them in the form of taxation.

This is the basic political-economic fact about the role of the government—an instrument for increasing the exploitation of labor on behalf of monopoly capital. One consequence of the increasing scale of this extra exploitation is the declining share of consumption in the national income (brought out earlier in this chapter).

It is necessary to stress this point, if only to counteract the stream of apologetic propaganda concerning the role of the government. The liberal version claims that the government acts as a syphon to redistribute income from the "haves" to the "have-nots." The crude reactionary version is that "people of substance" are being ruined by "welfare loafers." And the puerile ultra-left version claims that the masses are being "force-fed" by Establishment "consumerism."

Yet, despite their class bias, government budgets do buttress mass consumption. Here we subtract from the relevant government payments only the direct taxes, withheld mainly from workers' paychecks, and not the indirect taxes. The difference represents a *net primary* addition to mass consuming power through government activities.* Ultimately, the primary addition may be cancelled out through indirect taxation and monopoly price gouging. But the primary addition is important in providing a degree of relative stability to mass consumption, especially in countering its cyclical swings. To clarify these concepts, consider the data in Table IV-2, which covers state and local as well as federal governments.

Government wages and salaries and those of government contractors, together, came to $158.3 billions (lines 1 and 2). These workers were being exploited, like all others. Some were providing profits directly through their labor for private contractors. Those on government payrolls were being paid a wage in line with that offered for comparable work in private industry—a wage indicating a high rate of exploitation. That is, they were being paid far less than the values they would create in a commodity-producing industry. The situation becomes clear when government enterprises, like the post office or the arsenals, are transferred to private or quasi-private ownership. The conditions of the workers do not change appreciably, but their exploitation to produce profits for the new employer immediately becomes obvious.

An additional $61.6 billion was paid out as transfer payments. Transfer payments are those not given as compensation for current

TABLE IV-2. NET GOVERNMENT ADDITION TO MASS CONSUMING POWER, 1969
(billions of dollars)

1. Government wages and salaries	104.0
2. Wages and salaries of government contractors	54.3
3. Government transfer payments	61.6
4. Total government additions (1+2+3)	219.9
5. Direct taxes on workers	117.8
6. Net government addition to mass consuming power (4–5)	102.1
7. Consumer expenditures	577.5
8. Percent 6 of 7	17.7%

Sources: See Table IV-1.

*The indirect taxes which workers pay are included in prices, and hence in the consumer price index used to compute real wages. For purposes of analysis, we have already taken them out in the calculation of workers' changing share of production in Chapter III, and cannot subtract them again without double counting.

goods or services. Examples are pensions, public assistance, and government subsidies. For the pensioners, who receive the largest share, this may be regarded as part of the lifetime wages owed them by the capitalist class collectively and now paid as a result of the successful struggles for social insurance waged by the working class. But the success, of course, is qualified, in that the pensions are inadequate and the workers pay half the cost directly.

Total government additions to mass consuming power, the sum of the first three lines of Table IV-2, came to $219.9 billion. More than half was financed by $117.8 billion direct taxes collected from workers. An estimated $81.3 billion of that was paid by workers other than employees of governments or government contractors. For the workers paying this sum, the $81.3 billion was sheer loss, except for the relatively small social benefits they derive from certain types of government spending, and what they may hope to get back later through old-age pensions. On the whole, however, they are big losers. Government workers and those employed by government contractors lose that part of their wages that represents their share of the direct tax payments.

All this refers to the social significance of government activities. And, over the long run, the economic significance is related to this. It is part of the process that builds up the contradictions between expanding capacity and relatively stagnant mass consuming power. But, in the short run, the immediate economic significance is to add $102.1 billion to mass consuming power (line 6, Table IV-2). This accounts for 17.7% of all consumer expenditures (line 8).

If this ratio has a long-term upward trend, it tends to encourage economic growth. To the extent that it fluctuates in a contracyclical fashion, it tends to smooth out the business cycle as it dampens booms and makes crises and depressions shallower.

The detailed calculations presented in Appendix Table II show the net government addition to mass consuming power rising from $22.2 billion in 1946 to $102.1 billion in 1969. But the dollar value of the economy was also multiplying during that period. The economic effect is measured by the relationship of the net government addition to total consumer income or outlays. In 1946–48, the first postwar cycle, the net government addition amounted to 13.2% of consumer expenditures. This ratio jumped to 17.1% in 1949–53 (dominated by the Korean War and its rapid expansion of the armed forces and military procurement).

The ratio dropped slightly, to 16.6%, in the next cycle, 1954–57 but thereafter increased gradually, to 18.4%, in the latest cycle 1961–69 (Appendix Table II).

Thus, in the first eight years after World War II, the activities of the government did much to offset labor's declining share in the fruits of its production. In the past fifteen years the additional offset has been relatively small. But within each cycle, government spending continued to play a significant moderating role. This can be seen by looking at the figures for the ten-year period 1954–1963. In Table IV-3; recession or crisis years are underlined and indicated by the letter *D*.

In the recession year 1954, government spending less taxes made a direct addition to mass consuming power equal to 18.1% of consumer expenditures. By the boom year 1956, this ratio was down to 15.7%. It returned to 19.0% in the crisis year 1958, declined again to 16.6% in 1960, increased to 18.3% in the recession year 1961, and then turned downwards again.

The upward swings in this government addition to consuming power help to check the cumulative effects of a downturn. In the traditional "deflationary spiral," workers laid off in one industry are unable to buy goods, which leads to layoffs in other industries supplying these goods.

TABLE IV-3. CYCLICAL FLUCTUATIONS IN NET
GOVERNMENT ADDITIONS TO MASS
CONSUMING POWER, 1954–1963

	Net Government Addition to Mass Consuming Power as a Percentage of Consumer Expenditures
1954 D	*18.1*
1955	16.4
1956	15.7
1957	16.3
1958 D	*19.0*
1959	17.3
1960	16.6
1961 D	*18.3*
1962	18.1
1963	17.5

D Recession Years.
Source: See Appendix Table II.

When the loss of income due to layoffs is partly compensated by increased government salaries and benefit payments and by a slowdown in the increasing tax bite, recessions tend to be shallower and shorter in duration. On the other hand, when the net government addition stagnates or turns downward during an economic upswing, this tends to top off the boom and contributes to a fresh downturn.

The mechanism is largely automatic; hence the economists' term "automatic stabilizer". In a crisis or recession year there is a sharp increase in unemployment insurance payments, old-age pensions of workers who retire when they lose their jobs, and welfare payments. On the other hand, tax deductions from workers' paychecks increase at a slower rate than usual and sometimes even decline slightly, owing to corresponding slowdowns or declines in total payrolls.*

Often these automatic responses are reinforced by special policy measures—increases in certain types of government employment and the acceleration of government contract-letting. This is discussed further in Chapter 9.

In the crisis year 1958, for example, a sharp jump in "transfer payments" accounted for nearly half of a $9.8 billion increase in gross government additions to mass consuming power, while direct taxes on workers increased only $0.7 billion.

In boom years the mechanism goes into reverse. Unemployment insurance payments are cut. Retirement rates are slowed when jobs are plentiful. Sometimes government contracting is held down as a means of relieving the financial pressures that develop at the peak of a boom. Simultaneously, taxes on workers soar, in response to higher employment and wages.

In 1963, for example, gross government additions to mass consuming

---

*In the textbook explanations of "automatic stabilizers," it is said that people's taxes decline more rapidly than their incomes owing to the operation of personal exemptions and the graduated rate scale of the income tax. This does apply to capitalists with rapidly fluctuating incomes and to individual workers. But for the working class as a whole, this theoretical version is destroyed by the chronic inflation of present-day American capitalism. This often results in stable, or even slowly rising, money wages per worker, even while real wages are declining in a recession situation. At the same time, social insurance deductions rise relatively when individual workers' wages decline, and periodically, regardless of the cycle, in accordance with a schedule set by Congress.

power increased by only $6.3 billion, while direct taxes on workers increased $5.1 billion, or nearly as much. There was little change in the net addition to mass consuming power and hence very little additional support for the flood of additional goods coming onto the market at higher prices.

During the early part of a war, the net government addition to mass consuming power increases simultaneously with other influences making for boom conditions. This adds to wartime inflation and to the accumulation of contradictions making for later economic difficulties.

During the Kennedy-Johnson administration there was an increase in the government's net addition to mass consuming power during a non-war prosperity period. This continued as the administration escalated its involvement in Vietnam into a full-scale war (Table IV–4).

The increase in net government spending in 1964 resulted essentially from the attempt of the administration in power, and those sections of big business backing it, to speed up the economic growth rate and to prevent a new recession or crisis from breaking out. It was in accord with the new capitalist theory that it was possible to eliminate the business cycle through government fiscal and monetary manipulation.

This attempt had temporary success, but with the cumulative stimulus of the Vietnam War and under conditions of the rapidly rising exploitation of labor, the problems of mounting inflation and lagging mass consuming power finally got beyond the government's power to manipulate. In 1969, under pressure of the extreme inflation and

TABLE IV-4. GOVERNMENT NET ADDITIONS TO MASS CONSUMING POWER, 1963–1969

	Percent Net Government Addition to Mass Consuming Power
1963	17.5
1964	18.4
1965	18.0
1966	18.1
1967	19.9
1968	19.6
1969	17.7

Source: Appendix Table II.

financial stringency, the government sharply reduced its net addition to mass consuming power, thereby helping to precipitate the crisis of overproduction which had become inevitable.

In one year, the net government addition to mass consuming power dropped from 19.6% to 17.7%. This decline of less than 2% seems small, but it amounted to over $11 billion. By and large, such a reduction of income is absorbed mainly in the curtailment of purchases of cars, houses and other durable items that have maximum impact on basic industry.

Financial and Service Industries

Financial operations and services, along with the profits and wealth of powerful exploiting classes, are traditional areas of rapid expansion. By 1968, when wages and salaries paid in manufacturing reached 343% of the 1947 level, they were 495% of the 1947 level in finance and 485% of the 1947 level in services.[3]

Expansion of services is referred to by Establishment economists as a source of economic stability and a symptom of the increasing welfare of the masses. There are *elements* of truth in these claims but basically they are distortions. The principal content of increased financial and service activity has nothing to do with mass welfare. Under certain conditions, the limited contribution to economic stability is converted into its opposite.

Most of the increase in employment and payrolls in financial industries arises from the need to account for and handle the enormous and constantly growing sums passing through and into the hands of the very rich and their companies; to coordinate the increasingly complex transactions of monopoly-financial-industrial groups, and to handle the increasing volume of speculation in a decaying society. A rising proportion of financial employees handle the overseas transactions of the multinational corporations and banks.

Workers do use banks more than formerly, but mainly to pay tribute on installment loans and mortgages and to cash the checks now preferred by employers in meeting payrolls. But, far from being symptomatic of the increased well-being of the worker, the overwhelming bulk of financial activity continues to be for the capitalist class.

The most rapidly expanding service industries are those that cater to the business and personal interests of the wealthy and not those that provide for the needs of the masses. Between 1947 and 1968 wages and salaries in business services increased ten times—faster than any other sector. This includes advertising and other essentially parasitic activities. Wages and salaries for legal service increased more than six times. On the other hand, wages and salaries in personal services and in amusements and recreation, essentially mass services, increased only 2.7 times.

Other service areas with big increases in wages and salaries were medical, which increased by nine times, and educational, with a 7.7 times increase.[4] The increase in medical wages and salaries reflects the growing institutionalization of medicine, the significant wage gains won by medical workers, and the increase in the medical requirements of the population. Some gains in mass access to medicine are also reflected in this figure. In the case of education, there is a mixture of some real gains in mass access to higher education, accompanied by increased educational requirements, and the increased use of private schools by the rich and the racists seeking to avoid the deteriorating, nominally integrated, public schools, along with the failure of government agencies to provide enough of the rising educational needs.

Finance and service wages and salaries have provided a constantly higher proportion of mass consuming power throughout the postwar period. In 1946 such wages and salaries amounted to 10.0% of total consumption expenditures, but by 1969 the ratio advanced to 15.2%. The most rapid relative advance in such wages and salaries occurred during the late 1960s—from 13.7% of consumption expenditures in 1966 to 15.2% in 1969.[5]

A substantial portion of the wages and salaries in financial and service industries represents a transfer of surplus value by capitalists in general to workers in these industries. As this transfer increases, it offsets part of the declining share of workers in manufacturing and other commodity-producing industries. To this long-run effect has been added a mild contracyclical effect since World War II, because there has been a certain continuing increase in wages and salaries paid in these industries during each downturn. The very rapid increase in financial and service wages and salaries during the Vietnam War years has been a signal of the increased parasitism and waste of the culminating period of a long boom.

There was a previous rapid mushrooming of financial and service activity during the 1920s. But when the deep crisis of the 1930s hit, these industries contributed to the general deflationary spiral instead of checking it. Wages and salary payments declined 38% in four years. It is instructive to compare the situation in 1969 with that 40 years earlier.

In 1929 wages and salaries paid in the financial and service industries reached one-sixth, 16.7%, of all wages and salaries. The percentage declined during the 1930s. In 1946 financial and service wages and salaries were 12.9% of the total. The percentage gradually increased but did not reach the 1929 proportion until 1967. In 1969, at 17.3% of the total, it went well above the 1929 ratio.[6]

This might well be taken as a danger sign, a warning of potential crisis. Indeed, in 1970, as the economic crisis developed, there were widespread layoffs in certain of the financial and service industries, notably brokerage houses and advertising firms. There were also layoffs among the corporate white-collar bureaucracy, which plays a similar economic role to that of the financial and service industries. But, on the whole, wage and salary payments in these economic sectors continued to increase, thereby playing a stabilizing role, as in earlier postwar declines.

Consumer Credit

Installment credit has become a major institution in American life, with important effects on consumption patterns and a significant economic impact. Most consumers' durable goods are now purchased on installments. For example, 70% of all new cars are bought through installment loans roughly equal to the price of the average car. The ease of buying on installments has encouraged a relative growth in the purchase of durable goods as compared with nondurables.

Consumer credit is highly regarded by capitalist economists as a means of stimulating consumer purchasing and general economic activity. Regulations governing its use can be amended readily for contracyclical purposes; terms can be tightened up to dampen inflation, as during the Korean War, or loosened to help stop a recession.

The volume of consumer credit outstanding has expanded fantastically during the postwar period—from $8.4 billion in 1946 to $122.5 billion in 1969.[7]

Most of this is installment credit. The total of consumer credit is turned over—repaid and borrowed—more than once a year. The critical figure is the net change in the amount outstanding. In most postwar years, credit outstanding has increased by several billions, with a peak increase thus far of $10 billion in 1965.

This seems a painless and profitable way of overcoming capitalist contradictions. Since the workers do not get enough to buy the output of consumers' goods destined for mass consumption, just lend them the difference and make an extra profit through collection of interest and other charges. So the bankers and their apologetic economists think. Actually, consumer credit has stimulated economic growth during the postwar period, especially in the durable goods industries. *But that stimulus has now come to an end.* Meanwhile, in the mounting consumer debt, American capitalism has set one of its most dangerous fuses for a potential financial crisis.

The first flaw in the capitalist argument is its failure to consider the interest burden. Despite all the advertisements about "low interest rates," a National Bureau of Economic Research study has shown that actual rates in 1959 averaged 13.3% per annum, in addition to various extra charges.[8]

This figure comes from reports of the lending companies themselves and obviously excludes the very high rates charged by some types of lending companies. Moreover, with the soaring level of interest rates generally, the average rate has probably increased during the past decade.

During the first postwar decade, when the outstanding debt was relatively low but increasing very rapidly, extensions of credit exceeded interest charges on the old debts, providing a net addition to mass consuming power. But now, when heavy interest charges are levied on a huge backlog of consumer debt, the total of interest collected exceeds the net increase in outstanding debt.

During five years of the Vietnam War, 1965–1969, consumer credit outstanding increased by $42.2 billion. But interest payments on the debt amounted to $66.9 billion, or an additional $24.7 billion.[9]

The balance is at its worst in recession years, when there is little or no increase in consumer credit outstanding and the interest burden continues. This burden tends to deepen a recession and makes its reversal more difficult.

American financiers have a tiger by the tail in consumer credit. Any attempt to curtail it seriously would lead to a drastic reduction in effective mass consuming power during the curtailment, since over $10 billion in payments come due every month. In the absence of replacement loans, this would precipitate a major crisis in consumers goods industries. Even to hold the amount outstanding steady would cause the full $16 billion of annual interest charges to become a drain on mass buying power.

But to let consumer credit continue to grow, not only absolutely but in relation to consumer income, creates an increasingly speculative situation that can eventuate in a collapse. In 1947 consumers had to use 6% of their after-tax income to repay installment debts. By 1950 it was 9%, and by 1969, 15%, of their disposable income.[10] That is just for installment debt and omits the other types of consumer debt, as well as mortgage debt and the interest on the debt.

Since most capitalists do not carry relatively large debts of this type, the percentage for workers is much higher. Virtually as much as one dollar out of five in the workers' pay check must by now go to pay debts, and the proportion is rising continually!

But bankers make so much money out of the high interest on consumer loans that they have thrown their customary caution to the winds and they continue to push consumer credit under conditions of very tight money, even at a time when they restrict other types of credit.

The Federal Reserve Bank of Philadelphia spelled out a typical banker's approach:

There are reasons to believe that future increases in income may be associated with even larger proportionate increases in consumer credit . . . installment credit outstanding in the next five years could easily repeat the 50% growth of the past five. . . . The ingredients are there for a significant upswing in consumer credit, which could dispel even further the idea that some natural lid exists on consumer repayments as a per cent of disposable income.[11]

But this theory of never-ending expansion of the credit chain is just as fallible in relation to consumer credit as it is in relation to the entire credit structure. Sooner or later, the overextension of consumer credit is bound to reach a point where it must be relieved in some drastic fashion. And at least a start of this process is to be seen in the wave of defaults on payments, garnisheeing of workers' wages, and repossessions by credit companies that accompanied the 1969–70 crisis of overproduction. All sections of the capitalist class, the courts, and the police cooperate in using the defaults as a means of further robbery of the workers and of further profiteering.

General Motors Acceptance Corporation alone repossessed 138,000 cars in 1969. The rate increased sharply in 1970:

> The other night Rick Civerolo and Jan Fisher stole a couple of cars [thus begins the Wall Street Journal's account of this racket]. Mr. Civerolo's clients—banks, finance company, and auto dealers pay him $40 a car, plus expenses, to snatch anywhere from 60 to 100 cars a month from under the noses of sleeping owners who have fallen behind in their payments.

The companies force the worker to pay the costs as well as huge amounts of alleged losses on the repossession, while collaborating dealers, in turn, sell the cars at a big profit.[12]

Credit Cards

The most rapidly rising form of consumer credit is the bank credit card. Up to the late 1960s, credit cards were limited to the well-to-do and rich business men who paid a fee for the privilege of using Diners Club, American Express credit cards, and others. The main purpose of these was to have automatic records of expenses for tax deduction purposes.

But in the second half of the 1960s, the biggest banks started mass distribution of free credit cards to a widening range of consumers. Essentially, anyone with a department store charge account or a modest bank account can qualify for a credit card. Millions of them were issued without application to people on "credit-worthy" lists.

These provide for relatively speedy repayment, so they add little to mass consuming power, even in the short run. They carry an interest rate of $1^1/2\%$ per month on the unpaid balance and so subtract even more than bank installment loans from long-run consuming power.

They are also a source of big profits to the banks at the expense of the small trading establishments and worker-consumers, including those who do not have credit cards. The banks discount credit-card payments by $4^1/2\%$ in most cases. Thus the retail store or restaurant loses $4^1/2\%$ of its gross income and 10 to 20% of its total markup. Yet a widening range of retail establishments are forced to join credit card schemes in order to keep those of their customers who have them. Even army and navy stores, which cater mainly to working-class customers, often accept credit cards nowadays. The inevitable tendency is for the stores to strive to increase their retail markups so as to cover all or as much as possible of the 4$^{1}/_{2}$%. Competition prevents complete realization of this goal, but the tendency is in that direction, just as the use of trading stamps led to a corresponding increase in consumer prices.

A huge racket has developed in stolen credit cards. Shopkeepers keep big books of "hot card numbers," and check every purchase against them. Literally hundreds of thousands of numbers are listed in these books. Customers using credit cards to simplify life find themselves held up while the shopkeeper painfully checks through his small-print book of numbers to make sure they are not thieves. The shopkeeper is offered a reward of $25 for every "hot card" he recovers.

Home Mortgages

The granting of long-term mortgages for home purchase was an even more powerful stimulant than consumer credit during the postwar period, and it lasted longer. By 1960 a substantial majority of working-class families owned their own homes. Usually, however, the "ownership" was practically vested in the mortgage-holding bank, which collected effective rent in the guise of interest and amortization of the loan.

For the first decade after World War II, the outstanding total of mortgages on small non-farm homes doubled every five years, and thereafter the total continuted to increase at a more moderate, but still substantial, pace. By the end of 1969, the total of such mortgages outstanding came to $263 billion, equal to 14 times the amount outstanding at the end of World War II. However, the costs of such mortgages have rapidly increased. The effective rate on new homes increased from 6.23% in 1965 to 9.40% in March 1970.[13]

Owning one's home became a trap for millions of owners as real estate taxes soared. Pressed by the relative curtailment of federal aid during the Vietnam War, and controlled by industrial and commercial interests that were able to avoid increases in taxes, the local governments put much of the increased operating expenses onto the small home owners. Taxes on such properties were increasing on the average by 10% per year during the late sixties.

Meanwhile, the pace of new home building slackened. The interest and amortization charges on existing buildings, not to speak of the taxes, far exceeded the net addition to mortgage credit by the decade of the 1960s.

Again, the resolution of this contradiction was at the expense of hundreds of thousands of working-class families. The number of foreclosures increased from a low of 10,000 in 1946 to 44,000 in 1959 and 117,000 in 1966, declined about one-third in the 1967–69 boom years, then turned upward again in 1970–71.[14]

The soaring volume of mortgages has been financed mainly through the savings and loan associations and savings banks. These banks are affected by the withdrawal of funds by depositors seeking higher interest rates in other forms of investment. In the tight-money "crunch" of 1966, several of the savings and loan companies went under. They are very vulnerable to massive forced closings if large-scale withdrawals and a new wave of defaults on payments by borrowers should coincide. Thus the development of a crisis of overproduction, curtailing mass employment and income, could reinforce a financial crisis.

In the late 1960s and 1970, the government took unusual steps to revive the stimulation of mortgage-backed housing construction. It set up the Federal National Mortgage Association (Fannie May) as a semiprivate corporation with authority to borrow many billions yearly to be used in rediscounting mortgage loans of banks and savings-and-loan associations. Through the Federal Home Loan Banks, it made big loans to the savings and loans companies to increase their lending power. And, finally, in 1970, Congress passed a law permitting government subsidy of mortgage interest payments, so that total returns on mortgages could be increased and funds attracted into the home mortgage market.

These measures had considerable if temporary success but at the cost of diverting funds from elsewhere and increasing the tensions in other financial areas.

Conclusion

The offsets to increasing exploitation discussed in this chapter, taken together, have had a significant effect in moderating the business cycle during the postwar period. But their potential has been considerably reduced and in some cases their effect has even been reversed. Meanwhile, those contradictions which they had neutralized have become more severe. Thus greater instability, more severe crises have become likely.

V.

The Profit Cycle

THE LAW of the declining tendency of the rate of profit is a crucial element in Marx's economic theory. This law follows from the analysis of the source of profit—surplus value derived from the direct exploitation of labor. The *amount* of profit depends on the number of workers employed and the degree of exploitation of each worker.

But the *rate* of profit on invested capital is something else again. If the only capital needed were that used to pay wages, the rate of return would be fabulous. Thus, let us consider a rate of surplus value of 200%, approximating current American conditions. And suppose the capital used to pay wages is turned over three times a year, then the rate of profit would be 600%.

Actually, much more capital is needed to buy materials, and especially to set up plant and equipment, than to pay wages. This part of the capital does not yield a profit in itself. Profits were reaped in the production of materials but they went to the capitalist who controlled that production. Similarly, the profits made in the production of machinery were taken by the capitalist who controlled that production and included in the price paid by our capitalist, who, let us say, owns a shoe factory. Marx called the capital that does not yield the shoe capitalist any profit *constant capital*. He called the capital used to pay wages *variable capital*, because that is the part which yields a profit, and hence increases. And he called the ratio of constant capital to variable capital the *organic composition of capital*. It is easy to see that the higher the organic composition of capital, the lower the rate of profit—all other things being equal.

Suppose a capitalist installs $40 of machinery and uses $10 to hire workers, who add $20 of value—including $10 to repay their wages and $10 of surplus value. The rate of surplus value, as calculated by Marx, is 100% in this instance, since the amount of surplus value is equal to the wages. The total capital is $50; $40 worth of machinery plus $10 of money used to pay wages. The rate of profit is 20%: $10 on $50.

Now suppose the capitalist substitutes superior machinery that costs $90. He continues to use $10 to hire workers, who now add $25 of value. Now there is $15 of surplus value and a 150% rate of surplus value. But total capital is increased to $100, so the rate of profit is 15%. The workers are more exploited than ever but the capitalist complains of a profit squeeze!

And there is no way to avoid this by sticking to old methods and old types of equipment. The economic history of capitalism knows endless examples of firms that fell by the wayside because they feared the expense of modernization.

But the very process of technical progress makes it inevitable that each worker handle more and more machinery, more and more raw materials. In many modern process industries, vast factories with costly complexes of machinery, equipment, and instruments, are operated by a mere handful of workers. It is not uncommon in new modern factories for the fixed capital per worker to reach several hundred thousand dollars.

The capitalists themselves will never recognize this whole line of analysis; they stoutly deny that only the capital used to pay wages really yields a profit. To them it seems that profit derives from all of their capital equally. Despite this conviction, they feel the effects of the declining tendency of the rate of profit, and they engage in strenuous efforts to counteract it.

Marx lists a series of "counteracting causes":

Intensifying the exploitation of labor by increasing the working day and other means.

Cutting wages.

Cheapening the prices of raw materials and machinery used in production.

Creation of a surplus population of workers, employed in labor-intensive, high-profit rate luxury industries.

Superprofits from foreign trade.

Raising of capital by sale of stock to outside investors, paid relatively small dividends, so that the rate of profit realized by the controlling capitalists is increased.

Additional "counteracting causes" are applicable today, including raising monopoly prices, shifting the tax burden from capital to labor, increasing superprofits from foreign investments and military orders.

In the long run, however, these methods end up by further accelerating the substitution of machinery for labor, further increasing the organic composition of capital, and bringing to the fore the primary tendency of the falling rate of profit.

This law plays a major part in the evolution of the capitalist cycle. During each cycle, the rush to accumulate capital leads to a rather rapid rise in the organic composition of capital.

During the boom phase of the cycle, additional factors besides the changing organic composition of capital tend to restrict the rate of profit. This is the stage where unemployment is at a low point. Workers are able to win substantial wage increases. With job competition less acute, they may be able to work less intensely. Soaring interest rates reduce the share of surplus value left the industrial capitalist, cutting his rate of profit. And the "counteracting causes" to rising organic composition of capital are largely inoperative at this stage.

Sooner or later, these influences invariably outpace or even stop any further increase in the rate of surplus value, and lead to a fall in the rate of profit on the total capital. At some point it is no longer profitable to expand production, no longer possible to sell everything produced at a rate of profit considered satisfactory by the capitalist.

This contradiction develops side by side with the contradiction analyzed in Chapter II centering around the relative inadequacy of mass consuming power, and around financial contradictions that we will examine later. In the long run, they all combine to precipitate a crisis. Marx writes: "Alongside the fall in the rate of profit mass of capitals grows, and hand in hand with this there occurs a depreciation of the existing capitals, which checks this fall and gives an accelerating motion to the accumulation of capital-values."

Listing this along with other contradictions, he concludes: "These different influences may at one time operate predominantly side by side in space, and at another succeed each other in time. From time to time the conflict of antagonistic agencies finds vent in crises. . . . "[1]

American experience confirms that fluctuations in the rate of profit play an important switching role in the cyclical process. Corporation profits were established as a "leading indicator" in the elaborate statistical analysis of business cycles carried out by the National Bureau of Economic Research during the 1950s. Geoffrey Moore writes:

> Some six to twelve months before these peaks in business activity or in aggregate profits, the number of companies with rising profits begin to dwindle . . . the turns in the diffusion of profits have usually preceded the turns in other diffusion indexes, and have been closely associated with those in new orders for investment goods. Diffusion of profits, therefore, is a most significant "leading indicator."[2]

This may be expressed in somewhat simpler language. At a certain point in the cyclical boom period, profits of many corporations begin to decline. These corporations, at least, stop ordering or reduce their orders for new plant and equipment. This, in turn, contributes vitally to a general downturn in business activity. Thus, the downturn in profits of a number of corporations, even if the total of profits for all corporations continues to hold up, is the danger signal for a threatening crisis.

In Moore's analysis, the absolute total of profits for all corporations would continue to increase—but obviously more slowly than formerly—after the "diffusion index" shows the profits of many individual corporations beginning to decline. Moore did not consider the rate of profit on invested capital, but it is obvious that in a period when many corporations are still rapidly expanding, the total sum of invested capital is still rising. At some point, therefore, in the late stages of a boom, the *rate* of profit would turn downwards for all corporations taken together, even before the total sum of profits began to decline.

Moore's conclusions were based mainly on conditions before and during World War II. But by carrying the analysis forward to the present time, it becomes clear that typically it is not only the rate of profit but also the total amount of corporation profits that changes direction before the major turns in business activity as a whole.

This is shown in Table V–1.

In the period through the end of World War II, the turn in profits led the turn in total activity about half the time and coincided with it the rest of the time. Since World War II, the turn in profits led the turn in total activity eight out of nine times and at every peak. There were exceptionally long leads of profit over general activity at two of the post-war peaks. The first of these was due to the special conditions of the Korean War. The second, from the fourth quarter of 1955 to the third quarter of 1957, was due to the artificial prolongation of the boom

TABLE V-1. TROUGHS AND PEAKS IN BUSINESS ACTIVITY AND CORPORATION
PROFITS, 1921–1969
(by quarters)

	Troughs			Peaks	
Trough of Profits	*Trough of Activity*	*Lead of Profits (No. of Quarters)*	*Peak of Profits*	*Peak of Activity*	*Lead of Profits (No. of Quarters)*
(quarter & year)			*(quarter & year)*		
II/21	III/21	1	II/23	II/23	0
III/24	III/24	0	III/26	IV/26	1
IV/27	IV/27	0	III/29	III/29	0
III/32	I/33	2	IV/36	II/37	2
II/38	II/38	0	I/44	I/45	4
II/45	II/45	0	II/48	IV/48	2
II/49	IV/49	2	IV/50	III/53	11
IV/53	III/54	3	IV/55	III/57	7
I/58	II/58	1	II/59	II/60	4
I/61	I/61	0	I/69	III/69	2

Sources: Peaks and Troughs of Activity from U.S. Department of Commerce, *Business Cycle Developments,* July 1965, App. A., p. 67, and June 1970.

Peaks and Troughs of Profits from Moore, Ed., *Business Cycle Indicators* Vol. II, Table 9.1. p. 106, U.S. Dept. of Commerce, *Business Statistics,* 1969 Biennial Edition and *Survey of Current Business,* June, 1970.

as a result of the steel strike, and the closing of the Suez Canal in 1956.

Actually, conditions in the latest boom, caused by the Vietnam war, were not too different from those of the Korean War boom. While the peak in total corporation profits was reached in the third quarter of 1969, it was only by a small margin over profit totals reached in 1966. Owing to the rapid expansion of capital during this period, it is certain that the peak in the rate of profits was reached in 1966 or even in 1965.

An economic crisis is a time of rapid reduction of profits. But Marx saw that its *function* was to restore the rate of profit. This paradoxical result comes about by destroying part of the capital, enough so that even a reduced total profit represents a higher rate on the smaller capital values. How this loss of capital is distributed, writes Marx, is determined by a bitter competitive struggle among the capitalists. Some of the capital is destroyed simply by closing down entire factories. Another part is destroyed through nonreplacement of depreciated equipment. Finally, there is a radical reduction in the market values of inventories of materials.

In the crisis of 1970, the process of destruction of capital values was widespread. Headlines and newspaper accounts tell the story:

MORE METALWORKING FIRMS GO UNDER HAMMER IN '70.
The auctioneer's gavel is being heard with increasing frequency in the land these days . . . at a rate up to 25 per cent more than last year.
The reasons vary . . . liquidations of metalworking shops and plants that succumb to the rugged economic climate . . . lack of funds . . . inability to collect receivables . . . .[3]

VACATED PLANTS SYMBOLIZE AEROSPACE DECLINE
The aerospace industry here is shrinking physically, in order to bring bloated capacity more realistically in line with dwindling demand.
While layoffs have been news for well over a year, an equally dramatic development is the actual abandonment or termination of a number of plant facilities.[4]

Vigorous attempts are made to cut working capital used along with fixed capital:

SHARPENING THE AXE. Firms Step Up Efforts to Reduce Expenses, Revive Lagging Profits . . .
The economy moves range from minor efforts like handwritten executive memos to such major steps as closing down inefficient factories. The intensity of the drive reflects concern over profits. Some companies report that belt-tightening has already enabled them to improve profits.[5]

Rising bankruptcies and sharp declines in stock and bond prices wipe out billions in capital values as well as destroying physical capital.

The bankruptcy of the $7-billion Penn Central Railroad was preceded by an accelerated deterioration of equipment, tracks and other facilities that have led to costly wrecks as well as many other disastrous results.

The bankruptcy, forced radical retrenchment, and forced merger of scores of brokerage and investment houses led to the vacating of considerable office space and facilities as well as to the firing of thousands of employees.

Under the inflationary conditions of the Vietnam War, the sensitive prices of industrial raw materials continued to rise for a time even after general economic activity turned downwards. But the Labor Department index of industrial materials prices finally peaked out at 120 in February 1970, and by October was below 110.

The cutting of wages reduces the amount of variable capital and, even more important, helps to restore the rate of profit by raising the rate of surplus value. Direct wage-cutting is relatively rare in modern conditions of swift price inflation, but the same effect is obtained by simply holding nominal wage rates steady.

In 1970 the average hourly wage for 662,000 Southeastern textile workers was only $2.34. Writes the *Wall Street Journal*: "It isn't easy to attract competent career workers to textile jobs because the pay is low. . . . This summer the appeal of textile mill jobs diminished even further. For the first time in nine years the industry failed to grant what had become a traditional yearly pay raise."[6]

Note that the previous freezing of pay was in the crisis year 1961. However, the rate of increase in consumer prices was several times faster in 1970, so the cut in real wages was sharper.

The textile workers are mainly unorganized and do not have union recognition. But even some groups of organized workers are persuaded to forgo wage increases, or even to accept wage cuts, on company threats to close down plants if they refuse.

Always a prominent part of crisis cost-cutting is the mass layoff of production workers, combined with the speeding up of the rest. In 1969–70 this was especially significant in the munitions industries, where cost-plus arrangements had permitted a profitable buildup of employment without regard to ordinary considerations of efficiency. Thousands of workers had been "hoarded" to be available for expected still larger contracts in the future—contracts that in most cases never materialized.

In addition to the firing of production workers, the 1969–70 crisis saw the laying-off to an unusual degree of salaried employees and executives, and the cutting of expense accounts, advertising budgets, etc.

During the long boom of the 1960s, the buildup of a parasitic corporate bureaucracy had surpassed the previous peak of the 1920s. This bureaucracy, especially the top executives, took over an increasing proportion of the total surplus value in the form of salaries, bonuses, pension schemes, stock options, open-end expense accounts, patronage to allied advertisers, lawyers, bankers, suppliers.

This has become an increasingly important share of the total surplus value—an addition to the traditional forms of the profits of enterprise (dividends and undistributed profits) interest, and rent. Under crisis conditions, however, the competition for a share of the profits between the top corporate bureaucracy and the large stockholders—to the extent that they do not overlap—becomes acute.

The bureaucracy is forced to give up part of its share in order to restore ultimately the rate of profit for the stockholders. This process was intensified in 1970, owing to the liquidity crisis of many corporations. It became necessary in such cases to radically reduce the payoffs to the top corporate brass and to slash clerical and research staffs in order to survive.

Both sides of this process were referred to by Federal Reserve Board Chairman Arthur F. Burns in discussing the 1970 crisis. He attributed the declining trend in the rate of profit during the years 1966–70 to the rise of interest costs "to astonishing levels," to the lack of serious effort "to bring operating costs under control . . . labor-hoarding . . . on a large scale, huge wage increases . . . granted with little resistance, and rash business investments." He referred to "the toll in economic efficiency taken by these loose managerial practices."

Burns rejoiced, however, that the slump was

now forcing business firms to mend their ways . . . . Business attitudes toward cost controls have of late changed dramatically. A cost-cutting process that is more widespread and more intense than at any time in the postwar period is now under way in the business world. Advertising expenditures are being curtailed, unprofitable lines of production critically reappraised. Layers of superfluous executive and supervisory personnel that were built up over a long period of lax managerial practices are being eliminated. . . . Indeed, employment of so-called nonproduction workers in manufacturing has shown a decline since March that is unparalleled in the postwar period.[7]

One aspect of this is especially relevant to the class struggle in the present period. From Burns' words it is clear that while the rate of profit accruing to stockholders' capital was declining for several years, there may well have been a continuing rise in the full rate of profit, expressed as the percentage of total surplus value to total capital. But more and more of the surplus value was going to bankers and bondholders, or was siphoned off by the corporate insiders and the bureaucracy, advertising firms, and other parasitic layers.

The depressing effect on economic activity of a decline in return to stockholders may be decisive, even if the real rate of profit—distributed among all groups of exploiters and parasites—continues to rise; even if the rate of exploitation of labor continues to increase.

Deliberately confusing the issue, however, the government sets up productivity and labor-cost indexes combining the productive workers with the executives, officials and bureaucratic layers. The very expansion of the share of surplus value going to these groups is used to claim a decline in labor productivity and an increase in labor costs per unit, and to justify a demand for the speeding up of work and cutting of real wages of the productive workers.

Indeed, Burns, in the very same speech, does just that. He refers to a decline in productivity growth to 2% in 1967 and its termination from mid-1968 to early 1970—just after pointing out the causes of this seeming decline, not in the productivity of the workers, but in the swelling of the bureaucratic and parasitic superstructure. He then expresses pleasure at the recovery of the rate of productivity gain to 5% following the curtailment of that superstructure as a result of the economic slump. Of course, this one factor would not bring about so much of a rise in productivity so quickly but it would contribute significantly.

This question is of quite practical importance. The government and the big corporations try to limit wage increases in relation to such synthetic "productivity indexes" and "labor cost indexes," which lump together workers and their wages with capitalists, their functionaries, and part of the surplus value they extract from the workers. Obviously, those workers who wish to uphold their class interests cannot accept statistics rigged against them in this way.

The role of profits in the business cycle and the determination of big business to restore the rate of profits in a cycle are expressed with brutal frankness in Gilbert Burck's lead article in the August 1970 *Fortune.*

During the past few years business hasn't been earning enough profit to do justice either to itself or to the public interest. This year corporate profits after taxes will be down about 12 per cent . . .

Profits are the driving force in the complex interplay of capital supply, interest rates, liquidity, employment, and securities prices. When profits are ample, expanding . . . both long- and short-term capital tends to be plentiful. . . . Anticipating still better business, corporations enlarge their operations and hire more people. . . . But when earnings begin to decline and their quality begins to deteriorate, this whole elegant process reverses itself. It is such a reversal, exacerbated by the government's anti-inflation policies that bedevils business today. . . .

How fast the economy itself recovers depends on how fast profits recover. . . . Once business has achieved something approaching normal profitability, however, it will still find its legitimate drive for profits hobbled.

Burck claims that owing to inflation profits are "overstated and overtaxed." He also claims ordinary profits will be insufficient, because "the demand for capital . . . will be staggering" in addition to the normal demand, which in itself "will be 'enormous'"; and "industry is under sudden compulsion to put in antipollution facilities whose cost will probably run into dozens of billions."

Where is the money to come from?

In part, says Burck, by cutting taxes on corporations through more depreciation allowances, and, even more hopefully, by substituting a value added tax for the corporation tax—that is, in effect, substituting a vast federal sales tax for the corporation income tax. But no matter how—so long as it was at the expense of the working people: "Any way you look at it, the country's enormous capital needs will have to be raised at the relative expense of consumption. . . . If business is going to raise all the money it needs to serve the public interest adequately, it has got to be more profitable—and profit-minded—than ever."[8]

This reveals with unusual bluntness the correctness of the charge leveled by the Communists in earlier crises—that big business was trying to climb out of the crisis on the backs of the working class. And whenever the workers refuse to take this lying down—and usually they do refuse—the result is a sharpening of class struggle.

One may agree with Burck that the "normal, healthy" way to restore the profits and prosperity of the capitalist class is at the expense of the working class and working people generally. But this way is most unhealthy for its victims, the vast majority. They strive to find ways of relieving their own crisis miseries, of improving their own conditions. Such ways can be found. Inevitably, if they are to have any lasting success, they must contradict the capitalist drive for profits, they must prevent the capitalist way out of the crisis.

It is true that any solution that decisively benefits the workers will be "unhealthy" for the capitalists, will deepen the general crisis of the system, will not restore "profitability," as Burck demands, and will give rise to even more intractable problems within the capitalist framework.

That will demonstrate, on a new level, the bankruptcy of capitalism and the need to replace it with socialism. But so, for that matter, does the very fact of crises prove this—with all the suffering they entail.

VI.

Financial Contradictions

HISTORICALLY, SEVERE economic crises in the United States have begun as financial crises, breaks in the money and credit system, massive bankruptcies, and stock market collapses. During the first two decades after World War II, crises did not extend to the financial sphere, except in marginal ways—an important reason why they were mild.

Indeed, rapid extension of the financial structure and the more flexible use of credits were the major levers for recovering from recession and for economic growth. But this very process meant a rapid accumulation of contradictions in the financial sphere—parallel to and, in some respects, more dangerous than, the corresponding contradictions in the area of production.

Marx analyzed in detail the use of credit accompanying the industrial cycle. In the wake of a crisis, when activity is low, money capital is plentiful and interest rates are very low. As economic recovery begins, money capital remains plentiful, interest rates remain low, and borrowing increases. Gradually interest rates increase and borrowing reaches a peak, mainly for the expansion of fixed capital. At the peak of the boom and the onset of a crisis, interest rates peak out, there is a surplus of commodities and a lack of money to borrow to carry them.

Marx finds a contradiction between money as a measure of value, a circulating medium, and money as a universal commodity, as the independent form of existence of exchange value. So long as everything runs smoothly, the first named is all that is noticed; the contradiction isn't apparent. But in difficult times, when money is "hard to come by," the situation changes. He writes:

> This contradiction comes to a head in those phases of industrial and commercial crises which are known as monetary crises. Such a crises occurs

only where the ever-lengthening chain of payments, and an artificial system of settling them, has been fully developed. Whenever there is a general and extensive disturbance of this mechanism, no matter what its cause, money becomes suddenly and immediately transformed, from its merely ideal shape of money of account, into hard cash. Profane commodities can no longer replace it. The use-value of commodities becomes valueless, and their value vanishes in the presence of its own independent form. On the eve of the crisis, the bourgeois, with the self-sufficiency that springs from intoxicating prosperity, declares money to be a vain imagination. Commodities alone are money. But now the cry is everywhere: money alone is a commodity! As the hart pants after fresh water, so pants his soul after money, the only wealth.[1]

And again:

During the crisis, forced cuts in prices and delays in selling goods . . . paralyze the function of money as a medium of payment, whose development is geared to the development of capital and is based on those presupposed price relations. The chain of payment obligations due at specific dates is broken in a hundred places. The confusion is augmented by the attendant collapse of the credit system, which develops simultaneously with capital, and leads to violent and acute crises, to sudden and forcible depreciations, to the actual stagnation and disruption of the process of reproduction, and thus to a real falling off in reproduction. [2]*

Strains in the Credit System

Unlike previous postwar crises, the crisis of 1969–70 was both financial and industrial. Conditions for a crisis had developed to an extreme degree before it erupted. There were some warning voices, but, characteristically, the capitalists as a whole, even their most prominent leaders and economists, assumed that these processes could go on forever without causing a crisis.

Traditionally, the growth of credit in boom times results primarily from the soaring demand on the part of capitalists for money capital with which to finance expanded activities. During the 1920s, a major new source of demand, consumer credit, was added. As noted in Chapter IV, it has been an outstanding method for temporarily papering

---

*Marx uses the term *reproduction* to represent the cycle of production following a primary cycle in which events occur determining the character of the next cycle. This is to project scientifically the dynamic, ever-changing character of capitalist production. Thus he often uses the term *reproduction* in senses that would customarily be referred to today by the simple term *production*.

over the difficulties of realization that arise out of the central contradiction between expanding production and relatively stagnant mass consuming power. An unprecedented burst of speculative activity in real estate and stocks gave rise to another multibillion-dollar source of demand for credit. These forms became still more prominent after World War II. There was also a major increase at that time in the demand for credit for governments on the federal as well as the state and local levels. Of course, the biggest surge in government borrowing was during World Wars I and II. But after World War I, federal debt tapered off, at least until the crisis of the 1930s; whereas after World War II, following a brief period of relaxation, the curve of federal borrowing turned upwards again, accompanied by accelerated borrowing by state and local governments.

Thus the strains on the credit/monetary system were accumulating from more directions and, as we shall see, to a greater degree than ever before. Further complicating the picture, there was a broadening outflow of capital to foreign shores for the purpose of seeking higher profit rates and simultaneously reducing the supply of domestic capital.

Why was it that the process could go further and last longer than before and still not precipitate a crisis? Certainly, in large part, the answer lies in the increased concentration of financial power in a handful of big money market banks and the Federal Reserve System, in the consequent ability to manipulate reserves flexibly to shore up weak spots, in the elaborate network of government institutions and systems of guarantees designed to avoid crises of confidence and back up the private financial institutions, and in government cooperation with the banking monopoly in budgetary and tax measures.

The institutions and mechanisms of state monopoly capitalism are potent but not omnipotent. Their successes were always at the expense of deepening underlying contradictions, of further complicating later regulation. Thus the problem of straightening matters out when the financial crisis finally appeared became all the more difficult, costly, and time-consuming.

An absolute growth of debt is not necessarily a source of financial strain, so long as it does not exceed the growth of real production. The makings of a financial crisis consist of the growth of debt far in excess of the growth of production.

Such was the case during the decade of the 1920s. In 1920, the cyclical peak year after World War I, the country's net debts reached

$135.7 billion, which equaled 172% of that year's national income. But by 1929, the peak year of the next major cycle, net debts had grown to $191.9 billion, 219% of the moderately higher national income of 1929.[3] Thus the relative net debt burden increased from 172% to 219%. This rapid rise contributed decisively towards setting the stage for the Great Crisis of 1929–1933.

Usually the burden of debts becomes heavier when commodity production and prices decline. Assuming that the total amount of debts remains unchanged, the values produced, from which these debts and the interest thereon must be paid, are curtailed. On the other hand, rising production and especially rapid price inflation, lightens the debt burden. In effect, a given increase in the price level means a corresponding decline in the real cost of servicing outstanding debts.

With that in mind, consider Table VI-1, comparing gross public and private debts in cyclical peak years over the past four decades. It shows the increasing debt burden during the depressed 1930s. Massive bankruptcies and foreclosures wiped out billions of debts. But the decline in current values and incomes was sharper, so that the relative weight of the remaining debts became heavier.

The U.S. financed World War II through huge budget deficits and a corresponding rise in the national debt. By 1948 gross debts were nearly $2^1/_2$ times the 1937 level.

But the war also resulted in an increase in the scale of U.S. production to a new plane, and in a near doubling of prices. Thus the money expression of the national income tripled, exceeding the growth in debts. By 1948 the Korean War inflation kept the relative debt burden at this reduced ratio, despite further sharp rises in indebtedness.

Since 1958, however, the relative debt ratio has moved upwards in every cycle. Particularly noteworthy is the continued rise in the relative debt burden during the Vietnam War, despite its inflationary character. This reflects the extraordinary degree to which the credit mechanism was extending during the 1960s. By the end of 1969, the ratio of gross debt to national income was noticeably higher than in 1929. The financial tensions had become as severe as those that contributed so much to the crisis beginning in 1929.

When debts are compared with commodity production, rather than with national income as a whole, the growth in the ratio is more

TABLE VI-1. GROSS DEBT,* NATIONAL INCOME, AND COMMODITY PRODUCTION
CYCLICAL PEAK YEARS, 1929–1969
(billions of dollars)

	Gross Debt	National Income	Percent Gross Debt of National Income	Net Commodity Production	Percent Gross Debt of Commodity Production
1929	215.2	86.8	248	44.5	484
1937	204.0	73.6	277	37.4	545
1948	493.4	224.2	220	121.1	407
1953	667.1	304.7	219	159.8	417
1957	836.1	366.1	228	182.0	459
1960	995.2	414.5	240	196.3	507
1969	1,963.7	763.7	257	337.1	583

Sources: Gross Public and Private Debt: *Survey of Current Business* May 1969, Table 2, p. 11; June 1972, p. 20.

National Income and Commodity Production, *National Income and Product Accounts,* Table 1. 11. Commodity Production is taken as equal to the sum of national income produced in agriculture, forestry and fisheries; mining; construction; manufacturing; transportation; electric, gas, and sanitary services.

*The Commerce Department publishes estimates of gross debt and of net debt. There is little difference in long-term trend between the two. On the whole, the writer considers the gross debts a more significant measure. Data on gross debts are not available for years prior to 1929.

dramatic. The non-commodity sectors of the economy, especially finance, services, and government, are peculiarly dependent on debt creation. One may say that these secondary sectors of the economy are in large measure the economic expressions of debt creation. But, in the last analysis, the whole structure of debt must be supported out of production of basic values, i.e., commodities.

In 1929 the gross debts of the country were 484% of the value of commodity production. By 1969 they had reached 583% of the value of commodity production. This means that the financial resources of the U.S. economy are employed today under very high pressure, un-precedented in the financial history of this country—a pressure which contributes strongly to economic instability, and which may prove as stubborn, as difficult to relieve, as any of those which held back the U.S. economy throughout the decade of the 1930s.

The combined total of private and public debts related to the country's total economic potential is the decisive figure. All borrowings draw on a more or less common pool of savings, and the degree of tension in the financial system depends on the total scale of drawings from that pool, rather than the drawings of any particular type of credit.

Nevertheless, it is pertinent to examine the course of particular types of debt, as shown in Table VI-2.

Corporation debts got way out of line during the 1920s, increasing by well over 50%, while the net value of their business increased only about 10%. In 1929 the ratio of corporate debt to corporate national income was 233%. But two decades later, in 1948, there was only a moderate debt, while corporate national income tripled. The result was that corporate debt had fallen to 113% of its national income. Thereafter the rise was rapid—corporate debts multiplied six times in the next two decades, far outstripping the gain in corporate national income. By 1960 the ratio of debt to income was 154%, and by 1969 it was 201%. This was still below the 1929 ratio, but the difference was more apparent than real.

By the late 1960s over $50 billion of corporate real estate was rented

TABLE VI-2. GROSS DEBTS AND RELEVANT INCOME RATIOS
ECONOMIC SECTORS, 1929, 1948, 1960, 1969
Billions of Dollars

	Corporate		Consumer		Home Mortgage		Government	
	Amt.	% of Corp. Natl. Income	Amt.	Pct. of Disposable Income	Amt.	Pct. of Disposable Income	Amt.	Pct. of Govt. Receipts
1929	107.0	233	7.1	9	18.0	22	35.3	312
1948	138.8	113	14.4	8	32.0	17	274.0	465
1960	361.6	154	56.1	16	137.4	39	372.1	266
1969	858.0	201	122.5	19	262.4	41	548.5	186

Source: Debts, as in Table VI-1. Other items from National Income and Product Accounts: Corporate National Income, Table 1.13. Disposable Personal Income, Table 2.1; Government Receipts, Tables 3.1 and 3.3. Federal grants-in-aid subtracted from state and local receipts to avoid duplication. Consumer debt includes installment, charge account, and all other non-mortgage debt.

through special leases that were substitutes for mortgages. The arrangement was made for tax reasons. Often the real mortgage was in the form of a municipal industrial development bond—which appears in the statistics as a part of government debt. But the real debtor was the using corporation.

Again, corporations in the munitions industries operated with large quantities of government fixed and circulating capital, which would not appear as a debt of the corporations but would be reflected in the total federal debt.

In 1929 less than half of all corporate debt was short-term, but in 1969 well over half was short-term and hence repayment requirements were relatively greater.

Last, but not least, interest rates by the late 1960s were at an all-time high. Undoubtedly the interest burden on corporations in 1969—and even more in 1970—was higher relative to income than in 1929. According to the Commerce Department tabulations, monetary interest paid by business in 1969 amounted to $82.8 billion, or 13.1%, of business national income, as compared with interest payments of $9.8 billion in 1929, or 12.4%, of business national income at that time.[4]

The rise in the relative burden of consumer debt, including mortgage debt, was discussed in Chapter IV. Note from the table that the burden of each by 1969 was about twice as heavy as in 1929. Most of the increase took place in the period up to 1960, but the ratio continued to increase gradually thereafter.

Owing mainly to World War II deficits, government debts increased nearly eight times between 1929 and 1949, by which time they amounted to well over half of all debts outstanding. Despite the permanent surge in government spending and taxes, government debts in 1948 were a higher percentage of receipts than was the case in 1929. The burden, however, was not serious in 1948 because of the very low interest rate prevailing. During the years since 1948, government debt has increased more slowly than any other major kind of debt, while government spending continued to rise rather rapidly. Thus, by 1969, government debts amounted to 184% of government receipts—a markedly lower ratio than that which prevailed in 1929.

But their burden to the public, that is, the size of the taxes that had to be collected to pay off the debts and interest on them, was a larger percentage of the people's income in 1969 than in 1929.

In every major area, the real burden of debt and interest reached a peak by 1969.

The debt-national income ratio has its own contracyclical movement. It increases during the downturn in the cycle and decreases during the upturn. The increase in the debt-national income ratio is particularly sharp in the early stages of a downturn, before most capitalists realize it has begun, when fresh debts are being incurred on a large scale. This was one of the factors that made the resolution of the 1929–32 crisis so difficult and prolonged. Beyond a certain point, the massive debt pile-up has to be cut down either through wholesale failures, or through monetary inflation that reduces their value.

Finally, both of these courses were adopted during the 1930s —adopted by the financial oligarchy and the government. The dominant bankers forced the liquidation of thousands of weaker rival banks so as to concentrate the country's wealth more completely in their own hands—besides foreclosing or driving into bankruptcy millions of private homeowners and small businessmen. The Roosevelt Administration devalued the dollar in order to induce an increase in prices and thereby liven up the economy somewhat.

Since World War II, a gradual price rise, combined with rapid government stimulation of a fresh upturn during each economic decline, has kept the cyclical rise in the debt-national income ratio within bounds. This was facilitated by the low relative indebtedness with which the United States emerged from World War II—an advantage that has gradually been spent and is now completely exhausted.

There is particular significance in examining the year-by-year course of debt ratios during the last (1960–69) cycle.

As usual, the debt/national income ratio increased sharply in the recession year 1961. There was no fresh decline, however, in the ensuing revival, since borrowing rapidly increased throughout the economy. By 1963–64 the debt/national income level was slightly above the 1929 level.

The radical escalation of the Vietnam intervention into a full-scale war in 1965, starting from a more dangerous degree of financial strain than the previous one, put off the danger of a new recession.

The experiences of World War II, the Korean War, and the Vietnam War demonstrate that a war economy has a particular effect on debt ratios. At first, wartime inflation reduces the debt/income ratio. The rise in prices causes a fall in the relative weight of all existing debts and

TABLE VI-3. GROSS DEBT/NATIONAL INCOME AND
GROSS DEBT/COMMODITY PRODUCTION
RATIOS, 1960–1969

	Gross Debt (billions)	Percent Gross Debt of National Income	Percent Gross Debt of Commodity Production
1960	995.2	240	507
1961	1,056.9	247	534
1962	1,128.1	246	530
1963	1,209.7	251	543
1964	1,300.0	251	547
1965	1,401.8	248	532
1966	1,517.0	244	524
1967	1,636.3	250	556
1968	1,796.3	253	565
1969	1,963.7	257	583

Sources: Same as Table VI-1.

a relative rise in the share of income going to capitalists. Simultaneously, anticipation of wartime orders causes a sharp spurt in private business activity and consequently in the national income over and above that consisting of price increases. Because of the extraordinary profits, the capitalists do not have to borrow as much, proportionately to the expansion taking place, as in other periods. The government, meanwhile, benefits from higher tax receipts, while its outpayments on account of military orders will mount at a later date.

In the later stages of the war, when deliveries of military products reach a peak far above tax receipts, the government debt rises correspondingly. Private activity ceases to grow, or it grows slowly, but with the early spurt at an end private borrowing increases. Thus the tendency is for a restoration by the end of the war of the debt/national income ratio in effect at the beginning—although at much higher dollar values for both debt and national income.

On the basis of this general analysis, an article written in February 1966 predicted:

The accumulated dangers of an overextended credit system will not put the economy to the test until the war in Southeast Asia draws to a close—insofar as we are concerned with the possibility of a crisis of overproduction associated with a financial crisis. But the rise in debts during the war, even if it is not as rapid as the rise in the gross national product, will be quite rapid absolutely and will be one of the ingredients of the inflationary fuel. This, in turn, will make it more difficult for the capitalists, even with the use of the most developed means of government intervention, to avert a recession at the end of the war, such as that which occurred in 1954 after the Korean War.[5]

Events followed this course through the first two years of the escalated Vietnam War, 1965–66. The debt/national income ratio declined, and the debt/commodity production ratio declined sharply in those years. But this war has dragged on longer than previous wars and has not represented so sharp an increase over previous levels of military spending. By 1967 its stimulating economic effect was largely exhausted. The buildup of debt accelerated in 1968–69 and with it the pace of price inflation. By 1969 the debt/national income ratio was well above the 1963–64 level and the debt/commodity production ratio was far above it.

Conditions for a financial and industrial crisis had fully ripened, even while the war still continued, although its economic effect was diminishing.

Declining Corporate Liquidity

Each capitalist strives to take advantage of a boom for maximum expansion. The longer the boom lasts, the fiercer the rivalry becomes. The scale of expansion for a single giant corporation has become enormous. It is not unusual for a score or more of major new construction projects in a dozen countries to be under way simultaneously. Those corporations which fail to keep up with the rate of expansion soon drop to second rank and become ripe for picking up by a stronger concern.

During the Vietnam War phase of the boom of the 1960s, the pace of fixed capital investment by U.S. corporations reached the highest sustained peak rate ever—in relation to the total scale of economic activity. This was described in Chapter IV solely on the basis of domestic fixed capital spending. At the same time, foreign fixed capital spending by U.S. corporations increased even faster.

Along with actual physical expansion, the long economic uptrend led to a merger boom. Expansion by acquisition is swifter than expansion by construction. The merger boom of the late 1960s reached an explosive pace, far outstripping anything previously seen. A whole series of new multibillion-dollar conglomerates arose, generally spawned out of armament profits. Simultaneously, the older corporate giants stepped up their pace of acquisitions and also diversified into wholly unrelated fields. The drive for expansion leads to putting every available cent into "growth." The modern variations on the cry of Marx's capitalist, "Only commodities are money," have become, "Only growth stocks are money," and, if he is powerful enough, "Only the control-block of shares in a company is money," for the latter is where the real superprofits, the huge hidden profits derived from corporate control are to be found.

Reserves of cash for a rainy day are spurned. More and more is borrowed and put to work immediately. Stock issues are floated to raise more capital; dividend payments are raised faster than profits in order to increase the prices of company shares and make it easier to sell more stock.

This reduces the share of profits available for investment and accelerates the requirement for outside capital. The escalated price inflation of the Vietnam War added another factor during the late 1960s. The cost of expansion increased without a corresponding increase in depreciation set-asides. Thus the requiremant for outside capital and its drain on remaining cash reserves accelerated both absolutely and in relation to the rate of real expansion in fixed capital.

With the surge in borrowing, interest rates rise, drawing in the market not only cash reserves of individual small capitalists and middle-class people, but also the reserves of those corporations which retain a liquid position. In the late 1920s, money poured into the call-money market, where stock market speculation pushed interest rates up to above 10%. In the late 1960s, there were similar flows of corporate funds, first into long-term certificates of deposit in banks, then into the Eurodollar market, and finally into the so-called commercial paper market. This last, representing short-term unsecured loans by one corporation to another, soared highest of all, to a total of about $40 billion early in 1970.

All this led to an unprecedented reduction in corporate "liquidity." A more-or-less standard measure of liquidity is the ratio of cash and government securities to current liabilities—payments due within a year or less and usually within a much shorter period. A "liquidity ratio" of

50% is regarded as ample. Here is how the ratio changed for all nonfinancial corporations during the postwar period.

The liquidity ratio of nonfinancial corporations changed as follows during the postwar period: 1945, 93%; 1950, 60%; 1955, 48%; 1960, 36%; 1964, 33%; 1969, 19%.[6]

Corporations emerged from World War II in an unusually liquid condition. By 1955, liquidity was down to a more or less normal ratio. By the early 1960s, liquidity was already low. Exactly comparable figures are not available, but apparently the ratio in that period was not too different from that which prevailed in the late 1920s and led up to the crisis that erupted in 1929.

During the Vietnam War years, however, the liquidity ratio has fallen very rapidly to an all-time low of 19% at the end of 1969, and to still lower ratios in 1970.

Simultaneously, the working capital of corporations, defined as the excess of current assets over current liabilities, declined—relative to the total scale of operations. Normally a working capital ratio of at least two-to-one is regarded as required for financial security. By the end of 1969, the *average* for all nonfinancial corporations was down to 1.64. For many individual corporations, current liabilities *exceeded* current assets, which is normally regarded as a key symptom of insolvency. The Penn Central, the country's largest railroad, on this basis was continually insolvent, from the moment of the merger of its two big component railroads until the formal bankruptcy in 1970.

Major airlines and munitions companies had substantial excesses of current liabilities over current assets. LTV Corporation, a multibillion-dollar conglomerate thrown together by Texas promotor James Ling, had debt, long- and short-term, exceeding its total assets.

So long as the volume of business continued to expand, this received little notice except from a minority of the more conservative bankers. Indeed, so long as the general volume of business continued to expand, it was generally possible for most companies to keep a step ahead of the bill collector. But the moment business stopped increasing and a downturn set in, the crisis in payments became inevitable. The *New York Times* financial commentators put it thus:

In Wall Street these days, the old-timers are worried. The unrelenting pressure of the worst bear market since the Depression has already driven a number of financial houses to the wall, and the Street is full of talk that other, far more serious problems are lurking just beneath the surface. . . .

Put bluntly, responsible analysts are beginning to ask whether there is a danger of a "liquidity crisis," perhaps even approaching the magnitude of those that periodically sent business through the wringer in the latter part of the 19th century.

They also quoted Tilford C. Gaines, Vice President and Economist of the Manufacturers' Hanover Trust, as saying:

It is obvious to anyone close to business finance that corporate liquidity, however, defined, is more seriously strained than at any other time since the second World War.

Short-term liabilities of business have skyrocketed in recent years while quick cash assets have been steady to declining. A similar process has been occurring in the banking industry, where increasing recourse has been made to highly liquid short-term liabilities to support increasingly illiquid assets.

In a disturbingly large number of companies in many industries, Gaines went on,

. . . survival questions have arisen. In most cases, these questions have related not to the fundamental long-term soundness of the company but rather to its short-term ability to service short-term debt, that is, its cash flow. . . . It might be an overstatement to refer to the present liquidity situation as a "crisis". . . . But if it is not a crisis, it is as close to one as any of us except our elderly colleagues are able to remember from personal experience.[7]

These remarks were made by Gaines in a speech at the end of April 1970. Two months later, he expressed the view that it would take five years to overcome the problem of illiquidity. He feared that banks would have to nurse corporations along while they gradually converted their short-term debts into long-term capital: "It's impossible to have a judgment on how long it would be necessary to walk this fine line before we get back to shore, but five years would have to be the minimum guess as to how long it might take to fund short debt and rebuild adequate capital."[8]

The implications are that for years to come corporations would be taxing the long-time bond market to the utmost in order to get more time to pay their debts. This would keep interest rates near their peaks and would leave little capital available for expansion.

There remained the Pollyannas, more concerned with trying to stave off alarm than with soundly analyzing the situation. Thus the First

National City Bank dismissed concern over liquidity as a "liquidity flap":

> . . . fears about the threat of a full-fledged liquidity crisis are likely to prove exaggerated. There are growing signs that corporations, in responding to the deep profit squeeze, are similarly working toward a more comfortable financial position. . . . It is conceivable that the current liquidity problems could intensify in the months ahead. But the recent concern about this scenario probably is misplaced.

The bank dismissed the decline in liquidity ratios by arguing that they had declined ever since the end of World War II and that lenders had become accustomed to accepting less liquidity on the part of borrowers:

> In each past year, there probably was some minimum liquidity ratio that would have triggered a substantial number of credit refusals by lenders and widespread business failure if the actual ratio had fallen below it. But that hypothetical lower boundary has declined significantly since World War II.[9]

This is much like the argument, five years earlier, of the Philadelphia National Bank about the indefinite expansibility of consumer debt ratios.

In the case of the First National City Bank, the fatuousness of the argument was exposed, only two weeks after publication of the June bank letter, with the failure of the Penn Central Railroad. Reputedly, First National City Bank was the largest single holder of Penn Central commercial paper—in amounts running into hundreds of millions of dollars!

The "liquidity crisis" of 1969–70 first hit with a wave of failures of brokerage houses, including some of substantial size. Others were kept afloat very temporarily only by extraordinary measures or were being saved from formal bankruptcy by absorption into a still-solvent firm.

By July 1970 the New York Stock Exchange had already used $55 million of reserve funds to pay off customers of bankrupt brokerage houses.

Next to appear in trouble were a variety of conglomerates. Ling Temco Vought hastily sold off sections of its empire in order to get cash to pay current bills. A number of lesser conglomerates—Four Seasons Nursing Homes, Commonwealth United, and others—went into bankruptcy.

A big international scandal followed the collapse of the shares of

Investors Overseas Services, a multibillion-dollar investment trust operating in Western Europe but promoted by American capital.

Early in 1970, Lockheed Corporation, largest of the aerospace companies, demanded government payments of more than $600 million in order to be able to keep operating through the year. Other munitions companies that had overextended themselves and diverted huge amounts from government payments for munitions to expansion in other areas, suddenly found themselves strapped for cash.

The Penn Central bankruptcy was expected to be only the first. At the time, it was known that six other railroads were on the verge of collapse. A number of airline companies were not much better off.

Many years earlier, the Wall Street bankers had taken over Trans-World Airlines from the lone-wolf financier, Howard Hughes, and had won a lawsuit charging him with mismanagement. But by the end of 1970 these Wall Street managers looked even worse. TWA was running a huge deficit and was begging the banks for cash in order to avoid bankruptcy. Chrysler Corporation, the number three auto-maker, passed through a tense cash situation in mid-1970, while American Motors was striving to stay alive at the end of the year.

Economist Eliot Janeway recalled Hoover's attempt to stem the 1929–32 crisis with huge bail-outs of giant corporations through the Reconstruction Finance Company. He writes: "He did so after the crash put him in the fatal position of being too late with too little. I regard Hoover's ghost as the most significant political figure in Nixon's Washington."[10]

The point is not that Nixon *wants* to be too late. He has demonstrated his readiness to give away billions of taxpayers' money to salvage the giant corporations. But public opposition to such a course has its reflection in Congress and impedes Nixon's efforts.

The AFL-CIO proposed nationalization of the railroads rather than the bailing out of their private owners. A group of Senators, headed by Proxmire of Wisconsin, proposed nationalizing Lockheed's munitions production while letting the civilian segment go bankrupt.

The balance of forces, however, was still against a democratic solution of the crisis. By the end of 1970 it seemed clear that Nixon and the financial power centers would have their way. The main bankrupt monopolies, in which these financial groups had the control stockholdings and also had tens and hundreds of millions at stake in loans, would be left in private ownership as a source of continued milking by the rich at the expense of very large federal subsidies.

Lockheed would be bailed out with the full amount of $600,000,000, to be doled out in smaller units that could be rammed through Congress. An initial $125,000,000 would be turned over to Penn Central to prevent forced nationalization of that railroad and of others to follow.

While similar to the 1929–32 crisis in some respects, the 1969–70 crisis differed from the Great Crisis in other important respects. The recent stock-market decline was not nearly so severe. There was not, by the end of 1970, a global crisis of overproduction. And there was, during 1969–70, only one major bank failure.

Thus it seemed likely that the acute crisis phase was passing and would not get cumulatively worse, as in 1931, 1932 and the beginning of 1933. Yet the financial contradictions remained severe, largely unresolved in 1970, and to a considerable extent focused on the banks.

The Banks

The largest and most serious bankruptcies of the great crisis beginning in 1929 were those of the banks. At the climax, early in 1933, the President had to temporarily close down all banks; many were never permitted to re-open.

Despite the small number of bank failures in 1969–70 crisis-breeding ingredients built up to an exceptional extent. Typical indicators are the ratio of loans to assets and of capital to loans and investments. Typically, during the 1920s, capital accounts amounted to about 13% of investments and loans, but in the 1950s and 1960s, the ratio declined to 8%.

For decades U.S. banks operated with between 55% and 57% of assets loaned out. This range was exceeded in 1920–21 and in 1929, just before the great crash, when the ratio went up a couple of percentage points. The all-time low ratio, and the all-time high of bank liquidity, was in 1945, with a loan-to-asset ratio of only 17%. By 1965 it was back to the normal 55–57% range and it stayed there for the remainder of the decade. This stability, however, was only apparent. The big banks "sold" tens of billions of their loans to holding companies set up for that purpose, and their asset base was inflated by a sharp increase in the "float" of checks in process of collection. By the end of the decade, the loan-to-asset ratio, in real terms, was at an all-time high. Overextension of credit was particularly notable among the giant money market banks. *Fortune* wrote of the First National City Bank as early as 1965: "The bank's ratio of domestic loans to domestic deposits has really been 70 percent, a level far above the historical norm; a decade ago a bank was considered to be 'fully loaned' at 50 percent."[11]

On April 15, 1970, loans of large New York City banks came to $42.6 billion, or 71% of gross deposits. But "adjusted gross loans" of $42.4 billion came to 138% of "adjusted deposits," which omit the float and certain other items. The float had increased to 40% of all demand deposits, indicating a feverish velocity of circulation. These banks operated by the grace of $8 billion borrowed from their foreign branches, $5 billion of "Federal funds purchased"—borrowings from the reserves of other domestic banks—and additional billions obtained through borrowings of affiliated holding companies.[12]

The commercial banks are closely interlocked with the savings and loan associations, savings banks, and consumer finance companies. The former institutions, which specialize in mortgage loans, also became severely overextended. During 1966–67 a number of them went through extreme difficulties, and a few were forced to close down. A wave of defaults because of increasing unemployment could create a much worse crisis among these institutions. Finance capital and the government have altered arrangements, relationships, and regulations, with a view to minimizing the danger of financial crises directly affecting the banks.

Banks are supposedly protected from depositors' "runs" by Federal Deposit Insurance protection. They are partly protected from massive losses on marginal debts through federal insurance of many mortgages and of certain classes of small business and foreign loans. Possible losses from stock market speculation are supposedly contained by regulation of margins and other SEC rules.

The banks have gained a fat "cushion," thanks to federal imposition of relatively low–ceiling interest rates on savings deposits. As the demand for credit expanded, permitting the banks to raise the interest rates they charged to record heights, the margin between interest received and interest paid expanded, thanks to the government ceiling on the latter. In addition, the big banks are recipients of multiplied income from handling the tens of billions in pension funds and other institutional trust accounts that have mushroomed in recent decades. Higher profits permitted absorption of substantial losses on "bad loans" and declines in prices of securities held.

During the crisis of 1969–70, the banks cut out lines of credit to smaller and less well-connected borrowers, precipitating many bankruptcies. At the same time, they relied on government handouts to save them from really huge losses. First National City Bank's outstanding loans to Penn Central Railroad at the end of 1969 amounted to $387 million. That amounted to 2.7 times the bank's profits for the year and to 28% of its capital funds. Obviously, only a few such collapses *could* put even the First National City Bank, with more capital than any other, in the deepest trouble.

The Fidelity Bank of Philadelphia had $65 million on loan to Penn Central—equal to 5.6 times its annual profits and 80% of its capital funds. The Penn Central bankruptcy alone would be enough to sink the Fidelity Bank—if the Fidelity Bank had to stand the loss. But the government bail-out of the Penn Central was designed precisely to protect the big banking interests, who were both creditors to Penn Central on a huge scale, and holders of the control blocks of its shares through their trust departments. The same principle applied to the bail-out of Lockheed Aircraft and the others, carried out or attempted by the Nixon administration.

All of these aids to the banks come under the general heading of state-monopoly capitalism. They not only preserved the big banks from serious danger in 1970, but also permitted them to raise their profits to record levels during the economic crisis.

It would be folly, however, to assume that a banking crisis is forestalled; this would be no more credible then the claim that a crisis of overproduction was ruled out by government regulation.

The ability to utilize the government to protect the banks from the consequences of their own excesses and to guarantee a permanant increase in their profits under all conditions, is subject to political limits. These limits cannot be defined in advance. They depend on the shifting balance of forces and the outcome of particular struggles. Some of these reflect conflicts of interest within the capitalist class. More basic is the conflict of interest between the working people and the financial oligarchy, as the former are forced to pay the toll of the banks' financial supremacy in enormous interest charges and in taxes used to bail out the banks' customers. These conflicts found reflection in attempts within Congress to prevent the Penn Central and Lockheed giveaways, attempts which were not successful but which developed considerable power, and cannot be dismissed as mere pinpricks.

Furthermore, the "protection" provided by the government results in the deepening of crisis-provoking contradictions. The aggressive financiers, confident in their power and in their ability to control and manipulate financial matters through improved state-monopoly coordination and control measures, have gone far beyond previous norms of financial "soundness" in the drive for speedier expansion of profits.

Central banking regulation, similarly, is much bolder and more permissive. Formerly the Federal Reserve Board aimed to make money "easy" in time of recession and increasingly "tight" as recovery moved into a boom stage. Now the policy is to make money "easy" under almost all conditions. Official "tightening" of money during the Vietnam War boom was rendered quite mild in its overall impact by a series of devices developed by the bankers, such as use of Eurodollar loans, bank holding companies, and "commercial paper." Nor did federal authorities seriously attempt to interfere with this. In April 1970, with the Nixon Administration scared by the deepening crisis, the Federal Reserve Board turned already to an easy money policy, even though inflation was still at its peak, as was the overextension of credit by the banking system.

In a famous speech (June 1, 1965), as the Vietnam War escalation took command of the economy, Federal Reserve Board Chairman William McChesney Martin warned of the similarities of the then prevailing financial and economic situation to that of 1929:

Then, as now, there had been virtually uninterrupted progress for seven years . . .

Then, as now, prosperity had been concentrated in the fully developed countries . . .

Then, as now, there was a large increase in private domestic debts; in fact, the expansion in consumer debt . . . has recently been much faster than in the twenties.

Then, as now, the supply of money and bank credit and the turnover of demand deposits had been continuously growing; and . . . this time monetary expansion has been superimposed on a dwindling gold reserve.

. . . Then, as now, international indebtedness had risen as fast as domestic debt.

Then, as now the payments position of the main reserve center—Britain then and the United States now—was uneasy, to say the least.

Martin noted that a number of features were worse than in the 1920s, but, offsetting this, some other features were less severe and various regulations had eased the situation:

And, finally, the experience of the twenties has strengthened the resolution of all responsible leaders, businessmen and statesmen alike, never again to permit a repetition of the disasters of the Great Depression.

But while the spirit is willing, the flesh, in the form of concrete policies, has remained weak.[13]

Conflict Between Policies and Practice

Mr. Martin's concern was well founded. During much of the Vietnam War, the expressed policy of banking leaders was to restrain the issuance of credit, to prevent wartime inflation and financial excesses. Representatives of these views were in positions of power. In 1966 they cracked down sharply on credit, in the so-called "credit crunch" of that year. Again, at the start of 1969, they shifted to a year-long "tight-money" policy. And yet, as can be seen from Table VI–3, each year the debts of the country increased more than the year before, or, in 1967, nearly as much.

Why? Partly because of the unwillingness to pay the price. The 1966 "credit crunch" resulted in a radical reduction in housing construction and a "minirecession." The governing groups feared the political and social consequence as Vietnam War opposition increased, and they hastened to reverse their tracks before financial tensions were reduced. The 1969 tight money policy contributed to the "unexpected" crisis of overproduction and to its consequences in major bankruptcies. By early 1970 the governing groups were again beset by the same fears as well as by pressures from capitalists with declining profits. Again the brakes were released while the chain of debts was still expanding dangerously.

An additional factor in both situations was the agility of the bankers to get around Federal Reserve regulations through devices permitting continued expansion of lending. The very largest New York banks, those with the dominant voice in Federal Reserve policy, pioneered in developing devices that minimized the effectiveness of that policy.

Thus, despite the extreme monopolization of financial power, despite the development of state monopoly capitalism, through which the biggest financial centers tried to coordinate their actions, the contradiction between the capitalist as an individual money-maker and the capitalist as part of a class remained unabridged.

As part of the top financial oligarchy, the heads of Morgan Guaranty, First National City, and Chase Manhattan wanted to see credit restrained, and encouraged regulations to that effect. As heads of their particular banks, they wanted to reap maximum profits from high interest rates, to insure the fullest flow of funds to the industrial corporations within their financial sphere of influence. In practice, the latter drive thwarted the former objective. At the same time, the contradiction itself was turned to particular advantage by the dominant banks. Only the very large banks with a network of foreign branches, which were able to set up holding companies and to deal in tens of millions at a clip with giant industrial corporations—only these banks could really take advantage of most of the loopholes. Thus the effect was to impose an effective credit freeze on the smaller banks while speeding the concentration of power in the giant banks.

Alfred Hayes, President of the Federal Reserve Bank of New York, in a speech delivered January 26, 1970, bemoaned the failures of anti-inflation policies during the Vietnam War. Praising the official policy of a budget surplus and tight money, he urged that it be maintained. He noted that a recession might be beginning and criticized those who considered "any recession" as "the greatest possible evil to be avoided at all costs." Inflation was the greater evil, he claimed, and must be stopped. To continue the restrictive policy would involve

a substantial slowing of economic growth, perhaps over a fairly extended period . . . . This will involve some hardships, such as employment opportunities lost and income foregone. However, I strongly believe that it is better to face up to these hardships now than to relax our stabilization efforts prematurely, thereby making necessary a much more difficult readjustment in the future.

The slowing of the economy has already commenced; but it is by no means clear that the slowing will be lasting enough to prove effective. . . . The biggest dangers I see on the horizon are (1) the danger that fiscal policy will be a weaker and weaker ally of monetary policy in the anti-inflation effort; and (2) the danger that pressures from outside the Federal Reserve and inside the System itself will prevent our maintaining a sufficiently restrictive policy for a long enough time to turn the trick. Skepticism on this point is unfortunately widespread.[14]

But within a few weeks President Nixon appointed a new chairman of the Federal Reserve Board, economist Arthur Burns, and at his very first meeting with the Board, it decided on an easier money policy. At the same time, the administration moved more and more clearly toward a large budgetary deficit.

Hayes himself expressed some of the contradictions in the policy he advocated:

I am well aware that maintenance of a firm monetary stance, especially in the event of weak fiscal support, will tend to keep markets in their highly uncertain state and may continue to cause serious problems for some financial institutions. But special facilities are available to assist the latter, and the Federal Reserve is always in a position to relieve market pressures if the need becomes acute.[15]

And this is exactly what did happen. By June, when the Penn Central went under and "serious problems" arose for key financial institutions, the Federal Reserve went all-out on its previously more cautious turn to easy money. Mr. Hayes' worst fears were realized, in part with his own participation, although he voted negatively on some of the moves to ease money.

Thus the financial crisis of 1970 was relieved by year's-end, but under conditions that made its reappearance likely in more intractable form—sooner rather than later.

VII.

Inflation

THE UNITED STATES, along with the capitalist world as a whole, has been in a stage of permanent inflation for the past three decades. This important new feature has a significant influence on the business cycle, the rate of economic growth, and on social and political relations.

During earlier U.S. history, prices moved upward in prosperity, downward in crisis and depression. In addition, there were longer upward and downward sweeps lasting one or two decades, and persisting through more than a single business cycle. The upward sweeps, usually shorter, were mainly in war periods; the downward sweeps began after wars and tended to last longer.

The first relatively long upward trend in prices began at the onset of the age of trusts, toward the end of the 19th century. It persisted, with significant interruptions, through World War I, until 1920. Thereafter, the long-term price trend was downward until 1933 and level until just before World War II.

The permanent upward trend began in 1940. The consumer price index has increased in all but two years, when there were declines of less than one percent. The "implicit price deflator" for the gross national product has gone up every year except for a fraction of a percent decline in 1949. Certain features of this long price rise should be noted:

1. Inflation is most pronounced in time of war but it is not limited to wartime.

2. Differentiation in prices is extreme. Retail prices go up the fastest; wholesale prices of finished goods more slowly; while wholesale prices of raw materials go up very little or even decline. Between the 1957–59 base period and 1968 the Bureau of Labor Statistics price indexes changed as follows: Spot market prices of basic commodities *decreased* 4.3%; wholesale prices of crude materials increased 1.2%, intermediate

products, 8.0%, and finished goods 11.3%; while the consumer price index increased 21.7% for all items, including 15.3% for commodities and 34.3% for services.

The differentiation is most extreme in the case of farm products and foods, where monopolies stand between relatively scattered, smaller farms and 200 million individual consumers. Between 1950 and 1969, wholesale prices of farm products increased 2%; processed foods and feeds, 28%; while consumer food prices increased 46%.[1]

3. More or less cyclical price fluctuations are limited to agricultural raw materials and some minerals. Prices of processed commodities, and especially retail prices, keep going up almost continuously. This characteristic is becoming more marked. In the crises or recessions of 1949 and 1954, consumer prices declined fractionally—and somewhat belatedly in the case of 1954. In the recessions of 1958 and 1961, they continued to increase, with some slowing of the rate of increase. In the crisis of 1969–70, consumer prices continued to increase at the peak rate reached in the first half of 1969.

4. Similar price trends have become a global phenomenon for the capitalist world. Consumer price indexes in industrially developed countries in the six years 1963–1969 increased in a range between 16% (West Germany) and 54% (Finland). Wild increases took place in a number of less developed and neocolonial countries, ranging from 126% in South Korea to 779% in Brazil and 61,183% in Indonesia.[2]

And almost everywhere price increases accelerated at the end of the 1960s despite official measures of restraint designed to curb inflation by slowing economic activity.

The Wells Fargo Bank commented:

We may derive some comfort, but not much from knowing that the U.S. is hardly alone in its dilemma. In all the major (capitalist) countries of the world, there has been a clear acceleration of price increases over the past few years. In 1969, for example, the lowest rate of price increase for a major country was for (West) Germany at 3.8%. In contrast, Japan hit 6.1%, and three countries, including the United States, ran between 5 and 6%, with the rest being above 4%. The situation has hardly improved in 1970 with (West) Germany showing a startling 8% rate of increase in the first quarter in consumer prices.[3]

Hiding the Meaning of Inflation

Inflation, properly speaking, is the depreciation of paper money, the issuance of currency beyond a normal ratio to the production and circulation of commodities. Webster's Dictionary, in its recent edition, still conforms to this meaning. It defines inflation as "an increase in the amount of currency in circulation, resulting in a relatively sharp and sudden fall in its value and rise in price." It defines an inflationist as a "person who favors inflation; especially, an advocate of an increased issue of paper money."[4]

Well-known examples of radical currency inflation were the issuance of "continentals" during the U.S. War for Independence, "greenbacks" during the Civil War, astronomical issuance of rubles during the Civil War and foreign intervention after the Russian Revolution, and the even wilder issuance of German marks after World War I.

Similar "runaway" inflation has been characteristic of many developing countries throughout the period since World War II. In the United States and other imperialist states, the pace of inflation has been slower and not so clear-cut, as the most conspicuous increase has been in deposit money rather than currency.

Capitalists and their economists, however, now call any increase in prices inflationary. For example, the Committee for Economic Development (CED), a grouping of leading figures of American finance and industry, wrote in 1958:

We use the term inflation to mean a persistent rise of prices in *general*. The term is sometimes used with other meanings. For example, inflation is sometimes used to mean an increase in the supply of money. But we believe that the identification of inflation with generally rising prices is common usage in the United States today.[5]

There have been periods of rising prices without inflation. Seasonal price increases and cyclical price increases are examples. Unusual curtailments of the supply of raw materials and foodstuffs owing to natural calamities have caused price increases, sometimes sustained. Longer-term increases have occurred when the value of gold, the basic money commodity, declined so that the values of other commodities, expressed in terms of gold, increased. This happened in the decade following the discovery of gold in California.

In fact, the persistent price increases of the last several decades *have* been inflationary. The disproportionate issuance of money has been a prime cause of the rising price trend, so it is valid to speak of chronic inflation.

Why quibble if both the bourgeois economists and Marxists agree that we have inflation? The fudging of the definition of inflation, its application to price increases "in general" has become "common usage" by choice of the capitalists, and not without reason. This makes it easier to hide the real causes of price increases, to attribute unreal causes that serve as justification for policies in the interest of the capitalist class. It aims to cover up the fact that inflation results in a redistribution of income and wealth in favor of the biggest capitalists and at the expense of wage-earners, elderly people on a fixed income, the petty bourgeoisie, etc.

Above all, it aims to obscure the increasingly decisive role of joint big business-government *policy,* of state-monopoly capitalism, in bringing about the particular pattern of price increases that has emerged, serving the most wealthy and powerful as instruments of such enrichment at the expense of the majority.

Moreover, in reality, monetary inflation has not been the sole factor involved in the rising prices of recent decades, nor the sole policy instrument designed to bring about selective price increases. Other factors accelerate and buttress the continuity of price increases and markedly distort the structure of prices. These factors, in turn, contribute to and interact with monetary inflation.

Accelerated Monopolization

Concentration of capital, already at a very high level, has become much more pronounced since World War II. In this country the process reached a climax in the merger boom of the 1960s, the formation of conglomerates, the tightened grip of the top banks on vast industrial empires. Similar processes are taking place in other capitalist countries.

In Japan, where the great Zaibatsu industrial-financial empires publicly flaunt their power, industrial cartel schemes are officially enforced. The European Economic Community (Common Market) accomplishes much the same thing through its industrial committees. Because of antitrust laws, such arrangements are not generally announced in the United States, but are quite apparent to the realistic observer.

Cigarettes provide an example. Owing to the revelation of associated health hazards, cigarette-smoking declined in the United States in 1969. Even previously, cigarette factories did not operate at anywhere near capacity. Tobacco prices increased only moderately. With even a modicum of competition, prices of cigarettes would have declined. Yet there were industry-wide increases of 35¢ per thousand in May 1969 and again in June 1970, the compound increase amounting to nearly 17%. All companies put them into effect virtually simultaneously. There were no other price changes at other times. As a result of the two price hikes, cigarette companies increased their profits at a time of decline in their industry's activity. The government did not utter a squeak of protest against this obviously monopolistic price collusion.

A similar situation can be observed in the regional markets for such a humble product as bread. The direct materials costs come to less than 10% of the retail price of bread today. Bread is manufactured by a substantial number of companies, and there is a great overcapacity. Bread consumption is not increasing, and there is no technological monopoly. It is a situation seemingly made for competition. Yet every year or so retail prices of most major types of bread are increased almost simultaneously by 2¢ per loaf in the New York area.

Monopoly pricing devices in steel, automobiles, petroleum, etc. continue unabated. Moreover, in contrast to earlier periods, price movements are always upward, even in face of declining consumption, or—as in the case of autos and steel—fierce import competition. Monopoly control of distribution, generally by the producing companies, has resulted in fantastic spreads between factory costs and consumer prices for drugs, petroleum products, packaged foodstuffs, and other articles of mass consumption.

The banking monopoly imposes soaring interest costs that directly and indirectly increase the price level all along the line. At the same time, the bankers, through their lending operations, have become the main emitters of *de facto* money and the main practical agents of monetary inflation, as well as the main forces in determining the inflationary bias of central banking monetary policy.

The U.S. government, as well as state governments, contribute substantially to monopoly price–fixing, as in the setting of allowable levels of petroleum production, crop restriction incentives, the application of price-jacking "fair trade" laws, and the dwindling of official regulatory bodies' restrictions of price-gouging by the public utility and transportation monopolies.

New forms of monopoly price-gouging have become important in the service trades, notably health and education. In the former, "non-profit" health insurance corporations, drug companies, hospitals, and doctors have combined in an apparently endless round of exceedingly rapid price increases, which have already brought the cost of medical services in this country "out of sight" in comparison with other capitalist countries. In education, local governments, through regressive taxes on homes; and colleges and universities, through soaring tuition fees, are the agents of monopoly price increases.

The importance of monopoly price-gouging is seen in the extreme differentiation of prices increases at the expense primarily of worker-consumers. It is absolutely necessary to take this into account in any scientific analysis of trends in distribution, rate of exploitation of labor, and other crucial economic-social measures. Bourgeois economists, failing to do so, present a bland, fundamentally inaccurate picture of modern capitalist economy. We have taken the effect of monopoly pricing into account—to the extent that available statistics make possible, in the fundamental analysis in Chapter III.

Permanent Militarization of the Economy

That wars are engines of inflation is well known; in fact, every substantial war in U.S. history has been accompanied by inflation. And the wildest inflationary periods in other countries have been associated with wars. For 30 years the United States has had a permanently militarized economy. The same applies, in lesser degree, to other major capitalist powers and, to an even greater degree, to certain small capitalist states.

Militarization provides corporations with a cushion of high-profit business, enabling them to set and maintain higher profit margins in civilian markets. Fantastic markups of four or five times factory cost are applied to the sale of products originally developed for military use, for example, electronics. Efficiency in production for the military is a fraction of that in civilian production, and the corresponding multiplication of costs inevitably is transmitted, at least in part, to civilian sales of armament manufacturers.

Military spending on a large scale generally involves a distribution of purchasing power to servicemen, and munitions contractors and workers, not offset on the supply side by production of civilian goods, nor on the demand size by an equal collection of taxes.

This last point usually signifies deficit financing of military spending, which translates directly into monetary inflation. The effect, however, can be similar even when there is no deficit. The federal budget was, on balance, in surplus during the Korean War—markedly so in the first year of the war,—yet prices soared. Deficits were not exceptionally high during four of the first five years of massive U.S. intervention in Vietnam, and yet there was a marked acceleration of price increases.

In part, this in due to nonmonetary factors connected with a military buildup, the strengthening of monopoly power already referred to, and the sudden increase in demand that surges throughout the civilian economy in a war situation. However, this also takes a monetary form—a rapid rise in credit money—even when the government does not issue money through deficit spending.

The pertinence of militarization might be questioned, considering that countries with relatively little militarization show just as much inflation as those with a high degree of militarization. There is, however, a high degree of militarization in the capitalist world as a whole, especially in its most powerful country, the United States. With the growing cosmopolitanism of capital, the effects are spread throughout the areas of operation of giant multinational firms, most of which are based on the United States.

Japan, which hitherto has devoted only one percent of its gross national product to its military budget, has had a higher rate of inflation than the United States. However, the Japanese military budget is increasing very rapidly, the economy is influenced directly by the extensive U.S. military operations on Japanese territory, and Japanese capitalists receive large military orders from the U.S. armed forces.

Deterioration of the Dollar

Historically, the country's money supply was linked to gold, a tangible commodity with intrinsic value that determined the value of paper and credit money, convertible ultimately into gold. This privilege, however, was ended gradually in the main capitalist countries, as central banks consolidated all gold holdings under unified control. This aimed to concentrate the gold stock in order to strengthen the position of each country's currency and big banks in international competition. Domestically, it aimed to strengthen the monopoly of the main financial groups, which, in reality, control the central banks.

The United States adopted one of the most rigorous laws to regulate gold in 1934. It forbade all private hoarding and circulation of gold. International settlements, however, continued to be made in gold. And there was a legally required gold reserve amounting to about 40% of currency in circulation before 1945, and 25% thereafter. These conditions provided a degree of stability to the dollar, but the discipline of international gold settlements was progressively undermined at U.S. initiative during the late 1950s and especially during the 1960s (see Chapter XI). At the same time, the gold reserve requirement became less meaningful as the currency in circulation continued to expand while the gold reserves shrank. Finally, during the Vietnam War, the legal reserve requirement was formally abandoned so as to free the remaining gold stock for possible use in international settlements and to avoid obvious violation of the requirement. By the end of 1970, in fact, the gold stock was less than 20% of currency in circulation.

These changes in the formal monetary framework were paralleled by a rapid decline in the practical gold basis of money. Before 1929 the U.S. gold reserve usually amounted to about 10% of currency in circulation and commercial deposits which, together, make up the effective money supply of the country.* When the gold reserve fell below 10% of the money supply, as in 1914, 1920, and 1928–29, it was a sign of impending trouble. Gold coverage of the dollar multiplied several times in the mid-thirties and early forties as a result of dollar devaluation, the flight of billions of capital from Nazi-occupied

---

*The traditional definition of the "money supply" is currency in circulation plus demand deposits in banks. In the past two decades, it has become customary to keep a rising proportion of deposits in interest-bearing time deposits, which technically cannot be drawn upon on demand, but in practice can be drawn, and which serve virtually the same purpose as demand deposits. To correspond with this practice and, with the growing custom of monetary analysts, we include in money supply currency and both demand and time deposits in commercial banks adjusted by certain standard exclusions. Savings deposits in savings banks and savings and loan associations, however, are not included as part of the money supply.

continental Europe, the purchase of armaments by Britain and France, and the U.S. near-monopoly of world markets at a time when normal communications with Europe were cut off by World War II.

The gold stock reached 40% of the money supply in 1940, falling to 15% with the subsequent inflation of the U.S. money supply in 1950. Since then the fall has continued steadily from the combined effects of gold losses and increases in money supply. By the early 1960s the gold coverage set an all-time low and by 1970 fell to 2.5%. (Table VII–1).

The central banking authorities have succeeded in greatly reducing the influence of gold on the domestic economy, so the decline in gold coverage is not the main content of domestic inflation. It is more relevent internationally, as being part of a process where the dollar has

TABLE VII-1 GOLD RESERVES AND MONEY SUPPLY
SELECTED YEARS, 1914–1970
BILLIONS OF DOLLARS

	Gold Reserves	Money Supply Including Time Deposits Adjusted	Percent Gold of Money
1914	1.5	16.0	9.5
1918	2.9	25.3	11.4
1920	2.6	34.2	7.7
1924	4.2	37.5	11.2
1928	3.9	45.7	8.4
1929	4.0	45.8	8.7
1937	12.8	45.2	28.2
1940	22.0	54.2	40.6
1945	20.1	121.3	16.6
1950	22.8	152.9	14.9
1955	21.8	185.2	11.8
1960	17.8	214.6	8.3
1965	13.8	314.8	4.4
1969	11.9	397.8	3.0
1970	11.0	443.7	2.5

Sources: 1914–1955: *Historical Statistics of the U.S.*, Series X-299, X-267 and X-271.

1960–1970: *Federal Reserve Bulletin,* December 1970, November 1971.

Money supply for 1914–1955 as of June 30. All other figures as of year-end. Money supply figures seasonally adjusted. Money supply figures for 1914–1955 not exactly comparable with those for later years.

been partly substituted for gold as an international currency, and has thereby become an international carrier of inflation. (Chapter XII).

The main inflationary relationship is in the expansion of monetary circulation versus the real volume of production. This applies to currency, and, even more important, to bank deposit money. Not only is the latter a substantial multiple of the former, but the relative importance of currency changes with customs in means of payment.

Table VII–1 sets forth this process of monetary inflation. Between 1929 and 1970 the money stock increased nearly ten times, while real production increased 3$^1/_2$ times. Thus the ratio of the money stock to production increased two and three-fourths times. *And the general level of prices increased in almost the same degree.* The relationship is brought out graphically in Chart II.

The first big inflationary surge since 1929 was during World War II and the immediate postwar period, when currency in circulation more than tripled, and the total money supply increased nearly three times. Since the real increase in production was only about 60%, this provoked a sharp increase in prices, partly and temporarily suppressed during World War II by price controls. A smaller inflationary expansion of the money supply during the Korean War is not brought out in Table VII–2.

The decade of the 1960s has been one of continuous monetary inflation, especially since the start of large-scale U.S. warfare in Vietnam in 1965. Between 1960 and 1970 the money stock more than doubled, while the real value of production increased less than 50%. This resulted in an even steeper rise in the ratio of the money supply to real production than the roughly 30% officially recorded increase in the price level. Particularly noteworthy was the development in 1970. In this crisis year, with production declining, there was an unusual, 12% increase in the money stock. Undoubtedly this provided much of the underlying content of the sharp price rise which took place in that year—the most pronounced ever in a year of economic decline.

Inflationary Policy

Secular inflation has a two-fold character. On the one hand, it is a specific feature of the increasing instability of capitalism in its stage of decay, of political crisis, of country-by-country disintegration. It tends

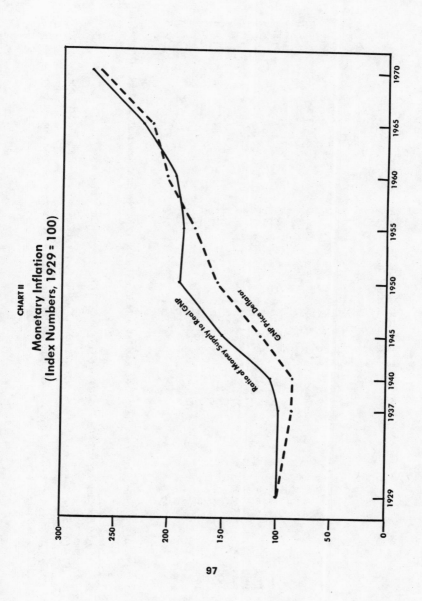

CHART II

Monetary Inflation
(Index Numbers, 1929 = 100)

Ratio of Money Supply to Real GNP

GNP Price Deflator

TABLE VII-2 MONETARY INFLATION IN THE UNITED STATES, 1929–1970
(dollar figures in billions)

	1. Currency in Circulation (dollars)	2. Money Stock (dollars)	3. Real GNP (1958 dollars)	4. Ratio of Money Stock to Real GNP percent	5. Ratio of Money Stock to Real GNP index nos. 1929–100	6. GNP Price Deflator 1929–100
1929	4.7*	45.8	203.6	22.5	100.0	100.0
1937	6.4	45.2	203.2	22.2	98.8	87.9
1940	7.8	54.2	227.2	23.9	106.0	86.6
1945	26.7	121.3	355.2	34.1	151.9	117.7
1950	27.7	152.9	355.3	43.0	191.1	158.3
1955	31.2	185.2	438.0	42.3	188.0	179.4
1960	32.9	214.6	487.7	44.0	195.6	204.0
1965	42.1	314.8	617.8	51.0	226.7	218.9
1969	54.0	397.8	727.1	54.7	243.2	253.0
1970	57.1	443.7	724.1	61.5	272.5	266.3

Sources:
1. 1929–1945, *Historical Statistics of the U.S.*, Series X-284, as of June 30. 1950–1970, *Federal Reserve Bulletin*, March 1971, A-16, as of year-end.
2. From Table VII-I.
3. *1929–1969 Economic Report of the President*, 1971, Table C-2 1970, Survey of Current Business, March 1971, Table 1, p. 9.
4,5. Computed.
6. *1929–1969 Economic Report of the President*, 1971, Table C-3 1970, *Survey of Current Business*, March 1971 Table 16, p. 12. Index numbers on 1958 base converted to 1929 base.
*There were also several billions of gold in private hands, so the currency figure is not comparable with that for later years.
Table IX-1. MS page 224

to become the rule, regardless of the wishes of the capitalists and governments of particular countries. On the other hand, it corresponds in time with the emergence of state-monopoly capitalism as a major, all-embracing feature of economic life, and becomes a key policy instrument of state-monopoly capitalism.

Inflation is never accidental, technically. The monetary authorities, representing the most powerful bankers of a country, can determine the amount of currency in circulation and can influence strongly the amount of deposit money through regulation of the lending activity of the banks. But sometimes they have little choice, since during all-out war or postwar devastation, governments have access to only a fraction of the revenues needed to finance activities needed for survival. In such cases, under capitalism, governments invariably turn to the "printing press" to pay their armies and munitions manufacturers and to buy supplies needed to avert mass starvation and to deal with other crucial conditions.

But after World War II a different type of situation arose—a conscious inflationary policy which the dominant financial-industrial groups execute through control of the capitalist governments. The emphasis is on "gradual," "controlled" inflation, as distinct from "runaway" inflation such as afflicts many neocolonial countries. This is seen as assuring a corresponding gradual rise in prices, which is considered an economic stimulant, encouraging capital investment, sale of consumers' durables, and the conversion of small savings into money capital through the purchase of newly issued corporation securities. Gradual inflation eases the pressure of existing debts and thereby creates additional leeway for credit expansion. It puts a penalty on hoarding, encourages the conversion into active capital of a larger part of surplus value, and thereby tends to accelerate economic growth and monopoly profits.

All these are subordinate to the main motivation—the use of selective price inflation as a means of increasing the share of capital at the expense of labor, and of monopoly capital at the expense of farmers and producers of primary materials in less developed countries.

Under modern conditions of strong unionism, it is no longer possible, for the most part, to directly depress wages, nor to prevent more or less regular increases. Capitalist economic strategy is to realize a higher rate of surplus value by obtaining increases in labor productivity and in retail selling prices which, in combination, exceed the increase in wage rates. Monetary inflation is a decisive lever (reinforced by monopoly power, military orders, and government regulation) for achieving the price increases.

Meanwhile, the draining of profits from developing countries, combined with the economic effects of backwardness and dependence, leads to chronic severe inflation in these countries. The imperialist banking centers use their power to force the periodical adjustment of this inflation with currency devaluations. This cheapens raw materials, labor power, and the properties that the imperialists buy up in these countries.

Inflation in the imperialist countries is accomplished through the government budget and through credit and money controls. Government deficits result in an increase in the money supply. Technically, the money isn't just arbitrarily printed; it is based on borrowings from private banks and individuals. But, in practice, deficit financing leads to an increase of several times the government deficit in bank deposits, that is, deposit money. Generally, central bank policy is coordinated with budget policy to achieve the desired result smoothly.

On the surface, a policy of encouraging price increases involves a contradiction among capitalists. It helps industrialists, provided they can hold down wages. But it hurts bankers, whose bonds and loans depreciate in real value. In fact, there have been severe quarrels within the ruling class over policy in this area.

Under modern conditions, however, that contradiction is more apparent than real. The key fact is that the same oligarchy of billionaire and centimillionaire families own control-blocks of shares in the biggest banks and industrial corporations. Their banks are not merely properties in themselves but also centers of industrial-financial empires.

Yet there remain specific institutional differences between the particular positions of banks and industrial companies and between particular financial-industrial groups which often lead to conflicts over inflationary policies.

The Roosevelt administration conducted its World War II monetary inflation in a way that kept interest rates at an extremely low level. The result was not favorable to the banks, whose capital increased by only a fraction of the increase in prices. In effect, they sustained a loss of real capital, although the huge stock of U.S. government securities they

were forced to take provided a basis for rapid expansion after World War II.

The bankers were hostile to Roosevelt's methods but subsequently they have been able to remove the elements of conflict that existed, by and large. They now regulate the money supply in such a way as to increase the rate of interest along with prices and to keep the rate of interest always well ahead of the pace of price increases. Today, inflation in the United States profits both industrial and financial monopolies, with the biggest accretion of power going to the great banks.

The minutes of the Open Market Committee of the Federal Reserve Board, which are now released three months after each meeting, reveal differences among the banker-members over the rate of increase in the money supply, but agreement on the principle of a fast enough increase to imply a continuous up-trend in the price level.

The policy of deliberate inflation is disguised by a rhetorical "war against inflation." But its gradual evolution can be traced in the writings of economists who supported the inflationary aspects of the New Deal during the 1930s to its fuller development by post-World War II bourgeois economists.

We leave aside here the various "funny money" advocates of outright inflation who flourished especially during the deep depression of the 1930s, but still continue active. Also the advocates of one-time dollar devaluation, whom President Roosevelt followed in 1933–34.

A "pioneer" among the advocates of "controlled" inflation was the late Sumner Slichter. In his book published in 1934, he advocated credit and investment policies designed to encourage price increases to stimulate recovery from economic depressions. Since strong labor organizations would not permit speedy cost reduction, he argues, it had become necessary to promote price increases in order to restore the "proper" balance between prices and costs—i.e., in order to restore the rate of profit.[6]

After World War II, he advocated constant price increases at a specified rate to help the domestic economy and as an instrument of the Cold War against the USSR. He regarded a "slow, creeping kind of inflation" as a logical result of rapidly rising demand, technological progress, and relative shortages of raw materials. And he associated this with the belief that capitalism was becoming quite stable, that "the present prosperity of the country is soundly grounded."[7] This was written less than a year before the beginning of a serious economic decline.

Alvin Hansen, a "liberal" economist, used the same rationale—that inflation would strengthen the U.S. economy for its anti-Soviet struggle, which Hansen strongly supported. Hansen wrote with particular enthusiasm of the "merits" of inflation:

> At no time in our history, nor indeed in that of any other country, can it be shown that price increases have injured the economy and the general welfare if in the period in question the increase in aggregate output has exceeded percentage-wise the increase in prices . . . . We should be prepared, in special circumstances, however, to go a bit farther. There are times when a tremendous forward push is urgently needed, when a choice has to be made between permitting a price increase substantially greater than my rule suggests or else foregoing the needed increase in aggregate output.[8]

By "special circumstances" Hansen meant a period of war or rapid military buildup by U.S. imperialism. Samuelson, whose *Economics* is the thoroughly eclectic synthesis of modern American bourgeois theory, the quasi-official standard textbook in colleges, wrote: "An increase in prices is usually associated with high employment. In mild inflation the wheels of industry are well lubricated, and output is near capacity. Private investment is brisk, and jobs are plentiful . . . . The losses to fixed-income groups are usually less than the gains to the rest of the community."[9]

The government, carrying out the will of leading big business groups, helps effectuate this policy of gradual inflation through the monetary and fiscal policies mentioned, as well as by its assistance to monopoly price-gouging.

An important acceleration in the rate of planned inflation has taken place in the last several years. This was associated with the deterioration of the position of the dollar as a world currency. In 1933–34, the government stimulated a one-time inflationary price increase by devaluing the dollar in relation to gold. Twenty-five years later, when the dollar again came under pressure, the U.S. Government strongly opposed any dollar devaluation, in order to maintain the dominant U.S. financial position in the capitalist world, and for other global political-economic reasons. But pressures mounted, especially during the Vietnam War. During the period 1968–71, the postwar monetary structure and the stable value of the dollar in terms of gold were destroyed in a series of moves culminating in the formal devaluation of the dollar and the ending of its international convertibility into gold (see Chapter XI).

With this, the rate of price increase accelerated along with the rate of price increase at which the capitalists aimed, as well as the degree of monetary inflation practiced in order to assure the faster increase.

Up through the mid-1960s the aim of the financial oligarchy was to keep annual inflation in the range of 1–3% per year, so as not to wipe out the interest return on bonds and loans, nor to cause excessive strain in the banking system, nor to unduly sharpen economic conflicts with labor. With the prolonged Vietnam War, and the general deterioration of the U.S. budgetary and monetary situation, that goal has been abandoned. Official and unofficial comment shows that the aim is to get the rate of inflation down below 5% and to hold it in the 3 to 5% range. The Nixon Administration, for example, publicly set a goal of a 3½% per year rate of price increase as an interim objective.

Similar policies are followed in other capitalist countries. Formal government statements have specified annual price increases in that range as desirable goals in France and Japan.

The French Finance Minister, Valéry Giscard d'Estaing, said in April 1970 that the government of that country was beginning to relax its austerity program because price increases were approaching the government's target of less than 4% per year. "Inflation has been strangled," he told a cabinet meeting.[10]

The Economic Council of Japan in the same month recommended an economic-social development program for the first five years of the 1970s which included a projected yearly increase of 4.4% in consumer prices.[11]

Here in the United States, Gaylord Freeman, Jr., chairman of the First National Bank of Chicago, put the matter on the line when he said: "The underlying trouble is that most of us like some inflation, no matter what we say. That is true of politicians, labor leaders, businessmen and, in occasional moments, even us bankers. We all like to show good report cards, and inflation makes our performance look better."[12]

The Nixon Administration, taking office at a time of rising discontent with inflation, emphasized the "fight" against inflation. Its policies helped trigger the economic crisis of 1969–70. Early in 1970, when it was already clear that unemployment would increase beyond the "normal" level in 1970, and while price increases remained above their "normal" level, the President's Council of Economic Advisers issued their annual economic report. Discussing this problem, the advisers wrote:

> It is impossible to state a target for reduction of unemployment and the rate of inflation in the years just ahead. As both are reduced, the costs and benefits of further reduction must be weighed. . . . But after 1970 we will have a clear guide for the *direction* of policy: lower inflation, and lower unemployment.[13]

Neither full employment nor full price stability, but *lower* "normal" inflation and unemployment—those were the goals.

But what actually emerged was the opposite. During President Nixon's first 36 months in office, the official rate of unemployment mounted from 3.3% to 6.0%. During the 36 months before Nixon, December 1965-December 1968, months of rapid Vietnam War buildup and maximum involvement, the consumer price index went up 11.5%. During the following 36 Nixon months, the consumer price index went up 15.7%, while interest rates soared to all-time highs in mid-1970.

The Phillips Curve

The fact is that modern bourgeois economic theory has rationalized permanent unemployment and permanent inflation with the scheme of the "Phillips Curve," which expresses the "trade-off" between unemployment and inflation. According to this curve, the higher the rate of unemployment, the lower the rate of price increase, and vice versa. In Samuelson's version, an unemployment rate of $1^1/2$% is associated with an annual price rise of $6^1/2$%, unemployment of 3% with an annual price rise of 3%, unemployment of 5% with no price rise, and unemployment of 7% with a price decline of more than 1%. The curve is hyperbolic—that is, actual full employment would require an infinite rate of price increase. Samuelson comments on this version:

> The indicated 'Phillips curve' shows by its downward slope that increasing the level of unemployment can moderate or wipe out the upward price creep. There is, so to speak, a dilemma of choice for society between reasonably high employment with maximal growth and a price creep, or reasonably stable prices with considerable unemployment; and it is a difficult social dilemma to decide what compromises to make.[14]

Typically, he offers the cost-push theory of inflation as an explanation for the Phillips Curve. His diagram is labeled "Cost-Push Phenomena," and shows wages always increasing 3% per year more than prices. Thus, the idea is that price increases are forced by wage increases. This masks the real cause of price increases and at the same time presents a propaganda platform from which to strive to hold down wages and to obtain working class tolerance of high unemployment.

Actually, there is no stable relationship between unemployment and the degree of price inflation. Historically, there has been a very rough inverse correlation, but the terms of that correlation have varied frequently and by wide margins, so that the Phillips Curve has no predictive value. Thus, in 1969 the unemployment rate was $3-3^1/2\%$, while prices were increasing at a rate of 5–6%, or well above the rate specified by Samuelson's version of the Phillips Curve. Establishment economists tried to save it by saying it had "moved upwards." But what about the situation at the end of 1970, when unemployment had risen to 6%, and prices were still increasing by over 5% per year?

More to the point, under conditions of state monopoly capitalism, the level of unemployment and the price level are both significantly influenced by relatively independent sets of government policies. A reactionary government can "prove" that the Phillips Curve works by raising regulated prices and following inflationary monetary policies at a time of low unemployment. But a government acting under pressure of a powerful and militant working class can provide jobs to most of the unemployed and simultaneously "roll back" the most outrageous monopoly prices.

Wages and Prices

The argument that higher wages result in higher prices and are, therefore, self-defeating, is as old as the organized labor struggle for higher wages. It is a propaganda standby for capitalists; it aims to "soften up" labor demands, to convince workers—especially trade union leaders—to be "moderate" in the "public interest." It also aims to mobilize the "middle classes"—merchants, professionals, pensioners, small security holders, and unorganized white collar workers—against unionized workers. It is a principal propaganda basis for wage-freezing laws, incomes policies, antistrike and antiunion legislation.

The essential theme is the "wage-push" theory of inflation that higher wages *cause* higher prices and are of benefit to nobody, and cut the living standards of people on fixed incomes.

The propaganda for the wage-push theory was rarely, if ever, as intense as it has been in the most recent period, when organized workers won substantial increases *and* prices continued to soar despite an economic crisis. Government, business, and academic economists, from right to liberal left, participate in the campaign. And key American labor officials make important concessions to it.

The basic theoretical answer to the wage-push theory was presented over 100 years ago by Karl Marx, at a debate before the General Council of the First International. An English workers' representative, John Weston, claimed that union attempts to get higher wages were self-defeating and actually hurt other branches of industry, because of the operation of the wage-push theory.

Marx countered that by relying on the labor theory of value. This predicates the *independent* determination of the value of labor power—around which wages fluctuate—and the value of other commodities—which depends on the *amount and quality* of labor going into them, and not on the price of the labor power from which that labor flowed.

Thus, he pictured a rise in wages as involving a redistribution of values between capitalists and workers—an increase in the workers' share, a decrease in the capitalists' share. Since, it was assumed, there would be no change in labor productivity, there would be no change in the value of commodities. But there would be a changed distribution of demand. There would be an increased demand for prime necessities, bought by workers, and a decreased demand for luxuries, bought by capitalists. The prices of prime necessities would rise above, and of luxuries would fall below, their values.

This would make it more profitable to produce necessities, and lead to a flow of capital from luxury industries to the production of necessities. Ultimately, the increased supply of necessities would bring their prices down to their original levels, while the diminished supply of luxuries would bring their prices back up to their original levels.

Marx illustrated the operation of the law of value in ways confirming his analysis and with practical data from then recent British experience.[15]

It is amusing to notice that no less august a capitalist institution than the First National City Bank virtually repeated Marx's analysis 105 years later:

> But, popular sentiment notwithstanding, there is no reason for rising labor costs in selected industries, however important, to lead inexorably to a rise in the general price level . . . when prices are increased in union-organized industries as a result of wage contracts, there will be an increase in the relative prices of some goods rather than an increase in prices generally. . . . Before a general rise in the price level can result from such increases, they must be validated by a monetary policy that fosters a general expansion in demand . . . if rising wages push up costs more rapidly than prices can be raised, profits will be squeezed.

The bank then goes on to express the opinion that more businessmen are espousing wage-price guidelines or controls because it is "increasingly difficult to offset excessive wage demands by raising prices." If the government followed an expansive monetary policy and therefore "inflation were expected to accelerate, they would not be so apprehensive about their ability to protect profits by increasing prices."[16]

Thus the cause of inflation is identified, in effect, as the depreciation of money through the expansion of its supply beyond that needed for increased commodity circulation, and not the increase in wages. The Marxist analysis presented earlier in this chapter is virtually conceded.

The actual history of the United States demonstrates decisively that causality has been in the opposite direction, with price increases spurring the fight for higher wages.

First, in every inflationary price upsurge in the United States, notably in wartime, the upward thrust of prices clearly *preceded* the rise in wages. Wage increases were fought for to catch up to the sudden increase in prices. Thus, in World War II, wage increases were limited by law to 15%, after prices had gone up by an even larger percentage.

The *Wall Street Journal* wrote:

> In the past 20 years there have been three distinct periods in which factory prices climbed substantially over a prolonged interval.
>
> In each instance, labor costs per unit of factory output were declining when the price climb began—and these costs continued to decline for a considerable period after the price rise was under way.[17]

Trade union contracts necessarily result in a lag of wage changes behind price changes, especially when contracts are for three-year periods. The lag is reduced when there are cost-of-living escalator clauses, but by the very terms of those clauses, there is a built-in wage lag of at least several months. It is typical of the self-serving hypocrisy of corporate executives that those who most bitterly resisted the restoration of escalator clauses in 1969–70, such as the General Electric and General Motors magnates, charged that the clauses would be inflationary.

There are two common arguments advanced to support the "wage-push" theory of inflation. One is the presentation of statistics claiming to show an increase in unit labor costs in the private economy and in manufacturing, in advance of, or exceeding a corresponding increase in prices.

This assumes that an increase in the real share of the working class in the values produced is impermissible and that to prevent this employers can and must increase prices. It is a modernized version of the Malthusian "wage-fund" theory—the very argument advanced by John Weston, against whom Marx debated in 1865. In practice, during most of the period of capitalism, including the recent period, the rate of exploitation of labor has increased, that is, the workers' share has been reduced. But there is nothing inevitable or desirable about this. Indeed, the epoch of the most social progress and concessions to the working people have been periods when there were temporary advances in workers' shares.

Also relevant, and perhaps more so to those who have theoretical doubts, is the fact that official statistics claiming to show causative labor cost increases are rigged. First, they are based on estimated "labor compensation in the private economy." The government statisticians have thrown "everything but the kitchen sink" into this statistic. They include the salaries of workers, employees, and even of corporation executives and officials, which include large elements of hidden profits. They cover all of the finance, service, and miscellaneous branches of the economy, for which the estimates of production are wholly arbitrary, and which are largely irrelevant to the main labor-management struggles over wages. They include estimates of the labor compensation included in the profits taken by employers—estimates, by the way, which are not separately published. They include employer social security payments, which are in no sense compensation to the workers currently employed. Finally, in 1970, the government statisticians introduced seasonal adjustments that yielded utterly unreasonable increases in labor costs. This is compared with the Commerce Department's gross national price deflator, which does not take into account the increasing margins between corporate selling prices and corporate prices for raw materials.

This latter point applies even more sharply to the index of unit labor costs published for manufacturing alone. It might seem more relevant to the big trade union wage issues, but here it is the price of manufactured goods that is used. However, official indexes show that there has been a rapidly widening gap between the prices manufacturers get for their finished goods and the prices they pay for raw materials. The value added per unit of product has gone up much faster than the prices of finished goods, and faster than even the rigged labor cost index published by the government.

The fundamental fact about wage-price relationships is brought out in Chapter III, which shows the sharp, continuing, and almost uninterrupted decline in the real share of manufacturing production workers in the value of their production throughout the postwar period. The workers would have to get enormous wage increases merely to restore their share of a quarter of a century ago.

There remains an argument "from the left," to the effect that monopolies are now so strong that they are able to raise their prices to offset increases in wages. Marx's argument was valid for competitive capitalism, it is said, but not today. Further buttressing this argument is the claim that giant monopoly corporations charge a fixed percentage markup over costs, no more and no less, so automatically they transmit into prices any increase in wages.

This argument has elements of truth, but overall it is false. The clearest example is provided by the regulated transport and utility monopolies. Their prices are fixed by commissions, on the basis of costs plus a set return on capital. To some extent, therefore, a wage increase in these industries not offset by productivity increases, will be reflected in prices. But even here this reflection is imperfect. Even the utilities, the most complete monopolies, are affected by competition— from other forms of transport, oil versus gas, and so forth. The pliability of public commissions to utility demands for rate increases varies with the balance of political forces. During the New Deal period, despite substantial wage increases going to utility workers, rates were held down or even reduced. On the other hand, in a period of reactionary political domination, rates are increased regardless of costs by increases in the allowable rate of profit.

As for the monopolies in steel, automobiles, etc., their *actual* practice, as distinguished from the formal models of the academic textbooks, is to charge prices leading to the highest estimated profit. When supply-demand conditions permit, they will charge prices that will yield a very high rate of profit. But in times of severe competition and weak demand, they also cut their prices. The growing internationalization of markets, and the growing intensity of competition between the monopoly corporations of different countries, render ridiculous the claim that U.S. big business can automatically and generally increase prices to offset wage increases because of a subjective desire to do so, or that it will refrain from increases it can get away with because there have been no labor cost increases to justify them.

Capitalist propaganda is never at a loss to find an argument against wage increases. Thus, when not the slightest case can be made for the cost-push argument, there is the argument that wage increases will lead to increased demand for goods, which will be inflationary. This is used most often in times of war or military buildup but not exclusively at such times. It claims that an increase of demand on the part of the working class, owing to their rising purchasing power, is inflationary, but implies that a similar increase of demand on the part of the capitalist class, owing to their rising profits, is not inflationary. The self-serving character of this line is evident, although that fact is often disguised by its projection through "liberal" academic economists whose identification with capitalist class interests is not publicized. The basic answer to it is provided by Marx in the analysis of the price adjustments following a general increase in wages.

To sum up, the level of wages is governed by the value of labor power—as determined historically under conditions of continuous class struggle and as modified by the success or failure of workers to reduce the rate of exploitation of labor and improve their living standards. The level of prices is determined by the amount of labor required in production, as modified by variations in supply and demand, and by government economic regulations that directly or indirectly influence prices. These two—wages and prices—are largely independent. There is a degree of dependence, however, inasmuch as changes in prices change the cost of goods that workers buy and thereby change the money expression of labor power, even when its real value remains unchanged. Thus, what causality exists is from prices to wages, and not vice versa. Naturally, in conditions of rapid price changes, the degree of causality is quite substantial.

The "wage-push" theory of inflation turns the real relationship upside down. Its operative purpose is to justify imposition of wage freezes or restrictions through "income policies," "guideposts," or "austerity programs," to justify anti-strike legislation and regulations, and the use of troops and police to break strikes.

Under the pressure of big business and the government, some labor leaders make serious concessions to the "wage-push" theory. Thus Leonard Woodcock, president of the United Automobile Workers, argues that cost-of-living escalator clauses, such as the UAW succeeded in reinstating in 1970, are "counterinflationary" but conceded that wage increases won in anticipation of coming price increases lead to higher prices. Such an increase, he says:

. . . tends to guarantee the onset or continuance of the inflation that it anticipates. It builds increased hourly labor costs into the system. To the extent that such cost increases are not offset by increased productivity, the result is higher unit costs. Employers pass those higher costs on in increased prices whenever they can—and often with an extra margin to increase unit profits.[18]

This tacitly accepts the idea of "guidelines" or "incomes policies" that limit workers to increases which government boards deem appropriate in relation to productivity gains and price increases. If this were followed by all unions, it would inevitably lead to a further erosion of labor's share in total output, and a further increase in the rate of exploitation of labor. Indeed, Woodcock specifically attacked construction workers' wage increases as "excessive" thereby helping to create conditions under which the Nixon Administration was able to impose an incomes policy on the construction industry early in 1971—a first step toward the stronger restriction on wages in all sectors of the economy imposed later in the year. (see Chapter IX).

Economic and Social Effects of Inflation

Inflation makes for great instability; for unevenness of change as between industries, areas, and countries; for continuous strain in industrial and financial markets. On the one hand, it tends to stimulate economic growth by putting a premium on converting money into commodities—especially into capital goods that can be used to produce more commodities. It puts a premium on buying consumers goods before prices get still higher, and on accumulating inventories and selling later when prices presumably will get higher yet. On the other hand, it tends to stimulate speculative diversions as the cost of real capital gets out of the reach of weaker capitalists, and as the sales of the goods turned out with added equipment become more difficult because of the inflation-cut real income of working people. On both counts, it dries up the relative supply of free money capital and hence raises the rate of interest. This concentrates more and more of the surplus value of society in the hands of bankers, cuts into the profits of industrial capital, and builds up the pressure for ever faster price increases to restore the rate of profit.

These phenomena contribute to the building up of the crisis-provoking contradictions described in earlier chapters. They contribute especially to crises arising from serious financial disturbances. Continuation of inflation during a crisis reduces the effectiveness of the crisis in accomplishing its objective—the restoration of the rate of profit by wiping out part of the capital values. Thus a crisis with a continuing high rate of price increase can be particularly intractable and particularly long-lasting.

Socially, continuous inflation makes for sharpened class conflicts and conflicts of broader sections of the population with monopoly capital. Almost everybody suffers from inflation. The working class is hardest hit. Prices are increased most sharply in working class areas, especially those of the lowest paid workers—and, again, most severe in the ghettoes of Black, Chicano and Puerto Rican people. Thus conflicts over wages tend to become sharper, and they continue even into periods of prosperity and boom.

The impact is particular harsh on workers in industries that are not unionized or who belong to very weak unions. Inflation tends, therefore, to bring new segments of the working class into economic struggle. Certainly it has been a major influence in the recently expanded organization and strike struggles of government workers, employees of schools, hospitals and other "nonprofit" organizations, farm workers, etc.

Pensioners, the army of people permanently excluded from the labor force and having no choice but to live on relief, ordinary farmers (as distinct from parts of corporate conglomerates), certain categories of small businessmen and self-employed persons—all these are hit by inflation. The many millions of students—a very rapidly growing social segment—suffer not only from the general inflation but also from the skyrocketing level of college fees, textbook prices, etc. Housewives, who may not feel the oppression of employers in factories quite as directly as do their husbands, feel it more sharply in the supermarket. Inflation results in a more-than-proportional increase in government costs; thus taxes increase faster than incomes. The progressive rate structure of the income tax has become a means of disproportionately increasing the rate of taxes on workers as they obtain wage increases to offset higher prices—disregarding the fact that real wages remain unchanged or decline.

Thus, as inflation evolves into a permanent feature and deliberate policy of the ruling Establishment, it becomes a target of struggle around which the overwhelming majority of the population can unite— one of the conditions against which a people's antimonopoly coalition can mobilize.

The rising inflationary trend of the capitalist world developed in a period of relatively rapid economic growth—a special symptom of the growing contradictions within the system and of its growing economic and political instability. What are the limits of accelerating inflation? In one sense, the limits are what the majority of working people, the victims of inflation, will tolerate; in another, the economic and financial effects of accelerating inflation are bound to take a severe toll. Already, inflation has become so institutionalized that it continues unchecked during economic declines or stagnation. The mounting contradictions involved, at some point, will result in a pronounced, and perhaps prolonged, slowing of the economic growth rate of U.S. and world capitalism, with the possibility of really severe world financial and overproduction crises. These may prove necessary to cool the inflationary fever of a decaying system.

VIII.

The Keynesian Theory and Its Application

IN THE 19th century and, to a considerable extent, in the 20th, economic crises were regarded by the capitalists virtually as acts of God. The individual, as he would in a hurricane, did his best to protect himself from the storm. Sooner or later it would blow over, and those who were most vigilant could pick up the pieces of salvageable property.

After 1932, however, the capitalists came to the conclusion that they had to act collectively to cope with economic crises, or their social system and rule would be overthrown. They turned to government regulation as a means to influence the business cycle, to avert its increasingly disastrous impact. The theoretical basis of present-day capitalist government economic regulation is provided by the work of the late English economist John Maynard Keynes and especially by his book, *The General Theory of Employment, Interest and Money,* written in 1935.[1]

We may group the development of economic theories of capitalism in this very rough chronological sequence:

1. The theory of young, crisis-free capitalism, reaching its most scientific development in the works of Smith and Ricardo in the late 18th and early 19th centuries.

2. The theory of capitalism as a system of exploitation, afflicted by crises and a growing class struggle—the Marxian theory of the mid-19th century, which became a weapon in the working class fight for socialism.

3. The "marginal utility" school of Marshall, Pigou, et al. of the late 19th-early 20th century. This concentrated on minute examination of supply-demand relationships, and of the psychology of individual transactions (micro-economics). It endowed the drive of each individual

for maximum personal profit with Godlike virtues, as an "unseen hand" which in the crucible of pure competition would bring about the greatest good and progress for all. It assumed the "natural stability" of capitalism, its eternal and harmonious character. Discarding Smith and Ricardo, it was aimed most directly at combatting the influence of Marxism.

4. The Keynesian theory of capitalism in its monopoly phase, afflicted by unprecedented crises, losing sections of the world to socialism, when instability and disharmony could no longer be ignored. While recognizing some of the real problems of the era of imperialism, it strove to find a way to create within capitalism the stability and harmony requisite for its survival. It relied less on the spontaneous competitive drive of capitalists; more on government intervention to create favorable conditions for them.

With considerable elaboration but little fundamental modification since World War II, Keynesism has emerged as the dominant theory among supporters of capitalism, as Marxism remains dominant among supporters of socialism. Marshallian economics provided ideological weapons for the struggle of the individual capitalist against his workers—for policies of wage-cutting, refusal of social services, outlawing of unions, etc., in the name of free competition, and the unfettered operation of the law of supply and demand.

Keynesism is adapted to a new situation, in which direct wage-cutting is usually impossible; in which the government budget has become of major importance; in which a certain level of public services has to be maintained; in which the capitalists increasingly combat the workers as a class, through the instrumentality of the government; in which the government must mobilize the power for a massive military machine to advance the overseas interests of monopoly capital.

Retaining essentially unchanged the Marshallian "micro-economics" and psychological approach, Keynes added models of the economy as a whole that had enough resemblance to present-day reality to be serviceable to the capitalist state in its attempts to cope with instability and the tendency to economic stagnation in ways that would not disturb the dominance or profits of the capitalist class.

Despite its resemblance to reality, Keynes' economics systematically evades or obscures the social essence of capitalist production as a system of exploitation; it thereby reduces the validity of his formulas, and the accuracy of their practical application in government economic regulation.

Besides "micro-economics" Keynes deals with the broad categories of employment, production, investment, and consumption on a national scale—with "macro-economics." The language of Keynes and the Keynesians is "neutral" as between capital and labor. Keynes himself had certain reform notions, and his formulas have been adopted as arguments in favor of particular reforms within the framework of preserving capitalism.

But the main thrust of Keynesian economics and its main application have been in support of monopoly capitalism and in support of the economic and political objectives of the ruling class.

Keynes Main Theoretical Structure

Keynes' important contribution to bourgeois theory consisted of a dynamic model of production, divided between investment and consumption. The influence of Keynes is reflected, for example, in modern gross national product statistics, which divide the country's output into consumer expenditures, capital outlays, and government spending for goods and services. In Keynes' model, the level of production and of its main components are determined by the categories of "effective demand," the "propensity to consume," the "multiplier," and the "marginal efficiency of capital."

Keynes defines the "effective demand" as the sum of the amounts of income that employers expect to receive as profits and pay out as wages from that level of employment and production which they calculate will yield them the highest profits. This definition, characteristically, confuses real events with psychological expectations. Thus, the *real* "effective demand," in the ordinary sense of the term, of workers for consumers goods is determined by the amount of wages they *actually* receive, rather than the amount the employer expects to pay them, an amount that may change considerably for a variety of reasons.

This confusion permits Keynes to strike a fictitious balance in his model. He thereby fails to grasp the contradictory essence of capitalist production, which leads to instability and crises.

Keynes' "effective demand" can be expressed either in terms of income received for production, or as the value of the goods produced.

On the income side, it is divided between savings and consumption funds. On the production side, it is divided between investment goods and consumers goods. Keynes' definition makes the savings fund equal to the volume of investment goods, and the consumption fund equal to the volume of consumers goods.

In Keynes' structure, the economy finds its equilibrium at that level of "effective demand," which always corresponds to the employers' estimates of maximum profits but rarely corresponds to full employment. Keynes' predecessors pictured capitalism as always operating at maximum efficiency, save for accidental violations of the norm. Keynes' theory faced up to the evident reality of permanent mass unemployment under monopoly capitalism.

Because of the direct relationship between the income and production categories, a change in one will force a change in the other. Thus, a change in the proportion of the total income that is saved will result in a corresponding change in the proportion of production devoted to capital goods. Moreover, a change in the total levels of economic activity and employment will bring a corresponding change in total income.

Keynes' "marginal propensity to consume" is simply the proportion of any increase in income that will be spent in consumption. If two-thirds of the increase is spent on consumption and one-third is saved, then the marginal propensity to consume is two-thirds, and the marginal propensity to save is one-third.

Suppose in this case that from some outside cause the funds available for consumption are increased by one dollar. Then, to keep the proportion, the funds available for savings will automatically be increased by 50 cents, and the total level of demand and production will increase by $1.50.

Now suppose that from some outside cause, savings (or investment) are increased by one dollar. Then, to keep the proportion, the funds available for consumption will increase by $2, and the total level of demand and production will increase by $3.

This effect of an increase in investment on total production is what Keynes called the "multiplier." He assumed that the multiplier was usually about five or larger, but most works dealing with the American economy assume—or estimate from statistical calculations—a multiplier of three it is equal to the reciprocal of the marginal propensity to save.

Whatever the figure, the concept is convenient to capitalist policy. A given change in consumption has only a moderate additional effect on total production, employment, etc. But a change in investment has a *multiplied* effect on the economy. Business spokesmen claim that an increase in investment "primes the pump" of the entire economy.

Or so it seems from a superficial view of the theory. But a more careful study shows that there is *no difference* between calculated economic stimulation derived from an extra $1,000 of investment and an extra $1,000 of investment and an extra $1,000 of consumption, even within the Keynesian theoretical framework.

The multiplication comes from the repeated disposition of the first $1,000 spent. If the marginal propensity to consume is two-thirds then the receivers of the $1,000 will spend for consumption $666.67, and save the rest. The receivers of the $666.67, in turn will spend two-thirds of that, or $444.44 and save the rest. This goes on until the amount involved becomes trivial. Simple algebra shows that the sum of extra spending ends up to $2,000, in addition to the original $1,000. The sum of extra saving at the various stages comes out to exactly this same $1,000, thereby paying for the original extra $1,000. It's all the same if the first thousand dollars is used to build a garage for investment (as in an example of this sort given by Samuelson), or is an additional welfare payment to apoor family given by the government, or an additional $1,000 of wages won by striking workers and immediately spent for added consumption.

Bourgeois economists often attribute to the "multiplier" an almost magical quality of creation—as if several times as many goods are produced as the effort put into priming the pump.

Of course, there is no such thing as getting something for nothing. All increases in production are the fruits of increased application of human labor and increasing rates of labor productivity. The "multiplier," in one sense, simply reflects the proportions in which various functional sectors of the economy increase. The pump-priming effect refers to a stimulus that starts off an upward trend in production in accordance with the proportions specified by that "multiplier." When the increase is more rapid than the compound of the increase in the labor force and the increase in productivity, this simply reflects the result of activating unemployed labor, idle equipment, and stockpiled materials.

Keynes' "marginal efficiency of capital" refers, approximately, to the lowest rate of expected profit which will induce a capitalist to invest his money. Since he envisages a capitalist using borrowed money, the difference between this expected rate of profit and the rate of interest becomes crucial. Therefore, in Keynes' system, considerable importance is given to policies that will increase the rate of profit and to easy money policies that will reduce the rate of interest.

Government regulation and supplementing of investment, according to Keynes, is the main road of intervention to achieve a more desired level of economic activity. This line of analysis is used by business spokesmen to justify demands for various types of government subsidies and tax concessions, and thereby "help the economy."

In the Keynesian framework, government spending has a role analogous to investment, and taxation's role is somewhat similar to saving. Thus, government spending can be urged as a means of stimulating the economy—whether it spends for armaments or for housing.

Other economists, who may for convenience be called "labor Keynesians," use the multiplier in reverse. They call for increases in wages, tax concessions to workers, more social security benefits, etc., as a means of increasing consumption and thereby "helping the economy."

Whether one begins at the consumption side or the investment side, the end result, according to the formula, is the same. Projections of the future economy by big business groups, such as the Rockefeller Brothers Fund, end up almost the same in sum and in detail as projections by the Conference for Economic Progress, a combination of some union officials and lesser capitalists. But, in practice, policies rationalized on the basis of Keynesian economics almost always end up by being those which advance the specific *class interests* of big capital, rather than those of the economy abstractly or of the "general public."

While Keynes seemed to depart from the old theory of harmonious capitalism, he ended with a new stabilization, a new harmony, albeit at a level of chronic mass unemployment. And, like his predecessors in bourgeois economics, he glossed over the class differentiation in society—the issue of *who* owned the savings and *whose* consumption was advanced or reduced.

He envisioned the level of wages and prices as if they were to be determined according to an ideal policy rather than through the outcome of the class struggle and the relation between monopoly and non-monopoly sectors of industry. Thus he failed to understand the real dynamics of capitalist economy—the contradictions that inevitably breed instability and crisis.

Keynes vs. Marx on Crisis

Although Keynes wrote his main work following the great crisis of the early 1930s, his theory dealt more with low-level stagnation than with economic crises. This is understandable in terms of the time and place. The British economy had tended to stagnate through much of the 1920s. The crisis there was less violent than in the United States, Germany, and some other countries. But after 1932, Britain, like the United States, suffered from chronic high unemployment, at a level of production between the crisis low and the previous high. This was the period referred to by Marxists as a "depression of a special kind."

Keynes saw that the demand for consumers goods increased less rapidly than total production or income, at a ratio equal to "the marginal propensity to consume." The Marshallians have assumed that investment would always increase sufficiently to avoid any gap and insure full employment. Keynes saw that this didn't happen, that investment tended to stick at a considerably lower level. There was a "widening gap" between potential output and potential demand. Thus "the economic system may find itself in stable equilibrium . . . at a level below full employment . . . " at which supply equals demand . . . . "This analysis supplies us with an explanation of the paradox of poverty in the midst of plenty." In a "wealthy community" the marginal propensity to consume will be relatively low. Therefore, "the richer the community, the wider will tend to be the gap between its actual and its potential production; and therefore the more obvious and outrageous the defects of the economic system."[2]

Notice that even in this formulation Keynes avoids the class essence of the question: The main point is not the average wealth of the community, but the share of it going to the capitalist class! The gap between actual and potential production is especially shocking in certain "poor" countries, where the lion's share of the income is appropriated by foreign capitalists and domestic compradores, who do not use it to provide needed investment goods. Here Keynes does not talk of actual overproduction in relation to the market but rather of production settling down to an equilibrium, with demand at a relatively low level. He assumes that this is achieved smoothly and gradually.

Marx, on the other hand, dealt with crises of *overproduction,* caused by actual production running ahead of demand at prices that would yield a sufficient rate of profit. Marx then dealt with it as the process of temporarily resolving this crisis through the more or less violent decline in production and prices and the destruction of some capital values.

Keynes dealt with demand as the result of the psychological attributes of "consumers," without any social differentiation among them. Marx dealt with demand as a social function determined by the different relationship to production of different classes in society. He assumed that workers spent virtually all of their incomes on consumption goods, while the capitalists divided their incomes between consumption and investment, with a drive to invest as much as possible in order to grow still richer and more powerful—in order to swallow up competitors and avoid being swamped by still richer capitalists. But this very drive of the capitalists invariably leads to overproduction, then to a crisis and to fluctuating employment and unemployment.

Thus the Keynesians avoid facing the essential question: *Whose* income is increased or diminished by a certain policy—which is the only way to determine its impact on consumption and investment. The U.S. Department of Labor, in a study of family expenditures, income, and savings showed a very marked change in the marginal propensity to consume with changes in income—ranging from 1.03 in the $3,000-$4,000 income group to 0.49 for those with incomes over $15,000.[3]

Thus, lower-income workers' families spent every cent of additional income on consumption, *and then some.* They were able to do so because with rising income they had more access to credit. On the other hand, the capitalists spent less than half of any increase in their incomes on consumption—and we may be sure that this proportion dwindled still further for incomes over $100,000—the scale of the really big bourgeoisie. Moreover, the bulk of the capitalists' savings is within the corporate framework and never distributed to individuals at all.

Keynes' analysis was geared to attempts to cope with crises and depressions by capitalist governments desirous of hiding the responsibility of the capitalist class and system for the difficulties faced by the people, and anxious to hide the class essence of the measures they take. Marx's analysis provides a theoretical framework within which the working class can develop programs of struggle for coping with unemployment, crises and stagnation in ways which correspond to the interests of the workers at the expense of capitalists.

To Marx, the gap between supply and demand was a real phenomenon resulting from the contradictory character of capitalist production, destined to be resolved in violent economic perturbations. To Keynes, the gap was a potential phenomenon resulting from people's psychology, to be resolved harmoniously in "stable equilibrium," although too often at a lower-than-desired level of activity. Despite these fundamental differences, Keynes accepted, in this distorted way, the concept of the relative inadequacy of consumer demand which Marx had explained 70 years earlier.

In view of this, Keynes' treatment of Marx is revealing. Historically, says Keynes, Malthus argued the possibility of inadequate demand but was not able to demonstrate it theoretically. Later economists, such as Marshall and Pigou, completely ignored the question, limiting themselves to the tautology that supply creates its demand. The issue of effective demand "could only live on furtively, below the surface, in the underworlds of Karl Marx, Silvio Gesell, or Major Douglas."[4]

It is characteristic of Keynes' limitations that he regarded Marx's work as something "furtive" and of the "underworld." Almost 20 years after the October Revolution, with advocates of Marx's theories numbering in the millions—a force to be reckoned with in all leading countries including England—this leading economist of capitalism continued to regard Marx not as a scientist worthy of serious study but in the category of the "funny money" cranks.

Whether it was the Fabian socialists in England, or the Technocrats and some New Dealers in the United States, or the then current and brilliant applications of Marxist economics on a world scale by Eugene Varga, knowledgeable students, including revolutionaries and reformers, placed the problem of inadequate demand in the center of the stage before Keynes "rediscovered" it. And all of them derived their approach, directly or indirectly, precisely or incompletely, from Marx and his theoretical followers in the epoch of imperialism—Lenin, Luxemburg, Hilferding, etc.

Keynes essentially represented the attempt to tame this new tide in economic thinking, to strip it of all revolutionary content while using it to fashion a more flexible instrument than previously existed for maintaining the capitalist social system.

Specific Weaknesses in the Keynesian Structure

Important parts of Keynes' theory have become more or less obsolete—such as his theory of the role of the rate of interest. Here we deal only with certain key features which have current application and which led to incorrect conclusions on the part of Keynesians.

One of them is the definition of savings as equal to investment. This seemed necessary for the construction of an equilibrium scheme, which Keynes regarded as necessary to establish capitalism as a potentially stable system. But this leads to inconsistency when applied to a capitalist economy in a real state of dynamic change.

This can be shown in Keynes' own terms. Effective demand is the *expected* income of employers plus the wages they *expect* to pay out. Savings, a component of that income, is further dependent on a psychological factor, the "marginal propensity to consume." Investment, the object of savings, is dependent on yet another *expectation,* the "marginal efficiency of capital." Yet in Keynes' scheme, effective demand determines *actual* production, while savings equals *actual, current* investment, a component of that production.

In reality, incomes do not always equal advance expectations. Hence the actual savings may *not* conform to investment at any given time interval. But, argue the Keynesians, the level of production will be adjusted so that savings will conform. They tacitly assume that this adjustment takes place continually and instantaneously. But, in actual life, it occurs over a considerable interval, following a long, gross buildup of nonconformity, whereupon the adjustment occurs spasmodically and sharply, that is, in the form of a crisis.

Marx explained this real difference between the creation of surplus value (including a given segment of investment goods), and the actual realization of surplus value, most eloquently, as already quoted in Chapter II, i.e., "the conditions of direct exploitation and those of realizing it are not identical. They diverge not only in place and time, but also logically." At times Keynes seemed to realize this. But his basic theory did not take it into account, nor do his followers.

The Keynesians also fall into error by covering up the exploitation of labor. Every capitalist starts out with a sum of money that he invests in buying machines, materials, and labor. In the process, the money capital becomes commodity capital. Marx divides the capital into constant and variable. The former consists of machinery and materials, the product of past labor; it is "constant" capital because its value does not change in the process of production. The variable capital is used to buy labor power. This changes in amount in the process of production, accumulating surplus value through the difference between the value of the worker's living labor and the cost of his labor power. It was this theoretical advance over Smith and Ricardo that enabled Marx to identify the real source of capitalist profits and to penetrate all the contradictions of the capitalist mode of production.

Bourgeois economists deny the special character of variable capital or the existence of surplus value in Marx's sense. Profits, in their view, are the return for the capitalist's contribution, defined in psychological and supply-demand terms.

The Keynesians, evading the issue of the origin of profits, tacitly accept the old bourgeois rationalization. In the process, they wholly discard the existence of variable capital, which leads to serious distortions in their economic analysis. Thus, Samuelson defines capital as follows:

Modern advanced industrial technology rests upon the use of vast amounts of *capital:* elaborate machinery, large-scale factories and plants, and stores and stocks of finished and unfinished materials. Our economy receives the name "capitalism" because this capital, or "wealth," is primarily the private property of somebody—the capitalist.[5]

The economy is not called "capitalism" because individuals own the machinery. Individuals also owned the means of production under feudal and slave systems. It is called capitalism because the owner of the machinery hires workers to operate it for cash wages, rather than using their labor power under the earlier forms of exploitation.

From Samuelson's definition, one might think that the machines and materials themselves put together the final product, without human intervention. The portion of capital used to pay wages is wholly omitted.

The accounts of the U.S. Steel Corporation illustrate the importance of this omission. At the end of 1963 it had capital funds of $4,150 million. Of this, somewhat over $3 billion consisted of plant and equipment; the remainder, a little over $1 billion, consisted of net working capital—the circulating capital that is turned over and over during the year. This billion dollars is used to pay for raw materials and wages.

During 1963 U.S. Steel paid $1.8 billion in wages and salaries, $1.4 billion in purchases of materials and supplies. The total, $3.2 billion, suggests that the circulating capital was turned over about three times a year. And the distribution of the total suggests that a little more than half the billion dollars was variable capital, the part of capital that yielded surplus value.

In the Keynesian model, only the inventories on the books of U.S. Steel, valued at $642 billion, are included.[6] The rest simply disappears.

U.S. government gross national product statistics handle savings and investments as strict identities, limited on the investment side to plant and equipment outlays and changes in the amount of inventories. Fitting into the Keynesian mold, these statistics distort reality. And this has a serious gross effect, for, in reality, year-to-year changes in the money capital of American corporations are quite large and closely associated with changes in payrolls.

Parallel to this omission, both government and private accounting cover over the exploitation of labor. Work in process and finished goods inventories are valued so as to include only actual costs incurred. The wages paid are included, but not the surplus value. This does not even exist in the bookkeeping until the commodity is sold. It is as if the profit is exclusively the creation of the salesman. Ideologically, however, the practice is meant to glorify not the salesman, but the capitalist himself. It is meant to convey the idea that the profits are created by capital as one of the "factors" of production; that these profits are "earned" by the capitalists just as wages are earned by the worker. Corresponding to this idea, the financial manuals speak of the "earnings" of a corporation rather than of its profits.

Opposing Class Interpretations of Keynes' Multiplier

As noted earlier, the Keynesian analysis states that an increase in demand stimulated by events outside the normal transactions of the private economy activates resources that would otherwise remain unused. It converts these into investment or consumption funds, setting in motion a cycle of increases that raises total production by the original increase in demand times the Keynesian multiplier.

Keynes himself, concerned with the profits of the capitalists, focused on stimuli that favor investments. Most bourgeois economists do likewise. Samuelson writes: "Modern income analysis shows that an increase in net investment will increase national income by a multiplied amount—by an amount greater than itself; investment dollars—like any independent shifts in governmental, foreign, or family dollar spending—are high-powered, double-duty dollars, so to speak."[7]

A miracle! exclaims the prophet of higher profits. Such reasoning is used to justify government policies that favor capital over labor on the pretext of the need to stimulate the flow of these "high-powered" investment dollars.

But in the parenthetical remark Samuelson gives the game away. *Any* independent event will have a multiplied effect. Economists call these *exogenous* events—outside of the previous chain of transactions. Examples of this are changes in government spending and taxes, special demands arising from wars, class struggles leading to a marked change in real wages.

The capitalists use the official Keynesian stress on investment to argue for legislation shifting the tax burden from themselves to labor, for restraint on wages, for direct subsidies to investment—all on the grounds that this will be good for the economy.

But reformist labor spokesmen, using the same Keynesian theory, argue for legislation increasing wages and social benefits, reducing taxes on labor, restraining profits—all on the ground that this will have a multiple stimulating effect on the economy.

Where does the truth lie? There can be no simple answer, because the assumptions are wrong. As we have seen, there is no single multiplier, but radically different ones for capitalists and workers. The "exogenous" event does not influence a smoothly developing situation but one that is beset by contradictions. Thus, the stimulus to investment may simply aggravate the contradiction between productive capacity and limited mass consuming power, helping to precipitate a crisis. Indeed, this happened in the 1920s. On the other hand, a shift of taxes from labor to capital might cut the rate of profit, which also can set off a crisis under some conditions.

Since the main cause of setbacks has been the relative shortage of mass consuming power rather than any lack of profits, actions benefiting the workers would seem to be "better for the economy."

But then one must consider the political complications. When labor makes a major gain in a given country, the capitalists may shift their investments to other countries, where there have been no labor gains, and thereby minimize or even reverse the advantages accruing to the economy of the first country. In extreme cases, the capitalists engage in economic sabotage by trying to topple governments that take measures which have positive social content. What statistical evidence is available on this supports the contention that events benefiting labor result in the most marked economic growth. Thus, in countries such as West Germany, Japan, France, and Italy, where there have been the biggest increases in real wages and social benefits in recent decades, there has also been the fastest economic growth.

Many other factors, however, contributed to the fast economic growth of these countries. So long as capitalists retain the power positions in the economy and in the government, nobody can guarantee that measures involving a shift from surplus value to labor income will stimulate economic activity. The measures are justified and necessary primarily because they benefit labor and curtail the extremes of exploitation of labor by capitalists. They do not require justification on the grounds of benefit to the economy, which is not under the control of nor is it the responsibility of, the working class.

To the extent that labor can combine the winning of concessions with winning influence on government policies and positions within the government, it may be able to combine socially beneficial measures with elements of state control tending to ensure beneficial economic impacts, preventing the flight of capital and economic sabotage by the capitalists, and ensuring government investment where private investment is lacking.

In the final analysis, the only guarantee of all-around economic improvement is the proper combination of advances in living standards, social welfare, and production levels in a socialist planned economy in which the workers are the collective owners of the means of production.

Political Evolution of Keynes' Theories

The "pure" Keynesian theoreticians make a pretense of political sterility. They say it makes no difference whether the government stimulates the economy through low-cost housing for workers, tax incentives for big business, acceleration of the arms race, or the random dropping of dollar bills from airplanes for people to pick up. In practice, such seeming indifference is generally a cover for support of pro-capitalist policies. In any event, their purpose, which is to iron out the contradictions of capitalism, is objectively pro-capitalist.

Keynes wrote his main work when capitalist governments were engaged in emergency economic intervention, under compulsion of the great economic crisis. His theory reflected the need for a theoretical framework to explain this intervention and, to some extent, to guide it. But while Keynes and his followers on both sides of the ocean were discussing problems of peaceful governments' economic intervention, German and Japanese imperialism were "achieving full employment" with all-out war preparation and aggression.

By the end of World War II, U.S. imperialism attempted to take over where the defeated Axis powers left off. The United States became the core of world reaction; its corporations strove for economic conquest, while its armed forces established unprecedented global power positions. It used Nazi-like genocidal methods against weaker peoples, and threatened a thermonuclear war for the destruction of the socialist world.

This political framework determined the evolution of Keynesian economic theory in postwar America. Economists retaining academic, government, or business positions tacitly or actively accepted the central anti-Communist political and military assumptions of the Cold War. Full employment and economic growth were viewed as goals not so much for their welfare values as for internal political stability, external propaganda advantage, and more economic power for military expansion in the contest with Communism.

Regarding military activity as being no worse than civilian, the Establishment experts developed programs with a mixture of armament expansion and spending for schools and other civil purposes that were most useful to capitalism, that is, the provision of the trained people needed in the epoch of the scientific-technical revolution. A particularly shameful game was played by those Keynesian economists who put on a liberal or pro-labor front but acted as "left-wing" propagandists for the arms race.

Thus, Heilbroner and Bernstein considered it a question of "philosophy" and "open to political argument" whether federal spending should be for milk for school children or for missiles and weapons. Rebutting the charge that military spending is socially useless, they wrote:

Yet, even here, new areas of technological progress, new industries, new horizons for human endeavor are opening up. Furthermore, the knowledge that the United States is a powerful nation, well armed and well protected, gives a much greater sense of confidence and leads to a much greater willingness by businessmen to assume the risks of enterprise. Business would not likely be as venturesome if we were in a state of continuous anxiety about the imminence of invasion, subversion, or bombardment. No, even defense spending makes some positive contribution to the economy.[8]

Thus these New School for Social Research liberals project the ideology of imperialism in a light, and with an eloquence, that surely please the avaricious arms contractor and piratical foreign investor, transformed by the authors into venturesome beneficiaries of the public welfare; and they turn the most genocidal Pentagon brass into Sir Galahads of freedom.

Similarly, Keynesian Leon Keyserling, known as a labor economist, argues for "guns and butter" against those capitalists who wanted to restrain wages in order to finance the Vietnam War. But he yielded nothing to them in his support for that venture:

founded upon dedication to a way of life and a record of performance which gear our free institutions to economic and social justice at home. We cannot marshal full support for the undertaking in Vietnam, if this were to mean telling more than 34 million people that they must abide more patiently in the cellars of poverty because some of their brothers and sons are in Vietnam.[9]

During the worst Cold War years, virtually the only economists who attacked the military orientation of Cold War economic policy, exposed its anti-labor essence, and demanded a policy of government economic intervention with a peaceful, pro-labor content, were the Communist economists, those associated with left-led unions expelled from the CIO, and a handful of others close to them in orientation, many excluded from government or academic positions by McCarthyism.

An outstanding work with this view was Hyman Lumer's *War Economy and Crisis,* written, characteristically, while the author was in imminent danger of arrest by McCarthyite authorities. Later he was, in fact, arrested and jailed for over a year.[10]

During the 1960s, and especially with the broadening opposition to the Vietnam War, a widening range of economists entered the lists against the militarization of the economy. Columbia professor Seymour Melman, for example, worked out and popularized reconversion programs within the Keynesian theoretical framework.

However, just as many of the people opposed to the Vietnam War have come to realize that the roots of the evil are in the entire system of American imperialism, so more and more of the progressive economists are coming to realize that the theoretical weapons with which to campaign for peace and people's welfare are to be found in Marxism, not in Keynesism.

IX.

The Government, the Cycle and Economic Growth

The relations of government to business and the phenomena of state-monopoly capitalism have grown immensely more complex and all-pervasive in economic life. The "self-reliant entrepreneur" no longer depends on his own "initiative" in crucial social relations, internally or internationally. His system of exploitation increasingly conflicts with the technical and organizational structure of production, is increasingly challenged by more progressive social forces. Countering these, he uses the state apparatus to reinforce and protect his profit-taking in a thousand ways.

The most powerful and influential tycoons use the government to raise their profits through armament orders, subsidies, and support for foreign investments. The class as a whole uses the government to hold down wages, manipulate price increases, impose limits on wages and union activity, shift the tax burden to labor, and conduct a foreign policy in their own interest.

Marxists include the entirety of these activities and the relationships they reflect in the broad concept *state-monopoly capitalism.* A characteristic short definition of state-monopoly capitalism is provided by the Soviet economists, Ostrovityanov and Cheprakov: "State-monopoly capitalism is a complex system under which monopoly capital uses the bourgeois state in its own interests. It includes, in the main, state property, state consumption, government control and regulation."[1]

It became significant as capitalism fell into a chronic, basically insoluble, political-social-economic crisis, from the time of World War I and the Russian Revolution. It has multiplied in importance and scope since, with especial rapidity during the past three decades. Here we do not attempt a comprehensive description or discussion of state-monopoly capitalism, but focus on aspects relating directly to the subject of this book.

Since World War II there has developed a relatively new set of functions of state-monopoly capitalism: to stabilize the economy and stimulate its growth. These functions are on behalf of all the top monopoly groups, and for the preservation of the system itself. The leading magnates support them and, to some extent, are willing to subordinate particular interests to them—although in practice little is done to impinge adversely on any major group.

More concretely, the new policy objectives are:

1. To minimize the business cycle and if possible to eliminate totally its downward phase.

2. To prevent or contain rising prices and costs.

3. To increase the long-term rate of economic growth.

By and large, these functions developed first in other capitalist countries, notably Japan, France, and West Germany, where capitalism emerged from World War II in a condition of acute political and economic instability, able to survive and revive only with extensive U.S. military and financial support. However, United States capitalism became deeply involved also, as its relative position deteriorated and it encountered increasingly powerful international and domestic opposition.

Technically, the first listed function is required by the Employment Act of 1946, which calls on the government "to promote maximum employment, production, and purchasing power," and to afford "useful employment opportunities, including self-employment for those able, willing, and seeking to work." The Act made it clear that it was not intended to stray beyond the bounds of capitalism or to undermine the system, for these objectives were to be attained "in a manner calculated to foster and promote free competitive enterprise and the general welfare."[2]

Practically, the motivation was not to meet any requirement of law, but rather the conviction that the survival of the system required a greater degree of stability than had prevailed prior to World War II.

The second objective was not derived from the Employment Act. Initially it stemmed from the desire of big business to hold down wages, which were assigned the blame for rising prices. To "fight against inflation" was almost a code name for the fight against wage increases.

But increasingly, as price rises accelerated and the money and credit system became shaky, the fight against inflation was also viewed, in a broader sense, as the need to hold prices generally within some kind of bounds in order to achieve the first objective of minimizing the business cycle.

The third objective, that of increasing the long-term growth rate, became part of official U.S. government policy only in the 1960s. It was stimulated largely by the awareness of the increasing economic, scientific, and political challenge of the Soviet Union, and by the realization that this increased relative strength in other fields necessarily had its military counterpart.

The federal government has become more deeply committed, and its involvement in pursuit of these objectives has become more intense with the passing of time and the worsening of all the political, social, and military problems of capitalism.

A rather pronounced shift in priorities is reflected between the 1957 and 1965 Economic Reports of the President. The earlier report defines government responsibilities as follows:

> First, government must pursue policies that give positive encouragement to the spirit of enterprise. . . . Second, government must exercise a strict discipline over its expenditures. . . . Finally, it must pursue policies that will help maintain high levels of production and employment. . . .
>
> But government cannot assume exclusive responsibility for the smooth functioning of our enterprise system, nor can it guarantee sustained economic growth. Even an attempt to do so would involve intervention on a scale incompatible with the fundamental character of our enterprise system, based on the belief that, when regulation is minimized, the energies and talents of the individual are more fully released.[3]

Here the duty of the government to accomplish Employment Act objectives is distinctly secondary to its duty to create a "favorable climate" for business, with a minimum of detailed intervention.

Contrast this with the 1965 Report, which states:

> In 1964, the United States passed a watershed in economic policy. . . . A new era for economic policy is at hand. A wide consensus of responsible opinion now recognizes that Federal fiscal policy must be geared to keep the economy moving ahead. . . . No law of nature compels a free market economy to suffer from recessions or periodic inflations. As the postwar experience of Western Europe and Japan already indicates, future progress need not be interrupted even though its pace may vary from year to year.[4]

This change did not take place because of the shift from a Republican to a Democratic administration, although the Democrats have always been more overt Keynesians than the Republicans. A visible change of attitude appeared while the Eisenhower administration was still in power, and there has been no retreat in the intensity of government intervention during 1969-70 under Nixon—the first president to pronounce himself a Keynesian.

The most dramatic spur to the change was the Soviet Sputnik, launched in 1957. The revelation that the world's first socialist country was ahead of the United States at the furthest frontier of scientific advance had implications concerning economic and military potential. This scientific event, which delighted most of humanity, aroused only panic fear among the rulers of the United States, warped by their unbounded hatred of Communism.

They set up a special big business committee, the Gaither Committee, to recommend actions to meet the "crisis." Among the upshots were recommendations, that were carried out, for a rapid increase in military spending and the launching of a huge space program.

Parallel to that official committee, the Rockefeller Brothers set up their own study group under the research direction of Henry Kissinger, now chief foreign policy adviser to President Nixon. Its reports, inflamed with belligerent rhetoric, were largely parallel to the recommendations of the Gaither Committee, on which the Rockefellers had considerable influence.

In addition, the Rockefeller Brothers proposed a much more active policy of government economic intervention, with the goal of a 5% growth rate in order to strengthen U.S. capitalism in economic competition with the Soviet Union.

The heightened alarm was already reflected in the language of the 1958 Economic Report of the President:

The latest challenge of international communism will require a further increase in the economic claims of national security, which are already heavy. . . . Whatever our national security requires, our economy can provide, and we can afford to pay . . . international tensions persist. This hard fact emphasizes the need for a sound and growing economy to assure our defense. A sound and growing economy is needed also to meet the requirement of our expanding population. . . . A huge expansion of educational personnel and physical facilities will be required to train increasing numbers of students for the higher level of technology on which our security and welfare depend . . . economic growth is needed to help meet our expanded international responsibilities. Although the rate of economic growth that is best suited to the Nation's capacity and requirements cannot be stated precisely, the low current rate would clearly be unsatisfactory as a continuing condition. . . . The proper objective of national economic policy, to the achievement of which private as well as public actions must contribute, is to strive to limit fluctuations in the rate of over-all economic growth to a relatively narrow range around a rising trend.[5]

At the time, the 5% per year projection of Rockefeller was deemed excessive by most big business groups. Many argued that 3% was all that the country could safely absorb. The Kennedy Administration set a goal of $4^{1}/2$% per year. The Johnson Administration estimated 4.3% per year as appropriate. Thus there is a consensus among the leaders of American capitalism in striving for an annual growth rate in the 4-$4^{1}/2$% range.

Another constant theme is the belief in the inevitable contradiction between full employment and price stability. The economists of modern capitalism consider both substantial unemployment and a continuous rise in prices as unavoidable. They see their task as preventing unemployment from getting too high as a result of a crisis or recession, and preventing prices from rising too fast as a result of excessive economic growth.

The 1956 Economic Report puts it this way:

The continuance of general prosperity cannot be taken for granted. In a high-level economy like ours, neither the threat of inflation nor the threat of recession can ever be very distant. . . . If our economy is to advance firmly on the narrow road that separates recession from inflation, the Federal Government must pursue monetary, fiscal, and housekeeping policies with skill and circumspection . . . [6]

At that time, the Chairman of the Council of Economic Advisers was Arthur F. Burns, later to be chief economic assistant to the president and then chairman of the Federal Reserve Board during the Nixon administration.

In the 1962 Report, President Kennedy wrote:

The task of economic stabilization does not end with the achievement of full recovery. There remains the problem of keeping the economy from straying too far above or below the path of steady high employment. One way lies inflation, and the other way lies recession. Flexible and vigilant fiscal and monetary policies will allow us to hold the narrow middle course.[7]

But six years later, President Johnson admitted failure in this respect: "Neither the United States nor any other free industrial nation has yet learned how to couple steady growth at high employment with reasonable stability of prices."[8]

Fiscal and Monetary Measures

Government economic regulation includes both fiscal and monetary measures. Fiscal measures refer to government spending and taxation. In the simplest terms, when the government spends more than it receives, this is expected to stimulate the economy by creating added purchasing power. When the government receives more in taxes than it spends, or has a budget surplus, this is expected to slow down the economy by draining off purchasing power.

A presidential report states:

The instruments of fiscal policy . . . are the Government's most powerful tools for expanding or restraining over-all demand. . . . The basic task of Federal fiscal policy is to help provide a total market demand for goods and services that neither exceeds nor falls short of the economy's productive capacity at full employment. Maintaining this continuous balance . . . normally involves two basic requirements. First, since total productive capacity grows steadily over time, total demand must grow. Second, since fluctuations in private demand occur independently of federal policy, these fluctuations must be offset in order to avoid dips or surges that could touch off recession or inflation.[9]

The term "full employment" in this quotation is a propaganda description of a given level of *unemployment,* to be described later. Monetary policy "operates by changing the availability and cost of credit to businesses, consumers, and governments. These changes are accomplished most directly by affecting the reserves available to commercial banks, but through its impact on bank policies and financial markets, monetary policy affects the general credit structure of the economy. Monetary policy's impact on expenditures and thus on employment, comes when businesses, consumers or governments—finding borrowing . . . easier or harder, less costly or more costly—are induced to spend more or less than they would otherwise have spent."[10]

By permitting the commercial banks to borrow more or less money from the Federal Reserve banks, by altering their reserve requirements, by changing the interest rates the banks may pay for deposits, and by "open market operations," the Federal Reserve Board often decisively influences the volume of loans the banks can make. Open market operations consist of the purchase and sale of government bonds* from the commercial banks. When the Federal Reserve banks buy government bonds from commercial banks, the latter can use this money to loan to business firms. On the other hand, the Federal Reserve can curtail the commercial banks' lending possibilities by selling bonds to them, thereby absorbing funds they might otherwise lend.

The Federal Reserve Board also influences the rate of interest by altering its discount rate, the rate at which it lends to commercial banks. Keynes attributed great influence to the rate of interest, thinking that an increase would markedly discourage investment, and vice versa. In practice, however, fluctuations in the rate of interest have not markedly affected the amount of investment.

Monetary policy, in effect, is also carried out by government and quasi-governmental banks that deal in mortgages, farm credit, small business loans, and export credits, and by the Pentagon in the scale of its advances to munitions contractors.

Every administration has reacted to recessions and crises with substantial and often massive injections of government deficit spending as a means of stimulating a new upturn. And always this has been reinforced with easier money policies—but with the fiscal moves leading.

The Eisenhower Administration, in its first years, stressed "traditional" concepts of budget balancing and monetary "responsibility." But it met the 1958 crisis with a record peacetime deficit. The Nixon Administration came into office with similar talk about budget balancing. Administration economists downgraded fiscal measures of economic regulation, and much prominence was given to the Friedman theory of economic stabilization through a steady 4% per year increase in the money supply. Like the Eisenhower Administration in 1957, so the Nixon Administration in 1969 followed a tight money, tight budget

*The transactions are generally in medium and short-term securities, referred to technically as notes and bills.

policy. But in 1970 Nixon reversed course even more thoroughly than Eisenhower had. By the second quarter of 1970, the "national income accounts" deficit reached a $14 billion annual rate, suggesting Eisenhower's 1958 record and the still-higher 1967 peak of Johnson's administration. The money supply was being expanded at a rate nearly double Friedman's 4%. And government officials were claiming that their expansive fiscal and monetary policies were the main factors to turn the economy upward again in the second half of the year. When this failed, they used both types of stimuli more intensively, promising that the delayed upturn would actually come promptly in 1971.

When 1971 passed without a significant recovery, the Nixon Administration went to further extremes, signified by the publication of a $39 billion budget deficit for fiscal year 1972, far higher than at any previous time except for World War II years.

The creation of the Federal Reserve System in 1914 represented the beginnings of systematic government attempts to regulate the economy. Until the 1930s, however, these were limited to the monetary measures of the Federal Reserve. Since the Great Crisis of the 1930s, both forms have been used with generally increasing intensity.

By and large, Democratic administrations have tended to emphasize fiscal measures more than monetary measures—as suggested by President Johnson's Council of Economic Advisors' cited reference to them as "the Government's most powerful tools." Republican Administrations have tended to place relatively more emphasis on monetary measures than the Democrats, although fiscal measures are at least as important to the Republicans.

In part, this difference results from the more direct leadership of the most powerful banking groups in Republican administrations. In part, it results from the historical fact that Republicans came into power at times when the pressure to curb inflation was greatest—a situation calling for monetary restraint. In any case, as with other issues, the difference between the two parties on this is secondary.

The record shows a rough correlation between the federal fiscal policy and the trend of the economy. Large federal surpluses often preceded a crisis, while large deficits marked the beginnings of an upturn. Thus, on the "national income accounts" basis, there was a surplus in 1929, big surpluses in 1947–48, before the first postwar crisis, surpluses in 1957 and 1960, before the ensuing downturns, and a big surplus in 1969. There were big deficits in the depression years of the 30s, in the crisis or recession years of 1949, 1954, 1958, 1961, and 1970.

The relationship, however, was by no means uniform or reliable. Even aside from the effects of wars, there were periods in which the correlation was unclear. Thus, there were surpluses for three years, throughout the 1955–57 revival, before the 1958 drop. There were deficits throughout the 1930s, without bringing about a real recovery.

There are considerable difficulties in even estimating the impact of federal fiscal policies. The official "unified" budget differs considerably from the "national income accounts" budget. Neither of them takes into account the powerful effect of big increases or decreases in government orders for munitions, which are reflected in spending only much later.

A big federal deficit may have one effect when there are ample private resources from which the Federal Government can borrow, another when federal borrowings remove funds from private uses.

Generally, monetary policy has been carried out in accord with fiscal policy. There have been exceptions, when the "independent" Federal Reserve Board has followed a different tack from the executive branch of the government. Although both the Executive Branch and the Federal Reserve Board are run by representatives of the financial-industrial oligarchy, sometimes different groups have the leading voice in the White House and in the Federal Reserve Board. This may reflect different regional interests or even differences in opinion among the top Wall Street banks.

The effect of monetary policy has not been as clear-cut as that of fiscal policy. Restrictive monetary policy, however, did contribute significantly to the declines of 1958, 1961, and 1970, as well as to the pause or "minirecession" of 1967.

It is difficult to gauge the impact of changes in monetary policy. There is a substantial range of financial activity outside the scope of the Federal Reserve Board, so to a certain extent its restrictions merely divert the flow to other channels. International money and credit flows have become more important. The statistical measures of the money supply and the credit base are even more varied than the budgetary measures.

Thus, at best, these are rough tools. Occasionally, in the Johnson and

Nixon Administrations, there was talk of "fine tuning" the economy with the aid of these tools. But such talk rapidly died out under the pressure of sharp changes that went far beyond the bounds of the economic strategy of the Administration in power.

Class Content of Government Economic Regulation

The general goals of faster economic growth and ending depressions are neutral. Like good weather, everybody is for them. The significant questions concern *how* the government will strive to achieve these ends, for whose benefit and at whose cost.

The capitalists wish to spur growth in ways that raise the rate of exploitation of labor and the accumulation of capital, especially abroad. They want lower taxes for themselves and increased spending for armaments and for business subsidies—with only a minimum of outlays that are of value to the masses. They want a monetary policy that provides ample credit to big business, high interest to bankers, while they gather in at low interest the savings of the middle classes.

The workers wish to spur growth in ways that increase their welfare most, that reduce their exploitation and suffering from unemployment. They want the tax burden shifted off their shoulders and on to those of the billionaires. They want higher federal spending only for welfare purposes and the public sector—such as health, education, and social security—and less spending for armaments and war. They want a monetary system to supply ample low-interest credit for housing and consumers durable goods. The Black people and other oppressed groups want special programs to meet their particular needs and to overcome and compensate for the damages inflicted by discrimination.

In practice, government economic regulation is wholly dominated by finance capital, restrained only indirectly by the potential resistance of labor and oppressed peoples. The aims have become more far-reaching, but the class essence is like that of Hoover's "trickle-down" policy—giveaways to big capital, from which, it is claimed, benefits filter down to the workers.

Fortune magazine graphically describes how the modern "executive committee of the ruling class" carries out its intensified economic regulation:

For while government is moving into an active role in the nation's economic affairs, it is moving with the advice and consent of business. Literally hundreds of corporate executives are on the president's famous telephone list, and find their counsel sought and considered on high economic matters; scores have ready access to the White House to argue their cases on matters of policy that might affect them. . . . Johnson has preached and practiced the gospel that the U.S. rides on its economy, and the economy rides on the state of American business . . . all over town the speech writers declaim fervently and almost gratefully on the creative power of the American business system.

President Johnson, says *Fortune,* constructed his economic management team like a corporation executive staff—Defense Secretary McNamara of Ford Motors, Commerce Secretary Connor of Merck (and the Morgan financial group), Treasury Secretary Fowler, the Wall Street lawyer, are cited as examples. Secretary of State Thomas Mann, in charge of Latin American affairs, "has won the complete respect of such international businessmen as David Rockefeller and J. Peter Grace." Fowler

is a "businessman's Keynesian" accepting as necessary and desirable the need for government to stimulate the economy toward full employment of all its resources, but holding with a ferocious tenacity to the faith that growth will be successful only as it removes the burdens from business and allows the private sector to fill an ever larger role in shaping the nation's, and the world's economic development.[11]

Needless to say, the big business domination was fully as complete under Eisenhower and Nixon, and the same forces occupied the key posts in Kennedy's administration, although he himself was personally less liked and less the confidant of the main men of Wall Street.

The pro-capitalist content of government economic regulation is evident in all major areas of operations.

Revenue Policies

Government spending can be financed by capital levies, taxation, or borrowing, or combinations thereof. The U.S. government has never imposed a capital levy, which is a radical reform measure.* The

*Except indirectly through estate and gift taxes.

controlling financiers prefer taxation, supplemented by borrowing, to cover expenditures. The borrowing is not fortuitous, resulting from errors in budget estimates. It is consciously planned. The huge debt, accumulated throughout the history of the country, has special advantages to the bankers. The institutions they control hold the bulk of government bonds. They get an interest return at the ultimate expense of the mass of taxpayers. The more the federal, state, and local governments borrow, the more interest rates are pushed up all along the line. Between 1949 and 1969, the net public debt at all governmental levels combined increased 90%, but interest payments on that debt increased 183%.[12]

Most of the federal debt is now short-term or medium-term debt which must be turned over in a few months or within five years. Each year new and refunding issues mount up into the hundreds of billions of dollars—with commissions and opportunities for trading profit accruing to the handful of banks and special Wall Street houses that act as brokers for these bonds.

Since government policy now calls for a deficit most of the time, the tendency will be to further accelerate the growth of the debt turnover and the interest tribute accruing to the handful of banks and special Wall Street houses that act as brokers for these bonds.

A big increase in interest payments is guaranteed as old long-term bonds mature and have to be repaid with higher-interest issues.

Taxes provide the bulk of revenues needed to cover outlays. Throughout the past quarter of a century, the tax burden has been shifted from capital to labor, from the rich to the poor. Virtually every revision of tax laws has moved in this direction. Also, the Internal Revenue Service has frequently amended its rules and procedures so as to reduce collections from capitalists. At the same time, the form of the individual income tax law, under conditions of inflation, brings about an automatic year-by-year increase in the effective tax rate on workers.

According to rough estimates, in 1941, capitalists paid 55% of federal taxes, workers 45%, but in 1970, capitalists paid only 32%, while workers paid 68%. This amounted, in terms of 1970 revenues, to a shift of $45 billion per year, at the expense of workers.[13]

To dramatize the shift in the tax burden, consider the income tax, originally enacted as a concession to the working people, to move in the direction of taxation in proportion to ability to pay. Prior to World War

I, almost all income taxes were paid by capitalists, corporations, and well-to-do middle class individuals.

But in fiscal year 1970, $77 billion of income taxes were deducted from workers' paychecks, while only $26 billion of income taxes were paid by other sections of the population, and only $35 billion by corporations. In that fiscal year alone, income taxes paid by workers went up $7 billion, while income taxes paid by other individuals and corporations went down $4 billion.[14]

Expenditure Policies

Keynesian economists place the matter as if the gross amount of spending is the only important concern. But socially, and to a considerable extent economically also, the question is how the money is spent, and for whose benefit. In the U.S. budget for fiscal 1969, 58% went for military and related purposes (including space spending, international affairs, and veterans' care, and interest on the federal debt, almost all of which was accrued during periods of war.) Another 8% went for various kinds of business subsidies and so-called "pork-barrel" projects; 24% went for social security benefits, mainly through insurance systems handled by the federal government but paid for with contributions by the workers and their employers. Only 10% of the budget went for welfare programs, defined in the broadest sense.[15] Actually, most of this contributed absolutely nothing to the welfare of the working people or of the poverty-stricken who are considered to be the main beneficiaries. The multibillion dollar housing program provides hardly any homes for those needing public housing. It consists mainly of subsidies for building contractors and mortgage bankers. The "anti-poverty" and "community development" programs support expensive government bureaucracies, providing posts for lesser supporters of the regime in power, and profitable "research" and "management" contracts for corporations. Relatively little trickles down to the poor, or to improving the deteriorating cities of the country.

This type of expenditure has had the special purpose of attempting to dampen liberation struggles in the Black community, and simultaneously buttressing consuming power—however little *overall*—for contracyclical purposes. Governmental efforts of this type are supplemented by expenditures of the billionaire foundations.

Incentives

An important type of government economic stimulation is through incentives to encourage particular types of activity. These also have a pronounced class bias in favor of the capitalists and particularly the biggest monopolies.

On several occasions, for example, the government has put into effect special tax concessions to encourage investment. In effect, such concessions transfer to the working class part of the costs of the capitalists' investments. Housing construction is encouraged by insuring, subsidizing, and providing additional loan funds to the mortgage bankers and to private developers, but rarely by lowering the cost of housing to workers. Direct public construction of low-cost housing for those workers most needing housing is kept to a bare minimum, and that is so located and rented as to increase racial segregation. Corporate foreign investments are encouraged by tax advantages, insurance against losses, and the enormous and expensive U.S. diplomatic and military establishment—again, in the last analysis, at the cost of working people. When it is desired to provide more money for the banks, for use in business lending, interest rates are raised for large deposits by the rich and the corporations with cash, but held down for small savers.

There are occasions when the weakest sectors of the economy are the consumers durable goods industries—autos, appliances, etc—because of the depleted consuming power of the workers. But their consumption is never stimulated by government action to make these commodities cheaper, or to reduce monopoly prices generally.

The "Full Employment Deception

Because unemployment has been a persistently severe problem for American labor, the slogan of full employment held top priority among its long-term objectives by the time of World War II. In deference to this, President Roosevelt, in his 1944 "Economic Bill of Rights" placed first the right of every person, able and willing to work, to a job at decent wages. Like the other parts of the Economic Bill of Rights, it was to apply regardless of race, color, or religion.

The full employment pledge was wholly ignored by Roosevelt's successors, although it was revived briefly by Johnson in 1964 as a demagogic election slogan. Particularly shameful was the increase of discrimination in employment, so that even at times when unemployment was relatively low for white, Anglo workers, it has been persistently much more severe for Black, Chicano, and Puerto Rican workers.

Establishment economists have supplied the employers with a slick formula whereby a certain level of unemployment is defined as most desirable. This level was gradually increased, along with actual unemployment, after World War II. For a decade, the officially desired level of unemployment has been 4%. The publicity experts for the government and big business refer to this level of unemployment as "full employment." This official figure makes no allowance for many millions who can get only part-time or occasional work and for millions more who are erroneously omitted from the count of the labor force. Calculations by liberal or labor economists have shown that the actual rate of unemployment at a given time is one-half again or twice as high as the official figure.

Labor Department studies show that with an official figure of 4% unemployed, 12–14 million workers, or close to 20% of the wage and salary workers, suffer unemployment for various periods during a given year.

According to Establishment economists, 4% official unemployment corresponds to operations at about 92% of capacity, which makes for the highest profit. With fuller use of capacity and a correspondingly higher employment percentage, workers are able to bargain for wider wage increases and to resist increases in the intensity of labor. The 4% official unemployment goal is designed to maintain a many-million labor reserve to improve the bargaining position of employers over workers.

On the other hand, when unemployment, as officially measured, rises to above 5%, the rulers fear the political consequences—possible mass action by the unemployed and a general radicalization of the working class.

Since 1948, the official unemployment percentage has never gone down to 4% except during the Korean and Vietnam wars. Moreover, in 1970, with the Vietnam War still raging, the rate of unemployment rose by year-end to 6% during the first wartime crisis of overproduction.

Wage and Price Control

The tendency throughout the capitalist world has been for workers to insist on, strike for, and win larger and larger wage increases. This is the product of enlarged and strengthened trade union organization, the growth of Communist influence among the workers, the pressure of faster-rising living costs, and the stimulating example of working class gains in socialist countries. Some of these causes seem more remote in the United States, but they are growing in significance here also.

Yet, as shown in Chapter III, wage increases in the United States have consistently lagged behind the combination of price and productivity increases. Anti-inflation policy, if consistent with its avowed aims, would be directed at pushing down prices, while encouraging a catch-up in wages.

However, pursuing the class interests of capital, so-called anti-inflation policy has become a screen for the attack on wages. The wage-push theory of inflation, discussed in Chapter VII, is the main propaganda weapon used to justify application of state power to prohibit or severely limit wage increases. Whether called incomes policies or wage-price controls, these schemes involve restrictions of wages by the government, with the collaboration of trade union officials and employer representatives. Prices, on the other hand, are wholly or largely unrestricted, and there are no restrictions on property incomes.

Such schemes have held up during wartime, when they obtained substantial social acceptance, and when there was also a significant degree of price control, excess profits taxes, etc. But peacetime application has foundered in the main capitalist countries, either immediately or after a certain period, during which workers became convinced that the policies were rigged against them, and forced abandonment of the controls through strikes or political action.

Beginning in 1962, as a fresh military buildup leading to the Vietnam War got underway, the Kennedy Administration adopted a "guidepost" formula to restrain wages. Similar devices were applied in a number of West European countries. The formula provided that wage rate increases should not exceed the average rate of productivity increase in the entire economy. Government economists calculated this at 3.2% per year. This formula was rigged against workers in three important ways:

1. Productivity gains were calculated for all persons employed in the

private economy. This included many in the economic superstructure, in corporate headquarters, in advertising and finance, and in service trades. It included executives and officials. Estimates of the "productivity" of these categories are quite arbitrary. Figures for the all-inclusive measure showed much smaller rates of increase in productivity than were achieved by production workers in industry. Even when the rigged figure went well above 3.2% the government economists stuck to it by using long-term average "productivity" increases.

2. No allowance was made for rising prices, so even if a worker got an increase in money wages proportional to his increase in productivity, his increase in real wages would lag.

3. Strongly organized workers were forbidden to get increases beyond the guideposts, while there was no provision for even these small wage increases for the millions of unorganized or weakly organized workers.

These "guideposts" did not have the force of the law, but they were largely operative so long as trade union officials cooperated with them and the rank-and-file workers did not prevent it.

But after two years of the Vietnam War, this tolerance came to an end. Faced with soaring living costs, seeing big business profiteering on the rampage, the workers acted to preserve their living standards. Starting with the airline workers in 1966, they began to stay out on strike until they won much more than the guideposts permitted. By 1968 the Johnson Administration was forced to abandon the whole approach.

But government pressure against wage increases was not relaxed for long. By late 1969 the Nixon Administration aimed to achieve the same result through the pressure of increased unemployment. This also failed when, in the first half of 1970, the workers, despite rising mass unemployment, won the widest wage increases in over two decades.

Congress passed a law giving Nixon the power to freeze wages and prices. As with all such laws, there were loopholes to permit the continuance of actual price increases. Nixon hesitated to apply the law. His main big corporation supporters preferred other methods of holding down wages, which would not involve any restraints on monopoly prices. Also the administration feared that wage-freezing edicts simply would not be obeyed by the workers.

The administration concentrated its efforts in two directions. It attempted to get passage of laws seriously restricting the powers of trade unions and the right to strike. And by late 1970, it launched a massive propaganda campaign against wage increases, designed to sufficiently isolate and split the rank-and-file workers to make possible the freezing of wages.

Following the propaganda barrage, President Nixon imposed a wage limitation on construction workers early in 1971, without any limitation on the level of contractors' bids or on prices of construction materials. He attacked in advance the demands of steel workers for wage increases and made obvious preparations to intervene against them after steel companies had put through big price increases.

In August 1971, using the immediate excuse of the dollar crisis, President Nixon invoked the most stringent restriction on wages in U.S. history—a complete freeze applicable for 90 days. There was a simultaneous freeze on prices, but with many loopholes that minimized its effectiveness, especially at the retail level.

Following this three-month interval, wages and prices were subjected to control by a Pay Board and a Price Commission, respectively. The employer-dominated Pay Board adopted a modification of the former "guidepost" formula, permitting wage increases of $5^{1}/_{2}\%$, equal to an arbitrary 3% allowance for productivity, plus one-half of the going rate of increase in the consumer price index. On the face of it, this was designed to insure that workers' real wages would not increase as fast as their productivity. In fact, the situation was still worse. A major feature of the new setup was a drive for higher labor productivity, mainly through reducing the number of workers, and speeding up those left. The objective was to push up labor productivity in industry to a rate far above 3% per year. Simultaneously, the restriction on workers' right to strike implicit in any system of wage controls was used by employers to reduce wages in many cases, either through arbitrary revision of incentive systems, or by use of threats to close down plants and move work elsewhere.

Meanwhile, the ostensible control over prices was farcical. Virtually all requests for increases—some of them for 20% or more—were approved without change by the Price Commission—and there were no specific controls over prices of individual items at retail. The Administration claimed that it aimed to get the rate of inflation down to $2^{1}/_{2}$–3% by the end of 1972. But any such accomplishment would be on paper only. J. Roger Wallace, the astute economist of the *Journal of Commerce,* wrote:

To be sure, the consumer price index of the BLS (Bureau of Labor Statistics) for 1972 may show an increase of 3 percent or even less over that for 1971. Meanwhile, however, the true rise in the cost of living might be considerably larger than the rise in the consumer price index, possibly twice as large or even more. It is axiomatic that, the longer any attempts are made to control prices, the less and less reliable will the consumer price index become as a measure of the true rise in the cost of living.[16]

Wallace mentions various reasons for this—quality deterioration, elimination of low-priced items, etc. But the main thing is the deliberate rigging of the official index as a weapon of state-monopoly capitalism against the working class.

The dominant trade union leaders, denouncing the "unfairness" of Nixon's controls, nonetheless supported controls over wages and prices "in principle," participated in the operations of the Pay Board, and tried to restrain their members from striking against this attack on their living conditions.

During 1972 the Nixon Administration turned its main attention to the attempt to get passage of anti-strike legislation, with which big business hoped to make wage control remain effective indefinitely. Consolidation of a system of wage controls and prohibition of strikes would constitute a serious move in the direction of fascism.

In effect, this is an attempt to accomplish through the back door what Hitler accomplished directly for German big business in the 1930s by physically destroying the trade unions and then rigidly freezing wage rates.

Racial Discrimination

The class essence of government economic regulation is nowhere more evident than in its handling of the issue of economic discrimination. Federal and state and municipal Human Rights commissions have been established. In 1965 a federal law was passed supposedly guaranteeing equal employment opportunities. The federal government is supposed to refuse contracts to companies engaging in discrimination.

But in practice virtually nothing is done to carry out any of these laws or regulations. In fact, the Defense Department, in particular, but other agencies as well, systematically violate the law by granting contracts to companies that engage in the grossest discrimination. Gains have been made here and there in reducing the degree of discrimination against minority workers, but the general pattern of discrimination remains decisive. There is not a single industry, not a single major company which does not engage in serious discrimination against minority workers in even the limited areas of employment to which they are admitted—in their wages or salaries, in their access to promotion, in the security of their jobs.

So long as this is true, regulation of the economy has a bitter taste to nearly one-fifth of the population. For them, the business cycle is not one of relative prosperity and depression, but permanent depression and crisis, varying only in degree.

The role of the government worsened in the Nixon administration. Nixon and a number of his top aides took openly racist positions. They acted in ways that encouraged discriminatory practices in every sphere and insured racists against reprisals or official condemnation.

In 1970 the mean earnings of white people with earnings was $6,100, as compared with $3,949 for Black people with earnings. The difference, multiplied by the 9.4 million Black workers, comes to $20.2 billion. [17]

This represents a very rough, minimum measure of the extra profits derived by capital from super-exploitation of Black workers. The amount of super-exploitation increases, as more and more Black people are drawn into industry, especially the basic industries of the country. Additional billions of extra profits are derived from super-exploitation of Chicano, Puerto Rican, Indian, and Asian workers.

During the economic crisis and depression of 1969–71, the old pattern of first-to-be-fired, last-to-be hired, operated with full force. Black unemployment continued to increase steadily throughout 1971 and into 1972, while unemployment among white workers levelled off or slightly declined. The Black unemployment rate went to well above its "normal" ratio of double the white unemployment rate.

Appraisal of Results of Government Economic Regulation

The class content of government economic regulation limits the extent and duration of what can be achieved through it. The common denominator—increasing the rate of exploitation of labor—continually reproduces the economic contradictions that created the need for regulation. Generally, a partial success in achieving one objective is at the expense of a setback with reference to another objective.

Some success has been achieved in the key problem of smoothing out the business cycle, reducing its amplitude, preventing a prolonged crisis-depression cycle. Over the past 25 years, cycles have been less serious than during the previous quarter of a century, but no less serious than in the previous 25 years (1895–1920). Improvement since World War II results from various factors, but certainly government economic regulation, with all its crudities and mistakes, has been a significant one of them.

True, a potent element in this regulation was manipulation of military spending. True, the prolonged period of reconstruction after World War II, and readjustment of economic patterns following the breakup of the colonial system, provided an objective basis for moderating economic declines throughout the capitalist world. In some ways, conditions are becoming less favorable for successful contracyclical regulation than they have been during this past quarter century.

Yet, when all is said and done, a definite degree of effectiveness must be attributed to this regulation. Considering the depth of contradictions within the U.S. economy, in the absence of government regulation, economic crises of catastrophic dimensions would be likely.

In understanding this process, it is important to avoid two extremes—that of the apologists for the system who attribute potential infallibility to government regulation of the capitalist economy, and those wishful critics of the system who see its rulers as completely powerless to influence its fate in the short and medium term.

The influence of fiscal and monetary manipulation on the economy varies considerably in timing and extent. After all, government regulation is a long way from government planning and control. The great bulk of all economic activity is carried out by separate private firms. Their decisions are based on calculations of what actions will yield the highest expected profit. Government regulation is only one of the many influences on these decisions, although an important one. The anarchy of capitalism remains in force but somewhat restrained by a rather long, loose leash.

Political developments increasingly interact with economic trends, as political struggles come closer to dealing with fundamental social issues. International economic developments, on which the U.S.

Government has limited influence, increasingly affect the economy as the activities of U.S. corporations become more international in scope.

Decisions on government economic regulation require knowledge of where the economy is, in what direction it is moving, and, above all, where it is likely to move. But knowledge, even of the present status and direction of economic developments, is far from adequate. Despite all the high-speed electronic computers, there is generally a lag of several months before officials recognize significant turns in economic trends.

The factors mentioned above make it inevitable that forecasts of the course of economic activity must have a substantial margin of error. In turn, estimations of the effects of any given set of regulatory actions have an even larger margin of error. Thus, forecasts of the future connected with the changing course of government economic regulation, are often quite wide of the mark.

Victor Zarnowitz studied the record of year-ahead forecasts made by business economists, corporation research departments, government agencies, and academic researchers. The forecasts were made over a ten-year period at about the end of one year for the following year. On the average, he found, forecasts were off by 40% of the annual change in gross national product and 47% of the annual change in industrial production. The results, however, were even worse than indicated by these averages, because at the time the forecasts were made, results for the coming three to six months were already pretty obvious.

Forecasts for four quarters or more ahead are generally not superior to extrapolations of the recent trend. . . . The record of year-to-year forecasts does not imply any greater accuracy than this because such forecasts are generally made late in the preceding calendar year, and a good record in the first two quarters will produce a moderately good record for the year as a whole.

Most crucial in forecasting is to see turning points coming: "The results here are, on the whole, negative: the record . . . does not indicate an ability to forecast the turn several months ahead. Not only were actual turns missed but also turns were predicted that did not occur."[18]

Federal regulation is influenced by forecasts that are certainly no more accurate than those reviewed by Zarnowitz, and probably less so, owing to the continuous pressure on the Council of Economic Advisers to bend their predictions in a direction suitable to the political needs of the administration in power—usually in an optimistic direction.

In practice, contracyclical measures are usually taken at the wrong time—either too early or too late. Their impact is usually delayed by from six months to a year. Meanwhile, the conditions they are meant to overcome are worsening. And failing to have apparent success in a reasonable time, government administrators add more fuel to the stimulating fires or put more pressure on the restraining brakes, as the case may be. The result is apt to be one of economic overkill—with an inflationary boom converted unintentionally into a serious decline instead of a slowing-down of growth, or a recession converted into an inflationary upsurge instead of a period of moderate and steady growth.

There have been five cycles since World War II. The first four were characterized by relatively short depression periods, and fairly rapid recovery from the bottom. However, the downturn beginning in 1969 was followed by a rather prolonged depression, which persisted despite the application of government stimuli more vigorously than during any of the four previous crisis-depression periods. This suggests that the deepening of the contradictions withing the system, brought out in earlier chapters, is reducing the effectiveness of the traditional methods of contracyclical economic regulation.

The worst fears of the capitalists are associated with deep crises of overproduction. Therefore the tendency throughout this 25-year period has been to stress economic stimulation more than restraint. There has been more success, therefore, in averting deep crises than in pursuing the other objectives of economic regulation. But the price has been the increasing failure of attempts to restrain inflation, the buildup of financial contradictions that create sharper crisis dangers, and the aggravation of political conflict that restricts the freedom of action of the ruling groups. (The acceleration of inflation was dealt with in Chapter VII.)

Government regulation has completely failed to prevent inflation. Instead, the overall content of that regulation has increased inflation. Moreover, this objective has become less important to the ruling magnates, as they become more conscious of the possibility of using inflation as a means of raising the rate of exploitation of labor.

The record of achievement in improving the economic growth rate has been only fair (Table IX-1).

TABLE IX-1. ECONOMIC GROWTH RATES SINCE WORLD WAR II

	Percent Annual Growth Rate of Constant Price Gross National Product
1948–1953 (Korean War cycle)	5.0
1953–1960 (Peace cycles)	2.4
1960–1969 (Vietnam War cycle)	4.5
All postwar period:	
A. Covering complete cycles, 1948–1969	3.9
B. 1946–1970	3.6
C. 1945–1970	2.9

Source: Computed from *National Product Accounts,* using preliminary estimate of $726 billion in 1958 dollars, of 1970 gross national product.

Growth rates of better than 4% per year were achieved only in cycles that included wars—the Korean and the Vietnam wars, respectively. Growth was admittedly very sluggish during the seven years after the Korean war.

For the entire postwar period, growth averaged considerably less than 4%. Even limiting the calculation to complete cycles, which omits the cross-currents of the immediate postwar years and the decline of 1970, the average growth rate is a shade below 4%.

Starting from a base of 1946, the first postwar year, however, and continuing through 1970, the growth rate is reduced to 3.6%. If one uses as a base 1945, the last year of World War II, the average annual rate in growth is sharply reduced—to 2.9%.

This low figure must be viewed with caution, since the figures for the World War II period are not strictly comparable with those for later years, even after price adjustment, owing to the radically different composition of the gross national product during the World War II. But it has some significance if one takes into account the operation of the economy at full steam in World War II. Then one can say the growth rate of production in the past quarter of a century has been 2.9% per year in relation to the virtually full employment level of production at the beginning of the period. The most realistic appraisal is to put the average growth rate over the post-World War II period in the range 3.5–4%.

While the government officially refers to a normal growth rate of 4.3%, there is a widely expressed view that it will be well below recent levels during the first part of the 1970s. In fact, the financial tensions in the economy, the persistent inflation, and the shifting balance of international economic power tend to restrain economic growth, and to constrain government regulators from acting to stimulate a faster growth.

From the time when the objective of speeding economic growth came to the fore in the late 1950s, American capitalism has had a limited success. It is not clear, however, that there would have been any overall improvement without the special—and very costly—stimulation of the Vietnam War.

And prospects are doubtful for continuation of even the limited success of the 1960s.

The trend toward an increasing role of the government in economic life is bound to continue. And with this the potential scope of government economic regulation will grow. More elaborate methods of regulation may be developed, but so long as this power remains in the hands of the financial oligarchy, its use will never have full or certain success; it will never be able to guarantee against severe economic crises; and it will increase rather than diminish the social, economic, and political contradictions that are undermining the capitalist system.

X.

Militarism, Economic Growth and the Business Cycle

WAR HAS been a dominant factor in the U.S. economy for much of the past 30 years. The World War II boom stimulated the most rapid industrial growth in American history, and its aftermath gave rise to additional growth. Soon after these stimuli were exhausted, the Korean War provided another substantial boost to the U.S. economy, although less than that of World War II. Military spending declined sharply immediately after the Korean War, but a year later there began the decade long uptrend in military expenditures and the space budgets related to them which also had a significant economic impact. Finally, the Vietnam War provided another surge in military spending, relatively less than the Korean War buildup but still sufficient to power the final four-and-a-half years of the 1961–69 recovery and boom.

Throughout the period since World War II, the United States has been overwhelmingly the largest military spender, accounting for nearly two-thirds of the total armament spending of the capitalist world. Since the Korean War, military outlays have taken about 10% of the U.S. national income, more than double the corresponding percentage for the rest of the capitalist world.[1] This represents a degree of sustained militarization unprecedented in the history of capitalism.

During most of this period, spokesmen for the government and big business—and especially for the munitions manufacturers and generals—have claimed that armament spending was good for the economy. They said it accelerated technical progress, primed economic growth, and helped smooth out the business cycle. In recent years, their public position has become generally more cautious. They deplore the economic waste of militarism and assert that the United States does not need armaments for prosperity. However, with the poor economic conditions of 1970, there were indications that the line of touting munitions spending as a panacea would again become prominent.

One of the more euphoric appraisals of the merits of militarism was by munitions-maker Frank Pace, Jr., president of General Dynamics Corporation, during the late 1950s, when it was number one contractor. He lauded the "civilian impact of military defense spending and its function as an economic growth stimulant in our society." He claimed it "results in the accession to our society of economic, scientific, and cultural benefits of enduring and nonmilitary value."[2]

The Truman administration made the most brazen use of the military budget for contracyclical purposes. Its cynical concept of economic planning was expressed as follows by the pro-Establishment journal, *U.S. News and World Report:*

> Government planners figure they have found the magic formula for almost endless good times. They are now beginning to wonder if there may not be something to perpetual motion after all. . . . Cold war is the catalyst. Cold war is an automatic pump-primer. Turn a spigot, and the public clamors for more arms spending. Turn another, the clamor ceases. Truman confidence cockiness, is based on this "Truman formula." Truman era of good times, President is told, can run much beyond 1952. Cold war demands, if fully exploited, are almost limitless.[3]

Exactly a month after this was published, the spigot was opened wide with the launching of the Korean War. But by the end of 1952, Truman was out of the White House on account of mass dissatisfaction with the Korean War, and within another year the country was in a recession and entering a rather prolonged period of relative stagnation.

In recent years such propaganda has been toned down. Establishment speakers usually pay lip service to neglected civilian needs, insisting they would welcome a cut in armaments so that more resources would be available for economic progress and for filling social gaps. They attribute to Marxists the view that capitalism would collapse without big armament expenditures. Having set up this straw man, they proceed to demolish it, thus trying to get propaganda benefit out of their position.

Needless to say, Marxists never held such a view, although some "New Left" radicals, far removed from Marxist ideology, did. Actually they were merely reflecting "from the left" the right-wing propaganda prevalent in the heyday of the Cold War and McCarthyism.

The changed public stance of Establishment spokesmen is in reaction to the influence of the antiwar movement and the fear that the antiwar majority will associate militarism with capitalism and turn against that system. But despite the new propaganda position, big business has no intention of yielding the extra profits from armaments nor of giving up the international investment positions which U.S. military power strives to open up for them.

Actually, the Nixon Administration has cautiously moved toward the earlier line of extolling the economic virtues of militarism. This has been done indirectly by claiming that soaring unemployment was mainly caused by military cutbacks, and by exaggerating the employment to be derived from this or that military or paramilitary project.

Regardless of shifts in the Establishment propaganda line, domestic economic motives have not been the decisive factor in determining the long-term trend of military spending. In May 1950, Truman was happy because his military buildup had been important in bringing about recovery from the 1949 crisis. But the many times larger buildup of the Korean War period was not needed for economic stimulation and in fact resulted in considerable overstrain in the economy.

The decisive factor has been the foreign policy objectives of U.S. imperialism. These are, in brief, to confront the Soviet Union and other socialist countries militarily, to prevent the formation of socialist and anti-imperialist governments wherever possible, to open up all areas possible for investment by U.S. corporations, and to establish bases from which to attack or threaten other lands—with the same ultimate ends in view. There have been changes in priority within that set of objectives over the past quarter of a century. Thus, during the period of U.S. atomic monopoly, high priority was given to preparing for "rolling back" Communism, that is, to preparing direct military aggression against the USSR and other socialist countries. However, as such a project becomes increasingly suicidal, it has been given relatively less emphasis in immediate preparations and put on the "back burner" insofar as propaganda is concerned. Similarly, increasing priority has been given to combating anti-imperialist trends in the developing countries, with Vietnam the symbol of the lengths to which U.S. imperialism will go, and the depths to which it will descend, in pursuit of its neocolonial objectives. Correspondingly, the composition of military spending consists essentially of two parts, preparation for thermonuclear world war against the USSR and other socialist coun- tries; and preparation for and waging of "local" or "limited" wars and interventions against the national liberation movements in the former colonial and dependent areas of the world.

Relative Scale of Military Spending

There have been sharp year-to-year fluctuations in the share of national output going to the military, corresponding to the timing of limited wars and major armament buildups, and also influenced by manipulation of military spending for purposes of regulation of the economy.

The share of "national defense purchases of goods and services" in the GNP, down to 6.8% in 1971, minimizes the importance of the military in the national economy. The Commerce Department, in compiling its GNP aggregates, leaves out several billions of actual Defense Department spending as falling outside its GNP definition. Moreover, these, and the budget figures, put into nonmilitary classifications items largely auxiliary to the military effort such as space and international affairs. Also omitted is the spending resulting from wars—the multi-billion dollar outlays for veterans and the soaring interest burden on the national debt.

Thus, in fiscal 1969, "national defense" expenditures for goods and services in the GNP statistics came to $78.6 billion, while actual "national defense" spending in the budget came to $81.2 billion, and the sum of military and related spending in the budget came to $112.6 billion*.[4]

On the other hand, the GNP includes a substantial number of items that are dubious additions to the values created during the year. The most obvious are depreciation allowances ($81.1 billion in 1969), and many tens of billions in "imputed" items that do not represent actual commodity transactions—such as the rental value of owner-occupied homes ($55.0 billion in 1969).

Thus the financial burden of the military on the country's income is considerably greater than that indicated by the officially published figures of the percentage of the GNP taken by the military. The total of

---

*Consists of "national defense," $81.2 billion; international affairs, $3.8 billion; space research and technology, $4.2 billion; veterans' benefits and services, $7.6 billion; and interest, $15.8 billion.

military and related expenditures in fiscal 1969, $112.6 billions, came to 15.2% of the national income of $742.7 billion. Similarly, calculations of the percentage of industrial production and durable goods output going to the military and related purposes came to 15–20% of the totals in these categories. However, owing to the large percentage of military spending absorbed by profits, interests, payoffs to high-priced executives, etc., the proportion of the country's employment due to the military is only of the order of 10%.

Omissions from military and related spending in the GNP figures, relative to the total, are increasing. Similarly, the proportion of fictitious items in the GNP are increasing. Therefore, the official statistics tend to show a declining weight of the military in the national economy that is more than any actual decline that takes place.

Roughly speaking, the burden of the military on the country's financial resources has been virtually constant over the past 15 years. This means it has been taking relatively larger and larger amounts out of working peoples' pocketbooks, in view of the constant shift of the tax burden from capital to labor.

On the other hand, there seems to have been a slightly declining tendency in the industrial impact of the military program. Thus, in the period 1956–1964, military prime contracts to U.S. companies came to 57% of the contracts and orders of U.S. companies for plant and equipment. But in the Vietnam War years of 1965–69, the proportion of military contracts to investment contracts fell to 48%.[5]

A decreasing proportion of military spending is going for the procurement of weapons and ammunition and related large-volume contracts. Relatively more is going into the pay of the armed forces, especially officers—in order to get and keep men in the increasingly unpopular army—as well as into soaring payoffs to puppet troops in Southeast Asia and elsewhere.

With this as background, we can try to appraise the economic impact of military spending, and its performance in relation to its claimed "benefits."

Militarism and Technical Progress

Rapid technical progress, in comparison with all earlier social systems, has been an essential characteristic of capitalism. It has made possible the swifter economic growth of capitalism by raising labor productivity, and it has played an important part in the business cycle which tended to develop around cycles of the wearing-out and technological (moral) obsolescence of equipment and its replacement with new and improved models.

With customary disregard for fact, present-day apologists for capitalism assert that Marx did not "foresee" the scientific-technical revolution and hence was "wrong" in forecasting the demise of capitalism. In fact, it was Marx and Engels who pioneered in stressing the role of science and technology in economic developments. Early in their revolutionary careers, they wrote:

> The bourgeoisie cannot exist without constantly revolutionizing the instruments of production, and thereby the relations of production and with them the whole relations of society. . . . The bourgeoisie, by the rapid improvement of all instruments of production, by the immensely facilitated means of communications, draws all nations, even the most barbarian, into civilization. . . . The bourgeoisie, during its rule of scarce one hundred years, has created more massive and more colossal productive forces than have all preceding generations together. Subjection of nature's forces to man, machinery, application of chemistry to industry and agriculture, steam-navigation, railways, electric telegraphs, clearing of whole continents for cultivation, canalization of rivers, whole populations conjured out of the ground—what earlier century had even a presentiment that such productive forces slumbered in the lap of social labor?[6]

The scientific-technical-industrial power of capitalism enabled its armies to conquer hundreds of millions of people living under earlier social systems. Technical progress was also important in wars between capitalist states. But in World War I, with both sides on an almost equal technical-scientific level, this factor could not tilt the scales one way or the other.

By the end of World War II, scientific and technical progress became of primary, decisive importance in determining the military balance of power. The United States, not damaged or impoverished by war, was able to go far beyond all other warring countries in devoting billions to the development of advanced weaponry. Atomic bombs, radar, automatic fire-control systems, were some of the outstanding results.*

---

*Radar was discovered by British scientists. European scientists provided most of the know-how for nuclear weapons. But the United States had the capital to fully develop these discoveries, and the wherewithal to mobilize the labor of most of the top scientists of the capitalist world.

These involved far-reaching scientific and technical breakthroughs that have had enormous applications to civilian production. One need only mention atomic power, computers, electronics.

After World War II, the United States, in trying to obtain and maintain military superiority over the USSR, devoted increasing sums to military, scientific and technical research. This has created for the first time in this country a general appreciation of the importance of research and development in industrial progress. Similarly, corporations find research and development essential for maintaining and increasing their profits, so private companies have rapidly increased their spending for these purposes. But they still can count on more from the military budget than they spend of their own money. In 1970, 55% of all research and development expenditures were financed by the federal government, 40% by industry, and 5% by other sources. About 84% of the federal funds emanated from the military and space agencies.[7]

War taught the corporate owners just how profitable science could be for them and thereby stimulated scientific and technical development. But it casts a sorry light on the nature of capitalism that only through the military route could it come to appreciate the importance of science, and that to this day its scientific-technical work is predominantly oriented to military uses. Certainly some benefit "spills over" to civilian uses, but with enormous social inefficiency. Sorely needed billions for research and development in health, environment, nutrition, housing and mass transportation are diverted by the military domination of research.

War was a catalyst, speeding the opening of the new era of the direct, large-scale application of science to economic life—a transition that was historically inevitable. But now and for the future, militarism has become a drag on the effective and socially beneficial execution of that transition.

The USSR, the first socialist country, from its earliest years, gave a high priority to scientific and technical development as a principle of progress in civilian and military fields. With a centralized, socialist-planned economy, it could allot and mobilize resources for this purpose. The decisive superiority of socialism over capitalism in research and development was proven by the ability of the USSR in the postwar years to approach the level of, or advance beyond, the United States at the main strategic frontiers of scientific and technical achievement.

This was accomplished *despite* the initial industrial and technical backwardness of the Soviet Union, *despite* the tremendous economic devastation wrought on that country by World War II, *despite* the strenuous and continuing efforts of U.S. imperialism to bar the USSR from access to any advanced scientific or technical knowledge within its control or influence.

On the one hand, this accomplishment was necessary for the Soviet Union in order to guarantee its security from the threatened nuclear assault by the United States. On the other hand, it today constitutes, more than ever, the conscious central principle of socialist planning in all of the industrialized socialist countries, a principle which is the most certain guarantee of the ultimate victory of socialism over capitalism in economic competition.

Militarism and the Business Cycle

War and militarism tend to *increase* cyclical economic fluctuations. World War I was followed by extreme gyrations in the U.S. economy. An inflationary boom in 1919–20 was followed by a sharp and deep crisis in the United States. But the real postwar boom cut this short, with the revival of economy in war-torn Europe. It was not until 1929 that the real postwar crisis—the worst in history—was required to liquidate the economic contradictions and financial excesses generated by World War I and its aftermath. Although World War II was followed by even greater booms in capitalist countries, so far no world crisis comparable to that of 1929 has resulted. Yet economic cycles since World War II have been more pronounced in the United States, the most highly militarized country, than in any other land.

In part, this results from the sharp fluctuations in military spending. "National defense" expenditures jumped from 3.9% of GNP in 1947 to 13.3% in 1952–53; dropped to 9.6% in 1956; increased to 10.3% in 1958; dropped to 7.3% in 1965, advanced to 9.1% in 1967, and declined again to 6.8% in 1971. These swings are considerably wider than those in that traditionally volatile component—plant and equipment investment.

Rapid increases in military spending have a doubly stimulating economic effect. At the start of a war or big peacetime arms buildup, the increased outlay usually far exceeds increased tax revenues. Civilian purchasing power is thereby suddenly increased, with no corresponding rise in civilian supplies. The resulting inflationary price increase initially stimulates productive activity. People buy consumers' goods, business enterprises buy capital goods and raw materials to beat higher prices and possible later wartime shortages.

The arms buildup also directly stimulates a surge in capital investment. Munitions manufacturers, hoping to get the maximum possible share of the arms orders, hasten to increase physical capacity and to employ additional workers and scientific-technical personnel. This process is highly compressed in time; to get in on the ground floor a corporation must get ready quickly. The process of general expansion occurring in the cycle is exaggerated in the munitions industries. It is encouraged by Pentagon collaboration with the companies through such devices as the government's supplying machines and buildings and the allowance of capital outlays as "costs"; loose accounting that enables contractors to profit on the purchase of hundreds of machines, and to hire thousands of workers to be kept in reserve for possible later contracts.

The stimulating effect, both in productive activity and investment, goes beyond the simple dollar rise in budgetary outlays. Orders for procurement, and for research and development, increase more sharply than dollar outlays. The munitions factories are activated by the receipt of contracts or orders. Further, every new military buildup involves a shift in the kinds of weapons produced. The increase in procurement of new weapons is greater proportionately than the total increase in orders, calling forth correspondingly enlarged purchases of capital goods, expansion of capacity, and hiring of workers.

At the end of the military buildup, and especially with the end of a war or any other decline in military spending, the opposite effects are equally marked. Capital spending and purchases of materials by armament manufacturers are radically reduced or completely ended. Workers are laid off as rapidly—in some cases, more rapidly than they were hired. The only asymmetry is in prices. The power of monopoly prevents any general reduction, and it is usually able to maintain the price uptrend, if at a slower pace.

In the long run, the stimulus of a military buildup is balanced by the reduction in private purchasing power through higher taxes and prices. And the tendency is for this negative factor to reach its peak just as the military buildup comes to an end, adding its direct negative impact. Thus, military spending and activity contribute in a major way to the business cycle.

The longer a war drags on, the less its stimulating effect becomes, and the more its deterrent effect comes to the fore. In World War II, production reached a peak in 1943 and remained thereafter at a high plateau until the end of the war, when there was a sharp reconversion recession. Economic activity during the Korean War reached a similar plateau in 1952 and was followed by a final surge in the last months of the war. This sequence was repeated during the Vietnam War with the "mini-recession" of 1967 and the final surge of activity in 1968. But Vietnam has lasted longer than any previous U.S. war; in economic terms, it has lasted "too long." And it was the first war in which the negative factors became so dominant that an economic crisis of overproduction erupted while the war continued.

The above comments relate to the cyclical consequence of fluctuations in military expenditures generated by political-military causes.

On the other hand, all postwar administrations have manipulated the military budgets for economic purposes—to smooth out the business cycle, as well as to throw business to favored arms contractors. Contracyclical timing of the placing of military orders partly—but only partly—offsets the overall unstabilizing effect of military spending. To some extent, such manipulation is independent of military-political developments, although it inevitably interacts with them. An increase in military spending, for any reason, increases international tension, while a reduction helps create a better atmosphere for settlement of issues, agreements on disarmament, etc.

There follows a chronicle of cyclical development after the Korean War, with corresponding fluctuations in new military contracts:

Trough of recession: III, 1954 (Roman numerals represent quarters.)

Military contracts built up from an annual rate of $6.4 billion in the fourth quarter of 1953 to $16.4 billion in the third quarter of 1954, contributing significantly to checking the recession and starting a new upturn. The big strategic weapons buildup of the post-Korea period was the underlying driving force behind this increase, although economic motives hastened it.

Peak of the boom: III, 1957.

Military contracts dipped from $20.8 billion in 1956 to $18.8 billion in 1957, as part of a deliberate program to cut government spending for anti-inflationary purposes. This contributed to the outbreak of an economic crisis in the second half of 1957.

Trough of the recession: II, 1958.

Military contracts jumped from an annual rate of $16.9 billion in the third quarter of 1957 to an annual rate of $29.6 billion in the second quarter of 1958, exactly countering the cyclical movement. The military contract rise far exceeded the shift in any other area of the economy. The increase in residential construction—another plus factor—started later and was not so sharp.

Peak of recovery: II, 1960.

Arms contracts drifted downward from $24.4 billion in 1958 to $23.2 billion in 1960. This decline was not sufficient to set off a slump directly. But the failure of the 1958 increase to carry through contributed to it.

Trough of Recession: I, 1961.

Military contracts increased from $23.2 billion in 1960 to $26.0 billion in 1961 and $28.5 billion in 1962. There was a more rapid buildup in space agency contracts. Thus, military and space contracts, combined, contributed significantly to the recovery of the early 1960s.

With all the fluctuations, there was a steady uptrend in military contracts between the Korean and Vietnam wars, with the amount more than doubling between 1954 and 1964. Annual, quarterly, and sometimes even monthly contracts fluctuated around this trend and at crucial turning points were often deliberately designed to reverse undesirable cyclical trends, whether inflationary-boom or recessionary. Rarely was this purpose explicitly and officially proclaimed, but unofficial comment, the statements of anonymous White House spokesmen, and other evidence confirmed the purposive nature of the fluctuations.

Beginning with 1965, the rapid Vietnam buildup of military contracts gave several years of extra life to the tired boom and raised it to new heights. This added stimulation was primarily for military reasons; its economic consequences were side effects. Military contracts jumped from $27.1 billion in 1964 to $39.7 billion in 1966. The rise slowed down in 1967, when contracts totaled $42.3 billion; and ended in 1968, with contracts remaining at the 1967 level. Simultaneously, overall economic activity stopped increasing for a year, and then slowly moved forward until mid-1969.

Peak of boom: III, 1969.

Military contracts dropped sharply from $42.3 billion in 1968 to $35.5 billion in 1969.[8] There was simultaneously a sharp decline in space contracts. These declines came about for economic reasons, as part of the Nixon administration's "anti-inflation" program. The decline in armament contracts preceded the reduction in U.S. military activity in Indochina that took place in 1970. The 1969 drop in armament contracts contributed significantly to the *timing* of the crisis of overproduction that began in the second half of 1969.

In fact, the main decline in activity, and the financial crisis, occurred during 1970, while munitions contracts remained at a level. No significant economic recovery occurred during 1971, despite an upturn in military orders in the second half of the year.

President Nixon and his aides distorted the significance of the decline in military orders and in the size of the armed forces, ascribing to it full responsibility for the increase and stubborn high level of unemployment.

Early in 1972, President Nixon signalled an intended fresh upturn in munitions contracts. His budget for fiscal 1973 called for new "national defense" obligational authority at an all-time high of $85.4 billion, up $10.2 billion from the authority actually granted during fiscal year 1971. Another $1.7 billion increase was called for in authority for spending for international affairs, much of which is in support of military actions.

Accompanied by a big propaganda barrage about the alleged Soviet military buildup, this administration move foreshadowed a possible new round in the nuclear arms race, and the renewed savage bombing of North Vietnam which soon followed.

At the same time, the timing of the move was influenced by Nixon's desire to prime the pump through the favored method of big business—a sharp rise in military contracts—so as to improve economic activity prior to the 1972 presidential elections.

To summarize, armaments spending has been manipulated in every cycle for contracyclical economic purposes, generally as one in a collection of measures. In that sense, it has contributed to the early ending of several economic declines. On the other hand, on two occasions declines in military orders designed to "cool off" inflation, actually contributed to cyclical downturns, and in that sense added to economic instability.

Appraisal of results over the past two decades permits the conclusion that the stabilizing effect of contracyclical manipulation of military spending has been insufficient to offset the unstabilizing effects of fluctuations in military spending resulting from wars and arms buildups.

Thus, on balance, the militarization of the economy has tended to increase cyclical instability.

The ability to manipulate military spending is increasingly inhibited by growing public resistance to militarism, and resulting congressional attempts to reduce the freedom of military maneuvering by the White House and the Pentagon.

A shifting balance of political forces that would compel a marked and lasting decrease in the relative weight of the military in the national economy is possible, and indeed must be a major objective of struggle of all progressive forces. This would not end state-monopoly capitalist contracyclical economic regulation, but would force a reduction in its military component, and facilitate a shifting to methods of stimulation which could include objects of benefit to working people. It would also reduce the overall unstabilizing economic effects of militarism.

Aside from the overall cycle, military spending fluctuations have been the most important source of local economic booms and busts in recent decades, the source of economic instability and insecurity affecting whole cities and states—indeed, millions of people. The business of individual armament contractors fluctuates violently, as does their employment and ordering of materials, components, and subcontracted items. Whole communities go through rags-to-riches-to-rags cycles with these fluctuations. While one armament manufacturer takes on tens of thousands of additional workers, another lays off as many. One town becomes overcrowded, prices soar, thousands of workers live in trailers. Another town becomes desolate, homes are vacated, thousands are left jobless, engineers become dishwashers, cars are repossessed and homes foreclosed. Thus, Boeing's employment dropped from 92,300 in 1959 to 81,700 in 1960; increased to 104,100 in 1962, declined to 90,900 in 1964; jumped to 142,700 in 1967; stayed about the same in 1968; then dropped drastically to 108,750 at the end of 1969, with the decline continuing through 1970,[9] and employment expected to drop to 44,000 by the end of 1971.

In Seattle, Boeing "has dismissed more than 55,000 employees since its 1968 peak local employment of more than 101,000. A further decline of 10,000 to 20,000 by the end of 1971 is indicated. Thousands of the laid-off workers are highly paid engineers whose white-collar poverty is a new kind of problem in this city. Seattle area unemployment is now about 12 per cent, more than double the national average, mainly as a consequence of the heavy aerospace cutback at Boeing."[10]

In part, such violent fluctuations in employment reflect shifts in the fortunes of individual armament contractors. They are also related to the structural distortions involved in a militarized economy. Hyman Lumer writes:

> The industrial expansion which takes place in a war economy is highly unstable. It is extremely one-sided, with the greatest expansion occurring in industries which at most play only a relatively minor role in peacetime. Moreover, as the instruments of war become increasingly intricate, this one-sided character becomes more and more pronounced.[11]

He focuses on the aviation and aluminum industries as outstanding examples of "war babies." In the recent period electronics is a striking example, and the aviation industry has grown into the huge missile-space vehicle-aircraft "aerospace" complex.

Effects on Economic Growth

Wars under capitalism create an extraordinary demand for basic industrial products and stimulate economic growth by releasing potentials that are otherwise suppressed by the contradictions of the system. However, the very enormity of the industrial consumption of the modern industrial machine is more than matched by the enormity of destruction wrought by modern war. The United States grew during World War II, at the expense of the devastation of much of Europe and Japan; and, to a lesser degree, it grew during the Korean War, at the expense of the flattening of Korea.

To the extent that World War II and its aftermath hastened the understanding of the modern economic role of science and technology, it stimulated economic growth—paying the unspeakable price of the nuclear bombardment of Hiroshima and Nagasaki, and the slaughter by fiery napalm, pellet bombs, and ordinary guns of hundreds of thousands in the Indochinese countryside.

To the extent that wartime destruction forced a complete rebuilding and modernization of industry in Japan and West Germany, it hastened the economic growth of these countries.

To the extent that wartime mobilization hastened the application of state-monopoly capitalist regulation of the economy, with economic growth as a prime motive, it contributed to growth in a number of capitalist countries.

At most, however, like the stepped-up application of science, these were inevitable steps in social development. Particular wars acted as catalysts to hasten this process to an indeterminate extent—at the cost of at least 100 million people killed in World War II and subsequent conflicts. Only in these dubious and even frightful ways did war stimulate economic growth.

And this is in the past. In the present, and indeed for the last 15 years, war and militarism have acted as brakes on economic growth, especially in the United States and Britain.

In the long run, the rate of economic growth of a country is in great degree correlated with the proportion of its resources that is invested in expansion and improvement of productive capacity. Under capitalism, that investment is financed from the surplus value reaped by capitalists out of the exploitation of labor. Invariably, a substantial part of the surplus value is used by the capitalists for their own luxurious level of consumption. And a significant part, collected through taxes, is used for governmental purposes. (This still represents surplus value and the exploitation of labor whether collected from workers or from capitalists for the use of the capitalist-controlled government). Part of the government spending is a necessary component of, or auxiliary to, economic growth—construction of roads, public transport system, the postal service, and education are examples. Military spending, however, represents nothing but a drain on resources that might otherwise be invested productively.

Throughout the past 20 years, 1951–1970, business spending for plant and equipment has been almost continuously less than direct military expenditures, of which a substantial proportion might well have been spent for investment purposes. The sharpening competition for surplus value between military and private investment is reflected in the soaring interest rates and the shortage of money capital for both government and private investment purposes.

In Chapter XI, the uneven development of production in the leading capitalist countries will be brought out. There has been a strong inverse correlation between militarism and the rate of economic growth during this period. The capitalist countries with the smallest military involvement have grown fastest; those with the largest military involvement have grown more slowly. This is shown by Chart III.[12]

The order of economic growth is exactly the opposite of the order of militarization. Japan, which has far and away the fastest growth rate, is

CHART III

Growth Rates and Militarization

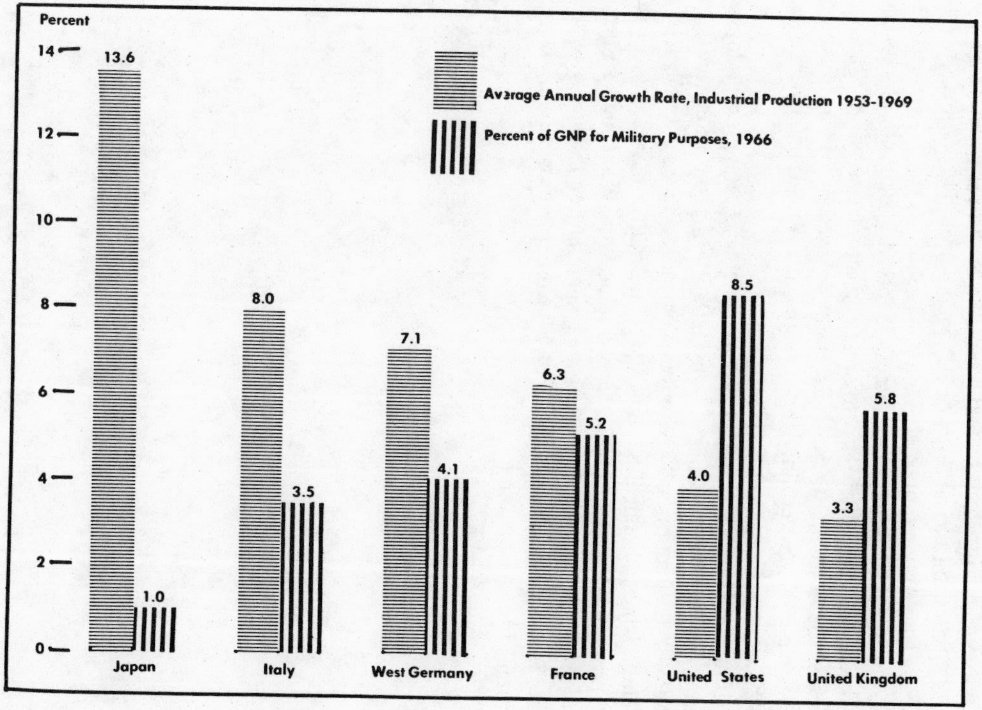

Average Annual Growth Rate, Industrial Production 1953-1969

Percent of GNP for Military Purposes, 1966

	Japan	Italy	West Germany	France	United States	United Kingdom
Growth Rate	13.6	8.0	7.1	6.3	8.5	5.8
Percent of GNP	1.0	3.5	4.1	5.2	4.0	3.3

far below any of the other countries listed in the percentage of militarism. Italy is second in growth, second from last in militarization, and so on. The only exception to the perfect inverse ordering is at the bottom of the list. The United States is next to last in economic growth and first in militarization, while Britain is last in economic growth and second in militarization.

Certainly, there are other factors involved in determining a country's growth rate. And there are complicated interactions of militarism with economic growth. Thus, the economic growth of Japan and West Germany have certainly been speeded by certain by-products of American militarization.

But the general conclusion is inescapable. In the present-day world, high military expenditures substantially impede economic growth. Would a reduction in U.S. military spending speed economic growth? There is no guarantee that it would, since many other factors as well are tending to slow down U.S. economic growth. What can be said is that with a radical reduction in military spending economic growth *could* be faster than it *would* be with the continuation of relatively very high military spending.

XI.

Uneven Development and the World Monetary Crisis

MOST MAJOR economic crises are international in character. Even the crises of 1949 and 1958, which were not expecially severe, made an impact on a large part of the capitalist world. There are usually differences in timing—the crisis begins in one country or a group of countries, then spreads to others—sometimes after a rather long interval. Thus, the great crisis of 1929–1932 didn't hit France until 1931.

The economic cycle is transmitted internationally through foreign trade, capital movements, and currency transactions. In the simplest form, a country in crisis buys less from other countries, thereby depressing markets in selling countries. Particularly serious are those financial crises in which a country does not have the international reserves needed to make payments that are due and demanded by foreign creditors.

In the postwar periods, a number of governments, faced with just such a crisis in their international payments, have followed policies designed to cause domestic recessions. A recession is supposed to cause a shrinkage in imports, while encouraging manufacturers to promote exports to replace smaller domestic markets. In this way, it is hoped, the international payments balance will be restored. European bankers have urged the U.S. government to do just this, but such advice has generally been ignored or carried out only inconsistently and temporarily.

A country's balance of payments is the summation of all the international transactions of its residents and government in a given period. It equals the difference between the country's receipts or credits and its expenditures or debits. Exports and imports are the largest items entering into the balance of payments; others include capital exports and imports, profits and interest on foreign investments, shipping and insurance transactions, tourist spending and the remittances of emigrants, and spending on foreign military bases. If a country's credits exceed its debits, it has a surplus. If the debits are larger, it has a deficit in its balance of payments. Temporarily, and within variable limits, balances can be carried as banking bookkeeping items. But from time to time they must be settled in some mutually agreed medium of payment.

Traditionally, settlements had to be made in gold, the one universally recognized money commodity. But the gold standard was seriously weakened by the wars and crises of the 20th century. At the end of World War II, the United States was the only really strong capitalist country, with most of the productive capacity and most of the gold reserves. One had to have dollars to buy many kinds of goods, and the dollar was considered to be as good as gold. Through the Bretton Woods agreements, the capitalist governments established the gold exchange standard, which recognized the leading position of the dollar along with gold. The parity, or value, of each currency was established in terms of gold or the dollar, while the parity of the dollar in relation to gold was fixed at $35 an ounce. The United States agreed to buy gold from, or sell gold to, all central banks on demand at that price. Governments agreed to try to maintain stable currency values and to change them only in accordance with specified rules. The International Monetary Fund was established as the organizational embodiment of these regulations. It had the function of providing temporary loans to assist in the maintenance of stable currencies and of exercising limited supervision over certain central bank operations.

One might say that these arrangements represented the most far-reaching expression of state-monopoly capitalism up to that time. International settlements between countries were the exclusive prerogative of central banks. Each government developed rules, varying in complexity and rigor, that controlled and limited the scope of private international transactions. Gold stocks of most countries were centralized, and in many countries private citizens were forbidden to own monetary gold. In addition, through the International Monetary Fund, elements of superstate monopoly capitalism became operative.

These procedures represent a most intensive, elaborate attempt to stabilize an important aspect of capitalist economy through government regulation, intergovernmental cooperation, and the creation of an international body with limited executive power over member states in the economic field. The attempt, however, has met with conspicuous failure. International financial relations have become more unstable over a prolonged period than ever before; acute currency crises have been increasingly frequent. The Articles of Agreement, By-Laws, Rules and Regulations of the International Monetary Fund are violated more and more by member states. Now, in 1972, many operations of the International Monetary Fund are suspended or in disarray, and spokesmen of leading capitalist powers are in a process of extended maneuvering and negotiations in an attempt to reconstitute and restructure the international monetary system.

This failure was inevitable in part because of the contradiction between the international planning of one aspect of capitalist world economy, and the anarchy of production in capitalist economy as a whole, between coordinated international regulation of one aspect, while other aspects were regulated independently by different governments, or remained unregulated by others.

The big banks and corporations continued to dominate international transactions, seeking private profit rather than national payments balance. Multimillionaires, controlling governments and writing their regulations, were always able to find ways to carry out their desires in international transactions, without regard to official policies. Driven by greed or by fear and by political events that created new openings or dangers, the biggest capitalists have caused sudden tidal waves of currency flow in the billions. These often broke through the protective dikes erected by the International Monetary Fund. In ironic contrast to the elaborate superstructure of regulation, the anarchy of capitalism here finds its most elemental, destructive expression.

Systematic tendencies in the economics of capitalism, and particular features of the attempted international regulation, made the international monetary structure especially crisis-prone. The universal inflation, proceeding at uneven rates in different countries, exerted great pressure on existing parities. The price of gold was maintained at $35 long after prices of virtually everything else had doubled or tripled. It became unprofitable to mine gold anywhere but in South Africa, where virtual slave labor prevails. The world supply of gold failed to expand with world trade. Reserves of gold became insufficient to provide adequate backing for fluctuations in payments balances.

The currencies of almost all capitalist countries were devalued after World War II, most of them several times. The most severe devaluations hit some of the developing countries. Devaluations provide temporary relief to a deficit in the payments balance. When the home currency becomes worth less than before, residents can buy fewer imported goods. On the other hand, prices that stay the same in the home currency become cheaper in foreign currencies, so the manufacturers can export more goods.

It doesn't always work out that way in practice. But, in any case, the workers of a country always pay the heaviest real price. Rising prices of imported goods influence prices of domestic goods. The cost of living jumps. Simultaneously, the capitalist governments impose "austerity" programs on workers, trying to freeze their wages and increase their taxes.

Thus there is a reduction in workers' living standards. But the increase in prices and the gains in foreign trade bring more profits to the capitalists. They profit by their country's loss. The biggest profits are garnered by the capitalists of stronger countries that do not devalue, and particularly by American capitalists, who did not devalue until 1971. Devaluation in other countries enabled them to buy up factories and mines and to hire workers for fewer dollars than formerly. It made foreign investments more profitable and cheapened the cost of imported raw materials.

Uneven Economic Development

The International Monetary Fund may be regarded, from one viewpoint, as a supercartel. The terms of international cartel agreements of big corporations in oil, electrical equipment, etc., have always reflected the distribution of power between the participants at a given time. Given the inevitable shifts in the distribution of power, these terms have always had to be revised after a number of years, or the cartels have broken up.

The terms of the International Monetary Fund reflected the overwhelming domination of U.S. imperialism within the capitalist world at the time of Bretton Woods. As that domination was eroded, it became inevitable that the one-sided terms of the Bretton Woods Agreement would be increasingly challenged, that they would either have to be revised or would collapse.

This is a particular example of a general cause of international imbalances, the uneven development of capitalism. This feature, elaborated by Lenin in his basic work, *Imperialism, the Highest State of Capitalism,* becomes increasingly serious in the epoch of monopoly capitalism, or imperialism.

There are different kinds of uneven development—between capitalism and socialism, between imperialist countries and dependent countries, and amongst imperialist countries. For the purposes of this chapter, the last-named is the most significant. Rarely, if ever, has the economic power balance among the major countries shifted so rapidly and so radically as in the years since World War II. This is brought out by comparison of the growth of industrial production in the six leading capitalist countries since 1953. By this time, the losses in production suffered by war-damaged countries had been fully made up, and something like the pre-war relationahip had been re-established—except for a still enhanced position for the United States. Thus, by and large, shifts in relative position since 1953 represent real changes and not mere recoveries from war damage.

The two capitalist victors of World War II showed a pronounced lag in growth. The three defeated Axis countries set the pace. Particularly remarkable was the record of Japan, whose industrial production increased nearly eight times in 16 years. Italy's production increased more than three times, West Germany's exactly three times, and France's production not much less than three times. In contrast, U.S. production failed to double, and British production increased by only two-thirds.

In annual growth rates, Japan achieved an unprecedented 13.6% per year (see Chart III, Chapter X). The Italian growth rate was double that of the United States; the West German and French growth rates about double that of Britain.

These sharp differences have made for unusually rapid changes in the balance of economic power. Japan has emerged as by far the second largest producer of the capitalist world. It has achieved world leadership in production of some important products and is rapidly closing the gap with the United States in others. Italy, West Germany, and France, combined with the Benelux countries in the Common Market, comprise a continental West European economic bloc of formidable and growing power. Traditionally third in industrial power, behind the United States and Germany, Britain will be in sixth place among the major powers within this decade if present trends continue. The United States has lost not only the extraordinary industrial dominance it enjoyed after World War II, but it plays a considerably smaller role industrially than it did 40 years ago. This has inevitably brought about a reduction in the U.S. share in world markets. Its share of world exports declined from 23.7% in 1948 to 18.5% in 1957 and 15.5% in 1969.[1]

U.S. big business, however, has not lost ground in proportion to the losses of the U.S. economy. For American capital has been expanding abroad on an unprecedented scale, and today the combined foreign holdings of U.S. corporations comprise a level of production equal to that of a major country. While highly profitable for U.S. monopoly capital, this further complicates the situation of the American domestic economy and is harmful to the economic interests of working people in the United States and in the countries where American corporations operate. In a number of ways, it worsens the imbalances in international transactions and contributes to the world monetary crisis.

By now most large U.S. industrial corporations have become multinational—with enterprises in a number of countries. They supply foreign customers mainly from foreign plants, less and less by export from the United States. Simultaneously, they use more and more of their foreign-made products for further processing or sale in the United States. This results in a built-in deterioration in the U.S. balance of trade and payments.

Since about 1875, the United States has systematically enjoyed a large favorable trade balance, or excess of exports over imports. In this century, as exports shifted from agricultural to industrial products, foreign trade became an important additional market and growth stimulant for U.S. industry. In 1957, exports amounted to about 10% of movable goods output.[2]

While lower than the corresponding percentages for European countries, this figure is significant, and changes in it can have a material effect on the domestic economy. The predominance of the United States in world manufacturing markets, especially for technologically advanced industrial products, became very marked during and after World War II. But the U.S. industrial trade balance has steadily deteriorated since then, as shown in Table XI-1.

During the late 1930s, non-farm exports were nearly twice as large as non-farm imports, a more or less "normal" ratio for the United States.

TABLE XI-1. U.S. FOREIGN TRADE IN NONAGRICULTURAL COMMODITIES, 1935–1971

Annual Averages, Millions of Dollars

	Exports	Imports	Balance	Percent Exports of Imports
1935–39	2,081	1,146	935	182
1940–44	7,486	1,652	5,834	453
1945–49	8,462	3,093	5,369	274
1950–54	10,892	5,911	4,981	184
1955–59	14,113	9,217	4,896	153
1960–64	16,904	12,409	4,495	136
1965–69	25,632	23,981*	1,651	107
1970	35,343	34,184	1,156	103
1971	35,824	39,870	−4,046	90

Source: Business Statistics, Supplement to the *Survey of Current Business,* various years, and *Survey of Current Business,* February 1972.

*Owing to changes in classification, imports for the period 1965–1969 are not exactly comparable with those for earlier years.

During World War II the ratio jumped to $4^1/_2$ times. But since then it has rapidly shrunk, and by the early 1960s non-farm exports were barely one-third more than non-farm imports. During the Vietnam War, the deterioration has been most rapid. In a five-year period (1965–69), the imports of non-farm products nearly doubled; the excess of exports over imports fell to only 7% and, in terms of dollars, to only one-third of the balance achieved in the 1950–54 period.

Finally, in 1968, for the first time this century, non-farm imports were slightly larger than non-farm exports. There were small positive balances in the next two years, but in 1971 there was a huge import surplus of over $4 billion, or 10%, in non-farm commodities. Despite a nearly $2 billion surplus in farm commodity exports—including a significant volume of grant-aid exports which did not help the U.S. payments balance—overall foreign trade was in deficit to the tune of more than $2 billion.

The inroads of foreign manufactures on the U.S. domestic market has been particularly spectacular. Imports of non-farm commodities multiplied 3.6 times in ten years, from nearly $11 billion in 1961 to nearly $40 billion in 1971. By the latter year, adding the cost of transportation and duties, the landed value of total imports amounted to over 15% of the value of domestic production of movable goods. This sharp increase resulted in a significant displacement of domestic production, with negative effects on employment. The AFL-CIO estimated loss of jobs owing only to the direct shifting of production from the U.S. to foreign countries at 700,000.

The 28% rise in non-farm imports between 1969, the peak year of the boom in the United States, and the depression year of 1971, was particularly significant. Normally imports stagnate or even decline in a period of lowered economic activity. The continued rapid rise fore-shadowed an even faster surge of imports when the U.S. economy recovered, barring far-reaching restrictions on imports, which could be counterproductive because of reprisals by other countries. This meant that an early restoration of the traditional positive U.S. trade balance was unlikely.

True, this decline in the U.S. trade position because of the shift to foreign production has paid off handsomely to American big business. A substantial proportion of the soaring imports were from subsidiaries of U.S. corporations. In part, the slower rise in exports represented U.S. corporations filling foreign orders from overseas plants in place of U.S. plants. Income from foreign investments has jumped from a billion dollars a year at the end of World War II to about $10 billion in 1970.

In the pattern of the old British Empire, profits from foreign investments could pay for an import surplus. In the case of the United States, however, the money coming in as income from foreign investments has been approximately balanced by the fresh outflow of capital for additional foreign investments.

But there are other multibillion-dollar expenses connected with these foreign investments, which the British imperialists of the 19th century did not have to absorb, and for which the U.S. imperialists have found no offset. These are the huge military-political expenses of maintaining an empire in the second half of the 20th century at a time when the national liberation movements, supported by socialist countries, be come ever stronger and more effective in their anti-imperialist struggle.

The $80 billion direct military budget isn't wholly involved in international payments, but several billion dollars of it are. This is the money that has to be paid in freely convertible dollars to governments and residents of other countries. No longer does imperialism enjoy the happy colonial paradise in which subject peoples had to pay the expenses of their occupiers. In the modern world of neocolonialism, big payoffs have to be made to the ruling classes and armed forces of occupied countries and allied countries that provide facilities and space for U.S. bases. Even helpless puppets of the Pentagon and the CIA, such as the "government" of South Vietnam, have to be lavishly bribed. Additional billions of supporting outlays have to be paid for economic, political and intelligence purposes.

The combined cost of all these operations came to $5 billion per year in the first postwar decade, increasing to $5½ billion yearly in 1955–64, and jumping during the Vietnam War to $8 billion in 1970 (Table XI-2).

Other factors tending to worsen the U.S. balance of payments are increased tourist expenditures abroad, and a shift from U.S.-owned to foreign-owned vessels and airlines in international shipping. These effects of aggressive U.S. expansion and the uneven development of capitalism have resulted in a mounting deficit in the U.S. balance of payments.

From a substantial surplus during the early postwar years, the U.S. balance of payments turned to a deficit during the Korean War (Chart IV). The annual deficit (calculated on the standard "liquidity" basis) increased sharply in the late 1950s, and again during the Vietnam War. The average annual deficit of $3.4 billion—for a cumulative deficit of

TABLE XI-2. U.S. CONVERTIBLE CURRENCY MILITARY AND
GIFT TRANSACTIONS, 1946–70
Annual Averages in Millions of Dollars

	Military Expenditures	Unilateral Transfers excluding Military, net	Total
1946–49	992	3,928	4,920
1950–54	1,831	2,965	4,796
1955–59	3,122	2,415	5,537
1960–64	3,007	2,554	5,561
1965–69	4,096	2,839	6,935
1970	4,851	3,148	7,999

Source: Survey of Current Business, June 1970, Table 1, pp. 34–35, and February 1972, pp. S-2, S-3.

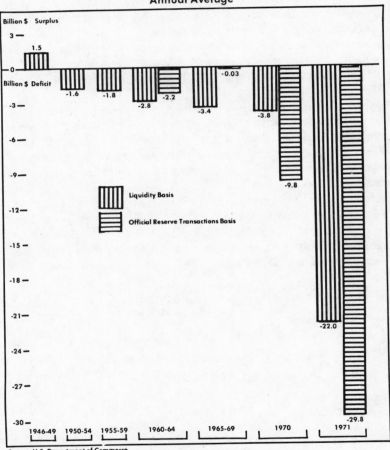

CHART IV

U.S. Balance of Payments, 1946 - 1971
Annual Average

Billion $ Surplus

Billion $ Deficit

Liquidity Basis

Official Reserve Transactions Basis

Source: U.S. Department of Commerce

$17 billion in the five years 1965–69—was sustained despite special transactions of the U.S. Government designed to make the balance-of-payments statistics look better than reality. This kind of "window-dressing" of the international books may have propaganda value to U.S. spokesmen but yields little practical relief.

The United States enjoyed a surplus in its payments in only two years of the past two decades: in 1957, as a result of the temporary trade effects of the closing of the Suez Canal; and in 1968, due to a surge in investment in U.S. securities and the issuance of a large volume of special "window-dressing" government bonds.

But in 1969 the deficit hit an all-time record high, for any country, of $6 billion. The deficit on this basis of calculation eased to under $4 billion—still huge by historic standards—in 1970. But on the alternative "official reserve transactions basis," the 1970 deficit hit a still higher record of almost $10 billion.

Finally, in 1971, the deficit soared to an incredible $22 billion on the liquidity basis, and to nearly $30 billion on the official reserve transactions basis, the final blow which forced the devaluation of the dollar and the substantial breakup of the old monetary arrangements.

Part of the U.S. deficits was redeemed with gold, and the U.S. gold stock fell from $24.6 billion at the end of 1949 to $10.1 billion at the end of 1971. But most of the deficits accumulated as dollar holdings by foreign central banks and private companies and individuals. After 1968, when the United States refused to pay out any but very small calls for gold, the giant deficits of the United States accumulated as foreign-held dollars.

U.S. liquid liabilities to foreigners, essentially the foreign-held dollars, jumped from $16 billion at the end of 1957 to $38 billion at the end of 1968 and $63 billion in November 1971. Of the latter sum, $45 billion was held by central banks and other official institutions of foreign countries,[4] and hence under the Charter of the International Monetary Fund could be presented to the United States for exchange into gold. Obviously, the bulk of such claims could not be met, as they totalled $4^{1}/_{2}$ times the U.S. gold stock.

In the years immediately after World War II foreign governments eagerly sought dollars, which were legally and practically as good as gold, as the only currency acceptable anywhere in the world, the best currency for buying needed commodities. But with the recovery of production elsewhere, the strengthening of other currencies and the weakening of the dollar, the eagerly sought after hoards gradually turned into burdens.

The role of the dollar as an alternative parity standard to gold placed on other countries a peculiar responsibility, one scarcely anticipated at the time of Bretton Woods. The International Monetary Fund Articles of Agreement required them to maintain their currency values within one per cent of parity. This meant they could not permit the value of the dollar to fall more than one percent below its parity. Thus banks, and through them individuals and corporations, could present unlimited amounts of dollars to the central bank of West Germany, for example, and demand payment in deutschmarks at close to the official parity. This effectively required the West German, Japanese, Swiss, and other governments with strong currencies to grant unlimited support to the dollar, especially after 1968 when the United States ceased to offer the option of converting the dollars into gold.

Since there was no prospect of ever redeeming most of the huge stockpile of dollars, the operation represented a drain on the national wealth of the countries with strong currencies. At the same time, the swelling flood of deutschmarks and other currencies paid out in exchange for the dollars became a source of mounting domestic inflation in these countries.

For a number of years they endured this situation. But finally it became intolerable.

The Dollar Crisis and Devaluation

The persistent, and increasing deficits in the U.S. balance of payments would, if suffered by any other country, have led to currency devaluation long ago. Under much less balance of payments pressure, the United States devalued the dollar in terms of gold in 1934. By the late 1960s, it became clear that the dollar was overvalued in terms of comparative prices in other countries. And yet the United States stubbornly persisted in retaining the $35-per-ounce gold parity. For many years, other countries with surpluses against the United States did not seek a showdown, and withheld demanding full payment in gold. The exception, the deGaulle government in France, was weakened by its lone financial warfare and was itself forced to devalue in 1968.

The two governments in the strongest position, West Germany and

Japan, realized gains in reserves corresponding to their gains in industry and trade, and yet, until 1971, they cooperated fully with U.S. tactics.

The "abnormal" actions of governments stemmed from the particular politics of this epoch—the politics of the Cold War. U.S. imperialism wanted to maintain the existing gold parity of the dollar for two essential reasons:

1. The second largest gold producer in the world is the USSR. Any increase in the price of gold increases the purchasing power of the USSR on world markets and hence, to some extent, helps it accelerate economic growth. True, an increase in the price of gold profits the United States even more in the short run, since it still holds the world's largest stockpile of gold. And U.S. capitalists have major investments in South Africa, the world's largest producing country. But U.S. imperialism has not yet relented in its economic warfare against the USSR—from its viewpoint, it seems, any damage to the USSR outweighs any possible harm this might do in the United States.

Absurd? Certainly. The same "logic" can be seen in the entire pattern of U.S. foreign policy.

2. Devaluation of the dollar would undermine its position as the key currency of the capitalist world, the main component, aside from gold, in the central reserves of governments.

In order to carry out that general policy, the United States required and received the cooperation of other imperialist governments.

Starting around 1960, the means of cooperation gradually expanded, along with the scale of the U.S. deficits. This is not the place to review them all, but particularly important steps were taken since the start of 1968. At that time, the dollar was in its most severe crisis. There was a massive run on the gold reserves of the United States, a veritable "gold hemorrhage."

The United States obtained agreement from the other leading capitalist governments to stop buying gold anywhere and announced it would no longer help Britain supply gold to the free market. In effect, the United States went completely off the gold standard. While itself buying gold when it could, the United States made it clear that it would no longer sell gold except in small quantities. A free market for gold ensued, with the price fluctuating above the $35 per ounce mark—at times well over $40 per ounce—while the "official" price remained at $35 per ounce.

Subsequently, the United States organized among the leading capitalist governments a boycott of South African gold until South Africa agreed to sell its gold on terms dictated by the major imperialist countries.

Then the United States obtained the agreement of the other leading capitalist countries to establish a new kind of advance from the International Monetary Fund, called Special Drawing Rights (SDR's). These can be used for international settlements in place of gold or foreign currency. And what is particularly significant is that about 70% of them do not have to be repaid.

The upshot of all these measures is that *in effect* the governments of West Germany, Japan, Switzerland, the Netherlands, and others were subsidizing expansion and aggression of U.S. imperialism to the tune of many billions of dollars per year.

Why did they do it? Primarily for the political reason that they regard the United States as the bastion of world imperialism, since big business in West Germany, Japan and other countries considers that the possibility of its expansion—let alone survival—depends on the Cold War policy of U.S. imperialism, on its domination of "third world" countries and military presence in Western Europe and Japan. And, secondarily, because concrete benefits went to the big monopolies of these countries in exchange for this support. They received handsome military orders from the Pentagon. They obtained an increasing share of markets and investment opportunities in countries occupied by, or otherwise dominated by, U.S. imperialism. And, as countries like West Germany and Japan built up handsome trade surpluses with the United States, their corporations derived big profits from the mounting sales to the U.S. market, even though this had to be paid for by the West German and Japanese people as a whole through absorbing the unredeemed accumulation of dollars.

At the same time, these governments sought to keep the cost down. They urged the U.S. Government to "put its house in order," to "stop inflation," slow down the economy, stop wage increases, improve its trade balance, and so forth.

And for many years the U.S. Government made certain minor efforts to improve its balance of payments, while loudly advertising its intention to achieve a complete balance by taking vigorous measures. Remarkably, just as the deficit reached record proportions in 1969–70, so did the talk of doing anything to reduce it seriously or to eliminate it come to a virtual end. In effect, Washington said to its allies: "Whatever the tab—$5 billion per year, $10 billion per year, or even more—you have no alternative but to pick it up. How you do it is your problem, not ours."

The gross imbalances in international finance constituted a major contradiction that could not remain without resolution indefinitely. By late 1970 a wave of speculation against the dollar, of unprecedented dimensions, erupted. At least $16 billion of flight capital was shifted from dollars into other currencies within a twelve-month period, a large part of it by U.S. capitalists. Almost every wealthy and many well-to-do Americans engaged in this speculation against their own currency, along with most of the U.S.-owned multinational corporations. Thus Americans were the main culprits among those "international" and supposedly foreign speculators whom President Nixon berated for the dollar crisis.

Temporary relief was obtained in May 1971 with the upward revaluation or the equivalent thereof of the West German deutschmark, the Swiss franc, and some other strong currencies. But the speculation against the dollar mounted to new heights, as the fact of a U.S. trade deficit became clear.

By August, according to rumors in financial circles, West European Governments demanded big gold payments of the United States, and informed Washington they would no longer support the dollar. On August 14 President Nixon formally abandoned convertibility of the dollar into gold, and currency values were permitted to "float" in international exchange markets, as central banks ceased regular support of fixed parities.

After several months of negotiations, a new set of more flexible parities were agreed on, with an average devaluation of the dollar by 12% against other currencies, and a U.S. commitment to raise the "official" price of gold from $35 to $38 per ounce.

The United States arrogantly sought to place the whole cost of the crisis on other shoulders. Its officials publicly demanded of allies huge direct or indirect contributions—a figure of $9 billion per year was mentioned—to support U.S. capital exports and military operations abroad. It threatened major import restrictions against other capitalist countries, that would lead to a trade war.

Simultaneously, the Administration imposed the freeze on wages, and the subsequent Phase II wage restrictions, in an effort to force American workers to bear the whole cost of the loss of position and value of the U.S. dollar. In essence, the attempt was to assure for big business a huge additional profit out of the national financial setback, to engage in a counteroffensive against U.S. labor and overseas rivals in the attempt to recoup and more than recoup from the losses involved in the devaluation of the dollar.

However, nothing was done to effectively stop soaring prices and corporate profits, nor to halt the export of capital, nor to remove special privileges from foreign installations of U.S. corporations. But only such measures could improve, or even halt the worsening, of the U.S. balance of trade. Nor did the United States do anything to reduce its overseas military operations. Instead, their costs increased because of the lowered relative value of the dollar.

The 12% average devaluation of the dollar was quite insufficient to overcome these handicaps. By May 1972, the price of gold passed the $50 mark, indicating a market belief that the real value of the dollar was about one-fourth lower than its already devalued rate. Speculation against the dollar resumed. Central banks were again put in the position of involuntarily supporting the dollar, and accumulating more dollars. It was clear that a long period of negotiations, and new crises, would have to be undergone before partial, temporary stability could be restored in capitalist world international finance.

It was also clear that the dominant role of the dollar, and of the U.S. multinational banks, would be reduced. Along with that there would be a rise in the role of the currencies and banks of Japan and of West Germany, or of the potential common currency of the enlarged Common Market of Western Continental Europe and Britain. And it seemed likely that during the 1970s a new currency would become a significant factor on world markets, the transferable ruble, the common international trade currency of the CMEA—the European socialist countries, (except Albania) Mongolia, and Cuba.

Meanwhile, the worsening crises, and partial collapse of the postwar capitalist world monetary system inevitably had negative effects on the course of economic activity throughout the capitalist world.

XII.

World Trends in Business Cycles and Their Political Setting

IN THE period since World War II, there have been significant changes in the pattern of economic cycles throughout the capitalist world. Simultaneously, production has grown much faster than in any previous period of comparable length. These changes have been more marked in Continental Europe and Japan than in the United States, having emerged under powerful political pressures more urgent in the other capitalist countries. In part they have been purposeful changes inspired by the financial oligarchs of the main capitalist countries and carried out principally through government actions.

A Soviet economist, G. Rudenko, compares this to the process of adaptation of biological species attempting to survive under adverse changes in conditions. He writes:

> Capitalism's adaptation to the new historical conditions has been carried out most intensively in the centers of world capitalism, the economically developed countries. This is quite natural. The dropping out even of a single big capitalist country from the chain of imperialism would have an incalculable effect on the entire bourgeois system. The tendency to adapt itself to the new conditions, to reduce the danger of such losses, is only natural for capitalism.
>
> The principal role in adapting the economy of imperialism to present-day conditions belongs to the government apparatus.

Rudenko acknowledges temporary successes for the process of adaptation: "Marxists cannot regard the process of adaptation of modern imperialism to the changing conditions as inevitably fruitless to capitalism. . . . Its immediate results are quite significant. . . ."

But in the long run, he asserts, it cannot save the system:

> Capitalism's attempts to resolve its contradictions can only result in the broadening and deepening of the sphere of their action. The attempt to resolve

them by adaptation is no exception. . . . The social consequences of the
processes of adaptation inevitably lead to the further weakening of the basis on
which the capitalist system rests.[1]

Some of these "processes of adaptation" have been analyzed in
earlier chapters of this volume insofar as they apply to the United
States. Some of these are examined again in this chapter in a global
context. Others discussed in this chapter have been less marked or are at
an earlier stage of development in the United States than in other
capitalist countries, but they foreshadow trends in this country as well.
These also must be understood, and require more exhaustive analysis,
in their application to U.S. conditions, than is possible within the
confines of this volume. Excellent work on some of these features has
been done by the group of economists of the Institute of World
Economics and International Relations in Moscow, headed by Stanislav
Menshikov. A summary of their views is contained in their collective
work, *Contemporary Cycles and Crises.*[2]

All of the changes taking place in capitalist world economy are
influenced, in greater or lesser degree, by the fact that capitalism is no
longer a unique, closed system. It is forced to coexist in a world
containing a powerful and growing socialist economic system. All of
the changes are impelled, in whole or in part, by the fear of
Communism and the revolutionary working class movement. The
countries of Western Europe and Japan are more directly influenced by
contact with socialist society and its economy than is the United States.
There are much stronger Communist movements in these countries, and
the possibility of revolution seems more imminent. That is why the
United States has lagged behind, in significant respects, in the intensity
of state regulation of the economy and in some of the other changes
affecting the course of the cycle and the pace of economic growth.

But the lag should not be exaggerated. The United States leads in
military confrontation with socialism and the world revolutionary
movement. This brings with it intensive militarization of the economy
and corresponding economic regulations. The social contradictions
within the United States have been greatly aggravated, while the
radicalization of important segments of the population proceeds apace.
This will certainly have an increasingly important influence on the
economy and on its regulation by the government.

Changed Course of the Cycle

Most cycles since World War II have been smoother than pre-war cycles. Instead of starting with a sudden crash, crises have been preceded by leveling off periods and have emerged relatively gradually. Declines have been comparatively shallow and not so long-lasting.

But the very mildness of declines has resulted in a failure to eliminate the contradictions that brought them about. The result has been the threat of a new crisis or recession soon after the ending of the last one. Also the cumulation of contradictions undermines some of the conditions that have made crises relatively mild.

Despite numerous international monetary crises, there have been no severe internal financial crises spreading from one country to another; only partial, localized financial ones in Japan, in Italy, and, most recently, in the United States. But in this sphere also, factors making for a severe international crisis have been cumulating.

Another important feature of the postwar cycle has been the difference of timing from one country to another. Thus the United States recession of 1961 did not spread to Western Europe. There were minor recessions in Japan in 1962 and 1965, a sharp decline in West Germany in 1966–67 and, finally, the U.S. crisis of 1969–70. If these declines had occurred simultaneously in all big capitalist countries, there would have been a major international crisis. But, as it was, continued rising trends in other countries helped pull the affected individual country out of its recession. The lack of synchronization of cyclical movements results in part from specific conditions in different countries after World War II; in part from the influence on the cyclical timing of government economic regulation, which varies from country to country; and in part from the extreme unevenness of economic development.

A number of factors are tending to counteract these causes. Most prominent is the rapid internationalization of capital. The Common Market is broadening the scope of its operations, making for a more uniform course of development throughout capitalist Europe. Other countries are catching up to the United States in technical level and in per capita output. Government economic regulation is more and more subject to the pressures of international groupings such as the "Group of Ten," central bankers of the biggest capitalist countries, the

International Monetary Fund, and the Organization of European Economic Cooperation. These trends make more likely than formerly a synchronized crisis in all or a number of major countries.

In fact, the stubbornness of the United States depression in 1971, combined with the effects of the dollar crisis, led to something at least approaching a capitalist world economic crisis. In four of the five leading capitalist countries, outside of the United States, industrial production either definitely turned downward or stagnated during 1971. Italy entered a full-fledged economic crisis, while Japan and West Germany went into what were officially regarded as recessions by authorities of those countries.

Faster Economic Growth

There has been a decisive speeding up of economic growth in the capitalist countries. Prior to World War II, the per capita growth rate in each of the leading capitalist countries ranged between one and two per cent per year. Moreover, the particular rate characteristic of each country was quite stable for a century or more.[3]

However, for the last two decades the annual per capita growth rate for each of these countries has exceeded 2%. In France, Italy, and West Germany, it has exceeded 4%, and in Japan it has reached the fantastic rate of 8 to 10%. (Table XII–1.)

Note that during the period prior to 1950 the United States led the capitalist countries in rate of growth. Although the difference was only a fraction of a percent per year, by the law of compound interest this was enough, continued over several generations, to propel the United States into a position of overwhelming dominance in capitalist world economy.

Since 1950 the tables have been turned. The United States has had the slowest per capita growth rate, except for Britain, and the margin of difference has been wider than prior to 1950. Should this continue, U.S. economic dominance will be ended much more rapidly than it came into being. This is especially true in relation to Japan. The Japanese government, in fact, predicts that it will surpass the United States in per capita gross national product by some time in the 1980s.

After two decades' duration, the stepped-up tempo of capitalist

TABLE XII-1. ANNUAL GROWTH RATES OF PER CAPITA
REAL GROSS NATIONAL PRODUCT
LEADING CAPITALIST COUNTRIES, 1870–1969

	1870–1913	1913–1929	1929–1950	1950–1964	1960–1969
United States	2.2	1.3	1.6	1.8	3.2
Japan*	*	*	*	8.7	9.9
West Germany†	1.7	0.0	0.7	5.9	3.6
United Kingdom	1.2	0.3	1.2	2.4	2.1
France	1.4	1.8	0.0	3.8	4.7
Italy	0.7	1.2	0.3	5.2	4.9

Sources:
1870–1964, U.S. Department of Commerce, Census Bureau, Long-Term Economic
Growth, 1960–1965, Washington, 1966, p. 101.
1960–1969, Computed from *United Nations Monthly Statistical Bulletin,* November
1970, Table 63 (real gross domestic product) and Table 1 (population).

*Source does not give per capita figures for Japan for periods prior to 1950, but shows
absolute growth in real gross national product at a rate slightly slower than that of the
United States, suggesting a moderately lower per capita growth rate.

†All Germany prior to 1945.

growth cannot be regarded as a passing or cyclical phenomenon. It must
be considered as a major change, valid over a relatively long period.

To some extent, the statistics distort reality. The destruction of World
War I and World War II distort the figures for the intervals in which
they occurred. Actually the tendency for the rate of economic growth to
speed up was evident even before World War I as a phenomenon of the
imperialist stage of capitalism. Characteristically, pro-capitalist economists claim that the speeded-up growth rate confounds Marxists, who
"expected" the opposite. And, characteristically, they exhibit ignor-
ance of what the Marxists really expected.

Here it is worth citing Lenin, the pioneer Marxist economist of the
epoch of monopoly capitalism, of imperialism:

The extent to which monopolist capital has intensified all the contradictions
of capitalism is generally known. It is sufficient to mention the high cost of
living and the tyranny of the cartels. This intensification of contradictions
constitutes the most powerful driving force of the transitional period of history,
which began from the time of the final victory of world finance capital.

Monopolies, oligarchy, the striving for domination and not for freedom, the exploitation of an increasing number of small or weak nations by a handful of the richest or most powerful nations—all these have given birth to those distinctive characteristics of imperialism which compel us to define it as parasitic or decaying capitalism. . . .

It would be a mistake to believe that this tendency to decay precludes the rapid growth of capitalism; it does not. . . . On the whole, capitalism is growing far more rapidly than before; but this growth is not only becoming more and more uneven in general; its unevenness also manifests itself, in particular in the decay of the countries which are richest in capital (British).

He then cites a German author, comparing the speed of growth of German economy in a then more recent period to that of a generation earlier, and the speed of an automobile to that of an old mail coach. Lenin then continues: "In the United States, economic development in the last decades has been even more rapid than in Germany, and *for this very reason*, the parasitic features of modern American capitalism have stood out with particular prominence."[4]

One can say that every sentence of this holds true with redoubled force today except that now the United States is at the low end of uneven development, and except that now the parasitism and decay of capitalism manifest themselves most in the United States, the richest in capital.

Another feature of Table XII–1 should be noted. The United States did not show any appreciable acceleration of growth until the decade of the 1960s, unlike the other capitalist countries, whose growth rate clearly had already accelerated in the 1950s.

This can be understood best by referring to Lenin's concept of the intensification of contradictions as the most powerful driving force of the epoch. This intensification, bringing mortal danger to capitalist rule, acts as a driving force propelling the financial rulers of these countries to use every means to strive to minimize crises and speed up economic growth. These contradictions reached the most acute state in the countries of Western Europe and Japan before they did in the United States, owing to the economic gains of the United States in World War II and the relative political stability of this country in the 15 years or so following the war.

But the pressures operating on other capitalist countries are also affecting the United States, and increasingly so. Examination of factors that have caused changes in the world cyclical pattern, in world-wide economic growth, and in the methods of government regulation involved, casts light on the potential course of development in the United States.

The changes have been partly due to the rapid strengthening of monopoly and, associated with that, the multiplied uses of state economic regulation. But the results of this regulation have been greatly conditioned by the vast social and political changes that have been and are taking place.

Government Programing

In a number of capitalist countries, government economic regulation has gone considerably beyond the essentially indirect influences of fiscal and monetary measures. The regulation includes direct programing of economic activity, often expressed in four-or five-year government plans. The term "programing" is used here to make a distinction between this and the planning in socialist countries. In the latter, plans are comprehensive—they cover virtually the entire economy; they are obligatory on all economic units; and they are carried out wholly in the socialist sector of the overall economy, that is, the execution of plans is fundamentally in the hands of their drafters.

In capitalist countries, government programing is far from comprehensive; it is not obligatory but merely an indication of what is desired; its execution is mainly in the hands of private companies, many of which will invariably be motivated to act in ways that are at variance with the program.

France has perhaps the most ambitious capitalist planning organization, including a large technical-bureaucratic staff and relatively comprehensive coverage. In broad terms, it is described thus: ". . . the plan is a summary description of the economy projected four years into the future, and accompanied by a set of commentaries and recommendations. As such it may be regarded as a giant marketing study at the national level."

Through active participation of private firms in the planning process "It is thus *hoped* that the projection, to the extent that it forecasts and influences their decisions, brings about enough consistency among decentralized plans and consensus among decentralized objectives to become substantially self-realizing."[5]

French economic programing has had uneven results. What successes it has had are largely attributable to the very large government economic sector in France, which includes the utilities, most of transport, a share in oil, all coal, aircraft, the four largest deposits banks, the Bank of France, Renault, and some other large industrial firms. Loans by the Economic and Social Development Firm—part of the programing operation—go mainly to the public sector. Public-sector purchasing and direct control over credits exercise significant influence on the private sector. As academic researchers put it: "The public sector is the basic element in the Plan both for drafting and implementation."[6]

Japanese government programing is different in formal structure but just as comprehensive in scope as that of France, although the state sector is not a large one. But programing is relatively effective, because of the extreme monopolization of the economy and the advanced organization of the government as the collective agency of the leading monopoly groups.

The Japanese economy is dominated by a handful of "former" Zaibatsu groups—Mitsubishi, Mitsui, Sumitomo, and others. While nominally disbanded after World War II, they have been reconstructed, with power and cohesion many times multiplied. Each of these groups has a compact financial-industrial empire embracing great banks, trading companies, and manufacturing firms in all basic industries.

The representatives of these groups meet in formal government bodies and government-sponsored bodies that program the course of the overall economy and *control* key decisions in particular major industries. For example, decisions are made as to how much steel capacity to add, and the added capacity is allocated among the several steel companies. In shorter-range regulation, when demand slackens, all textile companies, for example, might be ordered to cut production 20%.

The key element in government programing is the projection of investment, the most volatile element in the economy and the main determinant of long-term growth. Therefore, a key objective in government programing is the mobilization of funds for investment. This is equally true in countries like West Germany which do not have formal "plans."

In West Germany, the government programs the activities of a network of special mortgage banks, investment banks, as well as commercial banks in lending, so as to achieve investment levels consistent with long-term growth objectives and within conceived limits of inflationary pressure.

A common characteristic of investment programing is the high-pressure mobilization of savings. Thus, in Japan, which has surpassed all previous growth records, the multiplication of credit on a relatively narrow basis of money capital, and the extremely high ratio of debt to equity capital in industry, far surpass bounds of "traditional," "safe" financial practice. The Japanese monopolies have "gotten away with it" thus far, largely because of the relative effectiveness of their coordination.

The United States has lagged in programing. Under the Nixon administration, the President's Council of Economic Advisors prepared five-year projections of "what the future national output can be," and a rough breakdown of its composition.[7] The Chase Manhattan Bank prepared a ten-year economic projection, involving a number of key economic indicators. This, and other private and academic projections, were derived from computerized processing of algorithms involving far-reaching assumptions concerning control factors in the economy and national policy.

However, none of these projections, governmental or private, were in any real way connected with operative government regulation of the economy, nor could the underlying assumptions reckon with the complex of domestic and international contradictions which would inevitably cause increasing divergence from any given set of factor relationships.

Under these conditions, the speed, power, and objectivity of the electronic computer can give a totally unrealistic impression of precision. In reality, the computerized forecast is likely to be no more accurate than a simple set of linear projections of past trends, or of a crude set of assumptions worked out with equipment no more complicated than a slide rule.

At this stage, there are in the United States only primitive elements of actual programing, as in the manipulation of housing subsidies and stimuli in the attempt to realize desired overall levels of construction.

Effects of the Scientific-Technical Revolution

The extremely rapid progress of science and technique results in the rapid obsolescence of equipment and products. This tends to lead to a higher rate of capital investment and hence of economic growth as a whole. Certainly this has been a vital factor in the United States. In the present period it is even more important in other capitalist countries, which are striving to catch up to the United States in science and technique.

Taken by itself, rapid scientific-technical development might even aggravate cyclical tendencies. The well-known economist Joseph Schumpeter associated major cycles with the bunching of important technical innovations. This effect, however, is partly negated by two considerations:

First, the continuous massive expenditures on research and development assure a relatively continuous flow of new applications and techniques, as distinguished from fundamental scientific discoveries. It is through these new applications and techniques rather than directly through outstanding dramatic discoveries that the influence of the scientific-technical revolution on the economy is registered.

Second, there is the increased concentration of capital whereby at least half of the industrial output in the United States, for example, is carried out by corporations with scores and hundreds of separate plants and operations in many countries. Such monopoly corporations are better able to adhere to budgeted investment schedules, despite fluctuations in the markets for the products of this or that group of plants. They can pace the introduction of new techniques to derive maximum profit from the process.

International Mobility of Capital

There has been a marked acceleration of mobility of capital among the industrially developed capitalist countries. This carries with it a speedier international interchange of technology, enhanced flow of commodities, and more ready movement of the labor force. It also brings with it a tendency toward equalization of technical level, with those countries previously at a relatively low technical level, such as Italy, gaining on the more advanced.

The Common Market of six West European countries has been a major factor in the international mobility of capital. It has given continental Western Europe some of the advantages of a huge unified mass market previously enjoyed by the United States.

The multibillion dollar flow of U.S. industrial capital to Western

Europe has expanded the scale of electronics, computers, and other high technology industries. The flow of advanced know-how to Japan has been particularly liberal, accelerating the achievement of very high world standards in all major branches of Japanese basic industries.

The general effect of all this has been to speed up the rate of economic growth in the capitalist world. But the process has contradictory features. The internationally mobile capital remains national in ownership, the property of the banks, industrial corporations, and millionaires of the capital-exporting countries. U.S. capital, moving into Western Europe, installs a fierce competitor to West European capital on its own soil. Often it brings in advanced technology for its own use only, gaining a monopolistic advantage over locally owned enterprises. Through its use of Eurodollars, it strives for financial hegemony in Western Europe, with the New York money market vying with West European financial centers for control of that continent.

U.S. companies impose more intense working conditions and often prove to be the most bitter opponents of workers striving for needed wage concessions. These corporations play off the workers of one country against another, threatening or actually moving production from place to place in search of the lowest labor and tax costs.

Thus, all international and social conflicts are sharpened. The contradictions between the monopolies of different countries, papered over by economic and political-military alliances and by jointly owned companies, become more severe. This applies especially to the conflicts between the aggressive U.S. monopolies and those of other countries. The class struggle involving multinational corporations and the workers of the capitalist countries becomes more acute. This creates conditions for later economic setbacks, undermining the gains resulting from the vast flow of capital.

The contradictions are especially severe in the United States itself, the main source of capital export. Here, increasingly, the export of industrial capital involves the export of jobs to countries with lower wages. Initially this was concentrated in Western Europe and Canada, and these are still the leading recipient areas. But more and more of the capital goes to developing countries under U.S. political-military domination, where wages are especially low and many special concessions are offered to the U.S. corporations.

This process has reached a stage where it already impedes economic growth in the United States. It threatens virtual elimination of many traditional lines of output, and brings with it a tendency towards parasitism—reliance on the productive labors of other countries. It tends to increase chronic mass unemployment here, contributes to the rapid growth of the huge "surplus population"—dispossessed and cast out of economic life, reduced to subsistence on "welfare."

The anarchic international flow of money capital—on a scale of tens of billions yearly—parallel with, but largely independent of, the flow of capital used in production—is a virulent agent of inflation and speculative excesses of all kinds. It creates conditions for possible major international financial and industrial crises.

Strengthened Working Class Struggles

The multiplied strength of trade unions and working class political parties has a major effect on both the cycle and the rate of economic growth. Owing to this strength, workers are now able to win annual wage increases far exceeding any previous norm. Even though this has not resulted in an increased *share* for workers or in a reduction in the rate of exploitation, it has brought rapid increases in absolute real wages to workers in Japan, West Germany, Holland, France, and other countries. Over the six-year period 1963–69, real wages of workers in manufacturing increased at the following approximate annual rates: Japan, 7%; West Germany, 5%; France, 4%; Italy, 3%; United States, 1%; and United Kingdom, 1%.[8]

Such increases as were registered in the first four countries named resulted in a rate of growth of mass consuming power never before know in the history of capitalism. In Japan, to take an extreme example, the real wage of the average worker has almost doubled in the last decade.

Thus, in these countries, there is a substantial broadening of the domestic mass market, notably for automobiles and other consumers' durables. The density of cars in these countries is coming within striking distance of the U.S. level, while per capita production of automobiles now approximates that of the United States. This has contributed in a major way to the increased tempo of economic growth.

Cycles are smoothed down in other ways owing to labor's strength. Workers are able, by and large, to resist wage cuts and actually continue to obtain wage increases despite business slowdowns. Moreover, in France and Italy especially, they have succeeded in markedly limiting the ability of big employers to lay off workers when orders decline. The same is true in Japan for a significant sector of the working class, although here it is related not only to the power of labor but also to the survival of certain features of feudalism in labor-management relations.

The "automatic stabilizers"—notably social insurance payments and the progressive income tax, which tend to dampen cyclical fluctuations (see Chapter IV), are hailed by apologists as evidences of improved functioning of capitalism. But in fact none of them were yielded out of the wisdom of the capitalists, but rather as reluctant concessions to the increased organized strength and struggles of workers and other anti-monopoly forces. And the capitalists are always seeking ways to whittle down or do away with their concessions, as in the many changes in income tax laws and regulations which have eliminated much of the progressive rate structure and now put the main burden of income tax payments on wage and salary workers.

International influences have been very important in spurring more rapid and regular increases in workers' wages. Workers in capitalist countries are becoming more and more familiar with economic and social conditions in socialist countries: regular and manifest increases in real wages, varied social benefits, cradle-to-grave social security provisions, and extensive workers' rights and participation in factory management.

Western Europe and Japan are not the United States, where the bulk of the press prints only negative and distorted news about economic developments in the socialist countries, and where most trade-union leaders forbid contacts with the unions and workers of socialist countries. Major trade union bodies in Western Europe and Japan meet with the trade union bodies of the socialist countries in the World Federation of Trade Unions. Workers' delegations visit back and forth, and mass circulation newspapers of the Communist parties print details of economic and social progress in socialist countries.

Workers in capitalist countries are also influenced by the internationalization of capital and the mobility of labor. This has a tendency toward the equalization of labor conditions in Western Europe. Also, European workers employed by U.S. corporations see no reason why their wages should be a fraction of those of the U.S. employees of the same corporations. Recently, the leadership of the United Automobile Workers and of several other U.S. unions have begun to cooperate with trade unions of other countries in striving for international coordination of policies and actions of workers of multinational corporations.

Of course, it would be naive to claim that gains in the conditions of workers, if continued long enough, will stabilize capitalism, eliminate crises, create a "third way," etc. That is the kind of petty bourgeois consumerism advocated by labor economist Leon Keyserling and some of the West European Social Democrats. The gains are good for the workers but they are at the expense of the capitalists. They hold down the rate of profit. Capitalists often respond with such crisis-provoking actions as holding up new investments, transferring their funds abroad to countries with more docile workers, and so forth. And under conditions of monopoly capitalism, such moves are not necessarily mere automatic responses to economic law, but at least are supplemented by conscious decisions of the top financial oligarchy to use these economic and financial means for combating the working class. Moreover, such economic class warfare may be paralleled with political warfare, attempts to reverse the balance of forces through fascist coups or military adventures. Such political factors figured conspicuously in the Italian crises of 1964 and 1969 and in the French crisis of 1968.

Effects of the Struggle for Economic Independence

The countries of Africa, Asia, and Latin America—the majority of them recently freed from political colonialism—are now striving to achieve a more balanced economic development, to raise living standards, to become free from the drain on their wealth and income by imperialist banking institutions and industrial corporations.

They have made some progress in this respect. Between 1955 and 1970, industrial production in the developed capitalist countries increased 113%, but in the developing countries, the figure was 198%.[9] A number of these countries have become semi-industrialized and have reached a "take-off" point from which really spectacular advances in industrialization are projected and may be realized—barring political turmoil.

A decisive factor here has been the growing ability of socialist countries to provide industrialization equipment to the developing countries. For 15 years the Soviet Union and other socialist countries have played a significant, increasingly influential role in the process of global development.

They advance industrialization loans at nominal interest rates—typically $2^1/2\%$; they do not seek control over the enterprises, and they favor state-owned basic industry enterprises. They also encourage repayment in the raw materials and manufactured products of the developing countries on an expanding scale, without cyclical dips.

By contrast, imperialist banks make loans only at high interest rates and mainly for "infrastructure" projects that would provide power and means of transport for the oil and mining enterprises of imperialist corporations. They rarely helped, indeed generally sabotaged, attempts to set up nationally owned industry. Wherever possible, they favored private over state-owned industry. So-called economic aid was conditioned on agreements to permit the free transfer of profits by private investors and to provide a generally "favorable climate" for them. Such "aid" was also associated with the granting of military bases, as well as with support in the United Nations and elsewhere to imperialist diplomacy.

Socialist practices have undermined imperialist positions and policies. This has been true in countries like Egypt, which took a revolutionary, noncapitalist road of development when forced to choose between reliance on socialist or imperialist power. It has been true in countries like India, which have maintained extensive economic relations with both the socialist and imperialist camps, using the former as a lever to extract better terms from the latter. And it has been true of a number of Latin American countries, which until recently had little to do with socialist countries but obtained concessions from U.S. imperialism in exchange for refusing socialist aid.

Generally therefore, the United States and other imperialist countries have been compelled to modify their policies. They have been forced to advance some "soft" loans at low interest rates, to make some loans for state-owned basic industry in developing countries, and even to maintain economic relations with some countries engaging in the nationalization of imperialist properties. The oil companies and mining companies have been forced to concede increased tax payments to the governments of countries where they operate.

The economic gains in developing countries and their steps towards economic independence, however limited and halting, influence the capitalist world economy. The gains moderate the effects on developing countries of crises in imperialist countries and help prevent the deepening of world economic crises. They also contribute to a certain broadening of the market for industrial goods manufactured in the imperialist countries, although it should be noted that the main gainers have been the rivals of the United States which have made the broadest concessions to the developing countries.

On the other hand, as developing countries attain more freedom of maneuver, become more potent competitors in world markets for manufactured goods, curtail the profitability of imperialist corporations, and later nationalize critical investments, all of the economic and political contradictions within the imperialist countries will be intensified.

East-West Trade

The volume of trade between socialist and capitalist countries multiplied seven times, from $3.5 billion in 1954 to $25 billion, at an annual rate, in the first half of 1971, according to incomplete figures of the United Nations. The share of such "East-West trade" in total world trade increased from 4% to over 10% in the same period.[10]

Trade between the USSR and capitalist countries was delayed for a number of years after the Russian revolution by the world capitalist economic blockade, and never developed far prior to World War II, owing mainly to political reluctance on the part of capitalist countries.

After World War II, with a greatly enlarged socialist community, the promising possibilities for "East-West trade" were cut short by cold war restrictions imposed under the primary influence of the United States. It declined somewhat from the first postwar years to a low of under $3 billion before starting to expand as capitalist countries gradually relaxed their restrictions.

By the late 1960s most capitalist countries maintained trade relations with socialist countries that approached normal. They reduced the lists of prohibited items for sale to socialist countries, reduced the extent of discrimination against imports from socialist countries, and began to give more or less normal credit terms for sales to socialist countries. Sharp competition developed amongst capitalist corporations for this business.

The special advantages of East-West trade became increasingly evident. With their planned and crisis-free economies, the socialist countries were able to conclude long-term purchase and sales agreements providing for steadily growing trade in both directions. They concluded national agreements with capitalist countries for technical, scientific, and economic cooperation that tended to strengthen the industries of both sides. Trade and development deals on an unprecedented scale were concluded, such as those between the Soviet Union and some West European countries providing huge quantities of natural gas in exchange for large quantities of steel pipe and related equipment. A similar deal was concluded with Japan involving development of Soviet Siberian forest industries and huge shipments of forest products to Japan, with negotiations started on petroleum deals running into the billions. The Italian Fiat Company obtained a contract worth several hundred million dollars to participate in engineering and supplying equipment for the Volga Automobile Works. Canada and Australia concluded long-term deals for the sale of grain to socialist countries.

The volume of East-West trade became sufficiently large that its steady uptrend helped moderate downward cyclical pressures within the capitalist world economy, and to influence positively the long-term growth rate.

However, the United States continued to lag behind other capitalist countries, and to try to brake or slow development of East-West trade generally. Pentagon generals were conspicuous opponents, seeing military potential in everything from ladies' bras to commercial trucks. The powerful oil trust, fearing the competition of Soviet oil on world markets, was a particularly vigorous opponent, and the computer monopoly, IBM, sought to keep relevant technology out of socialist hands. Multinationals, with plants in Europe, were indifferent to bans on sales from the United States so long as they could evade them by sales from abroad. According to State Department estimates, such sales to socialist countries amounted to three times direct sales from the United States. Most fundamentally, the decisive sectors of U.S. big business calculated that the USSR and other socialist countries would make the most effective use of advanced technological equipment and processes purchased from the United States, and thereby more speedily catch up to and surpass the United States in economic strength.

The practical interests of most American manufacturers, especially in the machinery and metalworking industries, as well as millions of workers, dictated support for expansion of trade with socialist countries. Pressure for such trade became particularly strong during the crisis and depression of 1970-71, when production in the machinery industries fell to a low level. Secretary of Commerce Maurice Stans, reflecting these pressures, advocated easing trade barriers, and in 1972 expressed the view that U.S. trade with socialist countries could soon reach billions of dollars per year.

Trade between the United States and socialist countries expanded irregularly during the 1960s, but amounted to only $613 million in 1971 (with coverage comparable to the United Nations statistics), or a mere $2^{1}/_{2}\%$ of the total volume of East-West trade, and less than $1^{1}/_{2}\%$ of total U.S. foreign trade. Part of this expansion was due to the U.S. government policy of "bridge-building," opening up trade a little with socialist countries considered possible candidates for taking an anti-Soviet line and breaking with the Socialist community generally. Such a course was started with respect to China in 1971–72.

However, a real development of East-West trade is not possible on this basis. What is required is a general elimination of the various forms of discrimination against that trade practiced by the U.S. Government and some monopoly groups.

Economic and Political Crises—The General Crisis of Capitalism

The economic cycle is a significant factor, but only one of a number of major factors influencing the development of capitalism, as well as the struggle against it. The contradictions of capitalism—economic, political, social, national, and military—have become incurably deep.

The working class of the advanced capitalist countries, with trade unions embracing tens of millions and large contingents of Communists in the forefront of revolutionary struggle and guiding it, pose an increasingly ominous threat to capitalist rule. The national liberation struggle weakens the grip of imperialism throughout the former colonial and semicolonial areas of the world.

The socialist world exists side by side with capitalism. It grows relatively stronger year by year economically and in every other way. And it gains power as the peoples of more and more countries overthrow local capitalist and imperialist domination and take the path of pre-socialist or socialist development. It acts as a core of strength for the anticapitalist, anti-imperialist forces of the remaining world of capitalism.

All this comprises a mortal crisis of world capitalism which cannot be resolved except with the demise of the system. This crisis, continuous and deepening since the Russian Revolution, is known to Marxist-Leninists as the general crisis of capitalism. Attempts to suppress one aspect of this general crisis, when successful, lead only to the more severe eruption of another aspect.

Thus, in the simplest case, government economic regulation to stimulate the economy and counteract recessions on behalf of monopoly capital invariably leads to inflation. This aggravates social tensions as much as a crisis of overproduction. The cure is as bad as the disease. Militarism and foreign investments play a prominent part in the big business program of economic regulation and stimulation. But militarism leads to all the associated evils, and foreign investments lead to wars to protect them from the people exploited abroad. And who would dare say that the Vietnam War did less damage to the domestic political position of capitalism than a severe economic crisis would wreak?

Twenty years ago only the Communists warned that the suppressive foreign policy of U.S. imperialism would surely lead to international runaway shops taking jobs away from American workers. Now workers generally know about and condemn the loss of hundreds of thousands of jobs yearly, as U.S. monopolies engage in a massive exodus to lower-wage foreign countries.

The 40-million Black and other oppressed peoples in the United States are forced to fight racism by the hard pressures of life and are able to fight it more effectively than ever because of their large concentration in the main industrial towns. The working class becomes more militant and active year by year in fighting for its needs against the giant corporations.

All of these elements, including that of economic recessions and crises, draw the American people increasingly into the active struggle against monopoly capital. At the same time, in developing countries, from Vietnam to Chile, sharp blows are being delivered to U.S. imperialist interest and actions.

On many occasions I have heard radicals proclaim: "Just wait for the next depression!" The thought behind this remark is that a severe economic crisis will arouse the working class to a really revolutionary level of struggle.

But this slogan is a formula for passivity. Economic history will never repeat itself in the exact model of the 1929–32 crisis. There is a widespread belief that revolutions occur only in times of economic crisis; in fact, not a single one of the fourteen successful socialist revolutions took place during a crisis of overproduction.

The new crisis symptoms and the new contradictions of the general crisis of capitalism will surely spur the working class and its allies to making a revolution and seizing power in order to build socialism. Certainly, a crisis of overproduction always increases social tensions and the preparation and launching of a working-class revolution may be more likely to take place during such a period than otherwise.

While there will be no repetition of 1929–32, the developing economic contradictions make increasingly likely the eruption of crises that will be considerably more severe than any of the postwar period.

The attitude of Communists is not to rejoice at the arrival of crises but rather to fight against their harmful consequences for the working class. Such a struggle for immediate concessions and reforms is inseparably connected with the revolutionary struggle to end capitalism, with all of its contradictions and evils, and to substitute socialism.

XIII.

Outline of a People's Economic Program

As INDICATED in Chapter XII, the influence of labor and other anti-monopoly groups on the business cycle and economic growth has been of lesser degree in the United States than in a number of other advanced capitalist countries. This reflects the absence of an important labor-based political formation and the absence of a strong Communist movement to give an anti-monopoly thrust to labor pressures on economic issues.

The peak effort of the country's working people for this type of program was expressed in the full-employment legislation proposed by the main trade union centers toward the end of World War II. It established the responsibility of the government to provide jobs for all workers not employed by private industry. Introduced into the Senate in 1945, it declared as a policy:

All Americans able to work and seeking work have the right to useful, remunerative, regular, and full-time employment, and it is the policy of the United States to assure the existence at all times of sufficient employment opportunities to enable all Americans who have finished their schooling and who do not have full-time housekeeping responsibilities freely to exercise this right.

It called for policies that would encourage maximum employment by private industry, state and local governments. Beyond that, however, it stipulated:

"To the extent that continuing full employment cannot otherwise be achieved, it is the further responsibility of the Federal Government to provide such volume of Federal investment and expenditures as may be needed to assure continuing full employment; and "Such investment and expenditure by the Federal Government shall be designed to contribute to the national wealth and well-being, and to stimulate increased employment opportunities by private enterprise."[1]

The bill was full of assertions of its loyalty to "free competitive enterprise" and the supposed mutual interests of all classes in society. But, obviously, these "principles" are in basic contradiction to the full employment objective as stated in the bill, which is, fundamentally, one of working class struggle against capital. Enactment of such a bill could not lead to the harmonious progress its sponsors envisaged, but could set the stage for a higher level of struggle, from positions more advantageous to the workers.

Such a radical measure would have the effect of minimizing downturns in a way favorable to working people, that is, by taking up the slack in private production through government production. If administered by a government with important labor influence, it would be a major step toward weakening the power of large corporate employers and would tend to encourage the growth of an expanding state economic sector, oriented to providing for the social needs of the people.

This was a time of the war against fascism, a war waged in alliance with the socialist USSR. It was a period of relatively high progressive influence and minimized influence of the most reactionary big business circles. Thus such a proposal could be advanced and make considerable headway.

Even its opponents had to pay lip service to the idea of full employment. But capital remained in control of Congress and the administration. The trade union leaders were not anticapitalist and not willing to combat big business all the way. They went along with the Cold War anti-Communist ideology with which monopoly capital launched its postwar domestic and international offensive. The Full Employment Act was defeated. Instead, Congress passed the Employment Act of 1946. The word "full" was not only dropped from the title; it was dropped from the concept. The objective was shifted from attaining full employment to attaining a "high level" of employment. And no operative machinery was established nor responsibility assigned to attain that vaguely defined goal. The only action was to set up the Council of Economic Advisors to make studies and advise the president on policies for attaining the ill-defined purposes of the Act. Moreover, even the limited goal of "high level" employment was conditional—it was to be pursued by measures consistent with the preservation of private enterprise. This limitation could and would be used by the capitalists to oppose, and usually block, any measures which seemed likely to reduce their profits or to reduce their rate of exploitation of labor.

The real character of this Act has not prevented liberal apologists from eulogizing it as "Labor's Magna Charta" and a real guarantee of full employment. It is still referred to by them as the "Full" Employment Act, with much the same sort of shoddy, deceptive terminology as that calling 4% unemployment, "full" employment.

The prerequisite for substantial realization of a meaningful program is accession to political power of a party or coalition controlled by and clearly representing the working people including farmers and small businessmen, as well as wage and salary workers. A government so based could put some force behind the present Act and would, necessarily, formulate its own far-reaching program in the course of its struggles.

An essential component, it goes without saying, is peace. That means not only the end of any war that U.S. imperialism may be carrying on or supporting. It means also a withdrawal of U.S. troops from foreign bases, and a decisive cut in the military budget and in the size of the armed forces, to a point where these cease being major economic and political factors. It means agreement to outlaw nuclear weapons, and for their mutual destruction by all nuclear powers. With this kind of peace action, the resources can be freed and the social forces mobilized to carry out radical social and economic reforms.

Following are some principles that would be logical components of such a program, in terms of American realities. The objectives were expressed during World War II by President Roosevelt, in his "Economic Bill of Rights:"[2]

We have accepted, so to speak, a second bill of rights under which a new basis of security and prosperity can be established for all, regardless of station, race or creed. Among these are:

The right to a useful and remunerative job in the industries or shops or farms or mines of the nation.

The right of every farmer to raise and sell his products at a return which will give him and his family a decent living.

The right of every business man, large and small, to trade in an atmosphere of freedom from unfair competition and domination by monopolies at home or abroad.

The right of every family to a decent home.

The right to adequate medical care and the opportunity to achieve and enjoy good health.

The right to adequate protection from the economic fears of old age, sickness, accident and unemployment.

The right to a good education.

To move toward these objectives would require governmental measures of a radical character that would simultaneously tend to minimize the business cycle and stimulate economic growth. In this case, however, the stability and the growth would be by-products of the social objectives quoted rather than by-products of a drive for higher profits.

Here are examples of the kinds of measures that would be required:

Jobs or income. This includes provision for the government to provide "useful and remunerative" work to all those seeking work and not employed on suitable terms by private industry. There is now broad agreement that there exist huge unsatisfied social needs in housing, municipal services, health services, education, environment, culture, and recreational facilities. Calculations by researchers of the right and left alike show that the real fulfillment of these needs would absorb the country's resources for as far ahead as economists should reasonably calculate.

Not so long ago the "cyberculturalists," and others who made a veritable cult of the computer and automation, propagated the notion that their idealized and idolized machines would soon supplant virtually all human labor. The fallacy of this view has been amply demonstrated in practice, as well as in theory. Man's needs expand as rapidly as his ability to fulfill them. Consumption derives from production, and not vice versa.

Besides the limitless needs in the chronically underserviced spheres, there remain huge lacks in primary necessities—food, clothing, shelter—for millions of Americans.

"Free private enterprise" cannot provide the public services; adequate provision of these is, in fact, inconsistent with the highest rate of profit. By and large, government must organize and carry out provision of these services.

Services could be budgeted at a much higher level than at present, to start with. Any decline in activity in the private sector would be compensated by an immediate further upturn in the level of activity of the public sector. In part, this could be accomplished through activating the old proposal of maintaining a "backlog of public works projects" to be initiated whenever required. More important would be readiness to broaden the scope of the public sector, taking over activities abandoned by or not provided adequately by private owners.

Nationalization. Nationalization and government operation of major economic units are essential for overcoming monopoly domination of the economy to the extent necessary for realizing significant progressive reforms.

Plants abandoned by private owners, or left with substantially curtailed operations, are prime targets for nationalization. Conspicuous in this respect are enterprises in the aerospace and other armament-connected industries, whose private owners have proved unwilling or unable to shift to civilian production. Also there has been large-scale phasing out of electronic plants, as multinational corporations have shifted output to foreign lands. There continues a constant flow of industrial enterprises from urban areas, where workers are organized into relatively strong unions, into rural areas, and especially to open-shop southern areas offering special tax concessions and a prospect of low wages and no resistance to inferior working conditions.

The government should take over all such plants, fully maintain employment, and charge the corporation with all transitional costs.

It should take over munitions plants generally, thereby weakening the economic base of the notorious "military-industrial complex."

The transportation industry should be nationalized. It has deteriorated drastically under private ownership. Urban transit systems have been gutted and their costs have risen sky-high. Interurban rail transportation has practically vanished, and the United States lags far behind other countries in the quality and speed of train service. The entire system should be made into an integrated public system for freight and passengers, covering all modes of transportation, with lowered fares and rates, greatly increased and improved service.

The telephone system and other "public utilities" should be made really public, to end the superhigh charges and corresponding private profits now guaranteed by business-dominated regulating commissions.

Along with a system of socialized medicine, available without charge to all, there should be nationalization of the drug industry, hospitals, and related industries.

The construction of new housing should be nationalized. That is the only way to build quickly the tens of millions of units needed to decently house America at rents the ill-housed can afford, with adequate employment opportunities for Black and other minority workers. It is the only way to break up the segregated system of inferior housing for these 40 million people, enforced by a racist conspiracy of banks, real estate agencies, and old-line politicians. It would open up all areas to truly equal, unsegregated, housing.

Nationalization of industry should not be like that of the "public authorities" and some quasi-governmental corporations run by boards of directors and managers from the officialdom of the private big corporations and banks, for the profit of these enterprises rather than service to the public.

Democratic nationalization is required, involving direct, major participation by the workers of the nationalized enterprises in their management, and a real voice for the users of the services. It calls for boards of directors to be elected directly by the voters and by the enterprise workers, full application of complete equality in employment, at all occupational and salary levels.

Minimizing Unemployment. A whole series of measures would be directed towards cutting unemployment to vestigial levels. One cannot hope to completely end it so long as capitalism persists. A major element in the fight against unemployment is to win a shorter work week and the elimination of overtime. This, of course, would directly add millions of jobs.

A stronger labor movement could enforce concessions such as have been won by workers in some other capitalist countries, providing substantial protections against layoffs by large corporations.

Recently the demand has become popular among workers for continuation of unemployment insurance for the full term of unemployment. This should be accompanied by expanding coverage to all workers, minimizing the waiting periods, ending the exclusion of strikers and other categories of workers, and ending the humiliating compensation offices with their pressure on the client to take substandard jobs at substandard pay

A uniform Federal system should be substituted for the state systems, and the payments should be financed out of general revenues.

With the decay of capitalist society, millions of people have been cast out of productive life. In no other "advanced" country are there so many families without breadwinners, mothers without husbands, and disabled people not cared for by society. In no other country has the number of these people multiplied so rapidly. They survive on meagre welfare payments handed out under humiliating conditions, with their children facing no prospect but a lifetime of the same for themselves and their own children, in turn.

Most of the adults on welfare could be and would be productive workers, given the necessary conditions—child care centers for their children, decent jobs at decent wages, training in modern skills. But this cannot be accomplished overnight. Hence the demand for incomes now, for adequate incomes with which the people now on welfare can live a dignified life—incomes received as a right and not as a charity handout.

The National Welfare Rights Organization has encompassed this programatically with the demands for a minimum family income of $6,500 a year. This along with other provisions, will permit more and more of the people now on welfare to become productive workers. Naturally, minimum family incomes should be complemented by really adequate minimum wages, applied to *all* occupations and industries.

Social Reforms and Improvements. Socialized medicine has already been mentioned. Universal free health services, to be financed out of general revenues, would be at the top of the list. The construction of millions of publicly owned good quality housing units per year is envisioned in the proposal to nationalize construction of new housing. Maximum rents on such housing should be set at no more than 10% of the renter's income. The object should be to eliminate all slums, break down racist, and anti-working class zoning restrictions and patterns imposed by mortgage bankers. A specific objective would be to end both ghettos and lily-white suburbs. Such a program, within a few years, would create sufficient competition to force down the exorbitant rental charges of private landlords and to force improvements in their services. There would be a rapid expansion of educational facilities and training of teaching personnel, and broader educational opportunities for all who want them and are capable of taking advantage of them. There would be a multiplication of recreational facilities, measures to conserve nature, improve the environment, end pollution. The natural beauties of the country, the opportunities for rest for adults, and camp life for children, would become reality for the scores of millions of families of workers, and especially the Blacks and others now discriminated against in this respect.

Equality. Racism has become an all-pervasive evil of American life, poisoning everything. No lasting progress can be made in any direction without tearing out racist practices and ideology by its roots. And the most powerful root is economic—the realization of tens of billions of superprofits from lower wages paid Black and other minority workers, and from higher prices charged them for inferior merchandise.

So every economic reform must include special measures to achieve real equality in the given area. This must be attacked directly.

Every enterprise, private and public, should be required to employ Black and other minority workers at least in proportion to their numbers in the area's population at each occupational level, including the highest managerial and professional levels. The employers must pay the cost of any training or relocation necessary, and must be obligated to achieve this goal within brief specified periods—not more than one year except for advanced professional and technical jobs.

Black people and other minority people should have priority in all of the reform measures outlined in this chapter—access to new housing, education, jobs in nationalized enterprises, and so on.

Along with these economic measures, stern legal measures must be taken against racism. It should be outlawed, in every sense of the word. This should include racist expressions and deeds, and racist actions of all kinds. Racist and anti-Semitic propaganda and actions should be made felonies, punishable by severe terms of imprisonment as well as fines. And public officials shall be liable to punishment for failure to enforce laws against racism and discrimination.

Government price controls. Hitherto, price controls have been applied only in wartime. The freezing and rolling back of monopoly prices, together with noninflationary monetary policies, are the only sure means of stopping price increases. The scandalously expanded price spread between farmer and consumer should be narrowed, by cutting consumer prices, and increasing prices paid to farmers. Multibillion-dollar farm price supports now being financed by worker-taxpayers should be drastically reduced—at the expense of the profiteering corporations in between.

Price controls would *not* include wage controls. One of the purposes of price controls would be to permit workers to reduce the rate of exploitation by monopolies in order to restore some of their lost share in the products of their labors.

The series of measures thus far described would bring about a continuous and fairly rapid rise in mass consuming power. The basic contradiction between rising productive capacity and the relatively stagnant purchasing power of the workers would be minimized. One of the main causal factors of economic crises would be reduced and, in any case, mass suffering imposed by economic fluctuations would be minimized.

Simultaneously, the substantial and continuous increases in mass consuming power would make for steady economic growth.

Leon Keyserling and other reformers wedded to the capitalist system go a little way along this road and then stop. They present a shorter list of reforms designed to increase consumer purchasing power and government welfare spending and claim that this alone will insure steady economic growth and prevent depressions.

But history proves them wrong. To the extent that reforms benefiting the masses are really effective, they cut the rate of profit, one of the main factors bringing about economic crises. Monopoly capital, possessing great mobility, seeks greener fields. It "runs away" to countries without such reforms. Beyond that, investments are postponed or scratched as part of a campaign to politically discredit the reform government, to restore power to a reactionary regime, and to erase the most far-reaching reforms.

This was illustrated by the "strike of capital" against the New Deal Administration in 1937 which precipitated the crisis of 1937–38. It has been demonstrated repeatedly in Italy, France, and other capitalist countries with strong working class movements. It took place in Chile following the accession to power of the Allende Government in 1971.

Consequently, it is necessary to take steps to insure the continuity of investment and to prevent the flight of capital. Important in this respect is the following:

Control over investments. As indicated in Chapter XII, programing of investments is carried out, on a limited scale, in a number of capitalist countries. A higher degree of control over investment is necessary for the overall program contemplated.

A Government committed to radical reforms along the lines indicated herein would acquire a powerful lever to regulate investment. The large areas of nationalized industry, the massive government housing program, construction in all areas of social significance, would make the government the main generator of plant and equipment expenditures. This could be scaled to counteract fluctuations in private investment, especially any sharp decline in private investment regardless of whether or not the decline was politically motivated. The overall scale of investment could be planned ahead in appropriate proportion to projected expansion of consumption. Government investments could also be used to achieve geographical balance, as through investment in depressed areas such as Appalachia.

Exchange controls. A government following this general program, as one of its first acts, would have to put under strict control all international transactions. The "freedom" of giant corporations and centimillionaires to salt away tens of billions in tax-free havens would be ended. The "freedom" of multinational banks to shuttle billions back and forth across the Atlantic with every fluctuation of interest rates in this or that country would be ended. Simultaneously, foreign trade would be regulated sufficiently to insure an approximate balance in international payments.

These measures would aim at ending the unstabilizing effects of an internationally open system in a world of uneven development.

A Nonimperialist Foreign Economic Policy. All Government support for and privileges granted to existing foreign investments would be ended. New private corporate foreign investments would be completely prohibited or sharply curtailed. This would encourage economic growth in the United States, by making it no longer possible for big corporations to give priority to overseas operations while cutting back at home.

In place of private investments for extraction of raw materials in developing countries, the Government would provide long-term credits and arrange the sale of machinery, equipment, and technical know-how to developing countries to enable them to build up their own industries. This would immediately increase employment in the United States in production of the exported machinery and equipment, and provide more benefits in the long run as living standards and purchasing power in developing countries narrowed the gap separating them from the industrially advanced countries.

An especially important step would be the ending of all obstacles to and actively encouraging U.S. trade with socialist countries (See Chapter XII).

There are many obstacles to putting over the kind of program sketched in this chapter—or even major parts of it. A particularly formidable obstacle is the powerful military-industrial complex—the military cancer in the economy, the policy of foreign bases, interventions, and wars to establish neocolonialist domination, the policy of confrontation with the Soviet Union, and the pursuit of the nuclear arms race in preparation for a possible war of thermonuclear annihilation.

A decisive turn from this whole course is a prerequisite. An essential step is the decisive defeat of the military-industrial complex and of all sections of big business that support the militarized aggressive foreign policy.

This is necessary economically. The experiences of the Vietnam War have dealt a body blow to the guns-and-butter myth. It is even more necessary politically. It is inconceivable that the electorate can be won for, and organized to insure, the victory of a radical domestic economic reform program while it is not yet ready to oppose, and powerfully struggle against, an utterly reactionary foreign policy.

The main and fundamental obstacle is the inevitable bitter resistance of monopoly capital as a whole, of which the military-industrial complex is an integral part. To think that American big business will readily permit the organization, electoral victory, and radical legislative program of a political party or coalition that will turn around the whole social direction of economic regulation is to believe in miracles. Every weapon will be used to break up such a coalition before it gets started, and to sabotage its actions when it obtains governmental power. This includes the use of the police and the courts, the attempt to use the military, the use of legislative bottlenecks, an unprecedented use of the propaganda media and, finally, the use of economic sabotage.

That is why the necessary political basis for effecting this program is the formation of a very broad *antimonopoly coalition,* based on the working class, the Black, Chicano, Puerto Rican, Indian and Asian peoples, the youth and the women, who provide so much of the energy for social change, the professional and technical intelligentsia, small business people and farmers who are victimized by monopoly, and those nonmonopoly capitalists who see their future with such a coalition rather than as high-priced hired hands for a conglomerate that will swallow them up. But the leading role in this coalition, numerically and in terms of power, must be played by the working people. What form this coalition takes in terms of political parties, or whether it operates through an existing political party, are not decisive.

The aim of such a coalition should be to obtain power, set up a people's antimonopoly government, that would carry out the program outlined in this chapter.

The struggle for enactment and enforcement of the suggested reforms will surely involve the most intense, fundamental class conflicts in American history. In all likelihood, in order to maintain the gains that are made, more and more stringent measures will have to be taken to restrict monopoly capital. Either the people will advance politically to take stronger measures or they will retreat, and big business will again be in the saddle—more ruthlessly and in a more reactionary way than ever before.

The logic of an antimonopoly government is to serve as a stepping-stone on the way to the struggle for socialism. The fundamental issue for an antimonopoly coalition will have to be faced—either destroy monopoly or be destroyed by it.

To move to the stage of socialism will require much more far-reaching measures. Working class domination of the government will be necessary, as will nationalization of basic industry, finance, and international trade. The institution of a planned economy will follow. The problems of the business cycle will be eliminated along with big business itself. Economic growth, oriented toward the improved welfare of the working people, and toward long-range economic, technical, cultural, and moral growth, will be a natural goal of this planning. There will be no more fundamental political obstacles and no more major contradictions standing in the way of this goal.

Reference Notes

Chapter I

1. National Bureau of Economic Research, Ed., Geoffrey H. Moore, *Business Cycle Indicators,* Vol. 1, Princeton, 1961, pp. 670–671; U.S. Dept of Commerce, *Business Conditions Digest,* June 1970.

2. Wesley C. Mitchell, "Business Cycles," in President's Conference on Unemployment, *Business Cycles and Unemployment,* N.Y., 1923, p. 5.

3. Paul A. Samuelson, *Economics,* 6th ed., N.Y., 1964, p. 258.

4. James S. Duesenberry, *Business Cycles and Economic Growth,* N.Y., 1958, pp. 334–335.

5. *Economic Report of the President,* Jan. 1969, pp. 73–74.

6. *New York Times,* Dec. 5, 1970.

7. Benjamin Strong, speech in Atlantic City, Sept. 23, 1957.

8. Quoted by Studs Terkel in *New York Times Magazine,* Dec. 20, 1970.

9. Harry S. Truman, Speech to Better Business Bureau, June 6, 1950.

10. Samuelson, *Economics,* 3rd ed., N.Y., 1955, pp. 320–321.

Chapter II

1. Marx, *Capital,* Vol. III, N.Y., 1967, p. 244.

2. *Op. Cit.,* p. 244.

3. *Ibid.*

4. *Ibid.*

5. *Ibid.,* p. 245.

6. John Maynard Keynes, *General Theory of Employment, Interest and Money,* N.Y., 1936, p. 55.

7. *Capital,* Vol. III, pp. 257–58.

8. *Op. cit.,* p. 484.

9. *Capital,* Vol. II, p. 411.

10. Samuelson, *Economics,* 6th ed., 1955, p. 254.

11. Arthur F. Burns and Wesley C. Mitchell, *Measuring Business Cycles,* Nationaι Bureau of Economic Research, N.Y. 1946, p. 3.

12. Institute of Economics, USSR Academy of Sciences, *Political Economy,* London, 1957, pp. 264–265.

13. Frederick Engels, *Socialism: Utopian and Scientific,* in *Marx-Engels Selected Works,* N.Y., 1968, p. 425.

Chapter III

1. 1947–1960, *Historical Statistics of the United States,* and *Continuation to 1962 and Revisions,* Series p. 5, 7, 8; 1953–1957, *Statistical Abstract of the U.S.,* 1969, No. 1103, 1109.

2. *Electronic News*, Dec. 8, 1970; July 13, 1969.

3. *Conference Board Record*, Nov. 1967. See also Communist Party USA, *The Productivity Hoax and Auto Workers, Real Needs*, N.Y., 1970.

4. Calculated from *Economic Report of the President*, 1970, Tables C–28, 32 and 34.

Chapter IV

1. *Economic Report of the President*, 1970, Table G–38, p. 220.

2. *Ibid.*, and Federal Reserve Board release E.5, Oct. 26, 1970.

3. *Economic Report of the President*, 1972, Table B–38, page 238, and Federal Reserve Board release E.5, April 18, 1972.

4. *Ibid.*

5. *Op. cit.*, Tables, 2.1 and 1.1.

6. *Op. cit.*, Table, 2.1.

7. *Economic Report of the President*, 1970, Table C–60; and *Federal Reserve Bulletin*, June 1970, p. A 54.

8. Computed from Paul F. Smith, *Cost of Providing Consumer Credit*, N.B.E.R., Occasional Paper 83.

9. Interest payments from National Income and Product Accounts, Table 7.2; consumer credit outstanding from *Survey of Current Business*, May 1970, Table 1, p. 14.

10. *Economic Report of the President*, 1970, Tables C–57 and C–16.

11. Federal Reserve Bank of Philadelphia, *Business Review*, July 1965.

12. *Wall Street Journal*, July 21, 1970.

13. *Federal Reserve Bulletin*, June 1970, p. A 35.

14. *Federal Home Loan Bank Board Quarterly*, Real Estate Foreclosure Reports. Statistical Abstract of the U.S. 1971, No. 1126, p. 680; Survey of Current Business, June 1972, p. S-10.

Chapter V

1. Marx, *Capital*, Vol. 111, N.Y., 1967, p. 249.

2. Geoffrey H. Moore, Ed., *Business Cycle Indicators*, Vol. 1, Princeton, 1961, p. XXVI.

3. *Metalworking News*, June 29, 1970.

4. *Metalworking News*, July 20, 1970.

5. *Wall Street Journal*, July 20, 1970.

6. *Wall Street Journal*, July 29, 1970.

7. Arthur F. Burns, speech at Los Angeles, Dec. 7, 1970, mimeo.

8. Gilbert Burck, "The Hard Road Back to Profitability," in *Fortune*, Aug. 1970.

Chapter VI

1. Marx, *Capital*, Vol. I, N.Y., 1967, p. 138.

2. Marx, *Capital*, Vol. III, N.Y., 1967, p. 254.

3. *Historical Statistics of the U.S.*, Series X–423 and F–7.

4. *National Income Accounts*, interest paid by business, Table 7.2; business national income, Table 1.13. Interest paid by corporations not reported separately.

5. Victor Perlo, "Financial Contradictions and Government Regulation of the American Economy," in *(World Economics and International Relations)* Moscow, No. 11, 1966.

6. *Statistical Abstract of the U.S.*, 1969, Table 692, p. 476; and Securities and Exchange Commission Release No. 2452, June 23, 1970.

7. C. Erich Heinemann and Robert D. Hershey in *New York Times*, May 3, 1970.

8. Eliot Janeway, Interview, in *Weekly Bond Buyer*, June 29, 1970.

9. First National City Bank, *Monthly Economic Letter*, June 1970.

10. Janeway, in *Weekly Bond Buyer*, August 3, 1970.

11. *Fortune*, Sept. 1965.

12. Data from *Federal Reserve Bulletin*, June 1970.

13. William McC. Martin, speech at Columbia University, N.Y., in *New York Times*, June 2, 1965.

14. Alfred Hayes, in Federal Reserve Bank of New York *Monthly Review*, February 1970.

15. *Ibid.*

Chapter VII

1. *Economic Report of the President*, 1970, Table C–48, p. 232, and C–46, p. 230.

2. United Nations, *Monthly Bulletin of Statistics*, July 1970, Table 60.

3. Wells Fargo Bank, San Francisco, *Business Review*, July 1970.

4. *Webster's New Twentieth Century Dictionary*, Cleveland and N.Y., 1967, p. 939.

5. Research and Policy Committee of the Committee for Economic Development, *Defense Against Inflation*, N.Y., 1957, p. 17.

6. Sumner H. Slichter, *Toward Stability*, N.Y., 1934, pp. 50–51, 84.

7. Slichter, "A Look into Our Economic Future," in *N.Y. Times Magazine*, Nov. 4, 1956.

8. Alvin Hansen, *The American Economy*, 1957, pp. 43–44.

9. Samuelson, *Economics*, 6th ed., 1955, p. 270.

10. *New York Times*, April 23, 1970.

11. *Nihon Keizai Shimbun* (Japan Economic Journal), International Weekly Edition, April 14, 1970.

12. Clayton Fritchey in *New York Post*, April 8, 1970.

13. *Economic Report of the President*, 1970, p. 66.

14. Samuelson, *op. cit.*, p. 344.

15. Marx, *Value, Price and Profit*, N.Y., 1969.

16. First National City Bank, *Monthly Economic Letter*, Nov. 1970.

17. *Wall Street Journal*, Aug. 5, 1968.

18. Leonard Woodcock, *Wage Escalation is Counter-inflationary,* article reprint, UAW Education Department, Detroit, 1970.

Chapter VIII

1. Keynes, *The General Theory of Employment, Interest and Money.*

2. Keynes, *op. cit.,* pp. 30–31.

3. Computed from U.S. Bureau of Labor Statistics, *Consumer Expenditures and Income, Urban United States, 1960–61,* Table 1A, p. 10.

4. Keynes, *op. cit.,* p. 32.

5. Samuelson, *op. cit.,* p. 46.

6. U.S. Steel Corporation, *Annual Report,* 1963.

7. Samuelson, *op. cit.,* p. 232.

8. Robert L. Heilbroner and Peter L. Bernstein, *A Primer on Government Spending,* N.Y., 1963, pp. 87–88.

9. Leon H. Keyserling, *The Role of Wages in a Great Society,* Conference on Economic Progress, Washington, 1966, p. 3.

10. Hyman Lumer, *War Economy and Crisis,* N.Y., 1954.

Chapter IX

1. K.V. Ostrovityanov and V.A. Cheprakov in *World Marxist Review,* October 1958.

2. *Economic Report of the President,* 1962, p. 3.

3. *Ibid.,* 1957, pp. 1–2.

4. *Ibid.,* 1965, pp. 32–3, 38.

5. *Ibid.,* 1958, pp. iv., 2–3.

6. *Ibid.,* 1956, p. 11.

7. *Ibid.,* 1962, p. 8.

8. *Ibid.,* 1968, p. 19.

9. *Ibid.,* 1965, p. 62.

10. *Ibid.*

11. Louis Banks, "The Economy Under New Management" in *Fortune,* May 1965.

12. Net Public Debt from *Economic Report of the President,* 1972, Table B–62, p. 268; Net government interest payments from *National Income Accounts,* Table 7.2.

13. National Economics Commission, Communist Party, *The Big Tax Swindle,* N.Y. 1969, p. 8.

14. *Budget of the United States,* Fiscal Years 1971 and 1972.

15. *The Big Tax Swindle,* p. 23

16. J. Roger Wallace in *Journal of Commerce,* Sept. 22, 1971.

17. Computed from U.S. Census Bureau, Series P–60, No. 80, *Income in 1970 of Families and Persons in the United States,* Table 51, p. 113.

18. Victor Zarnowitz, *An Appraisal of Short-Term Economic Forecasts*, National Bureau of Economic Research, N.Y., 1967, pp. 6–7.

Chapter X

1. U.S. Arms Control and Disarmament Agency, *World Military Expenditures*, 1966–67.

2. Frank Pace, Jr., speech before American Bankers Association, Sept. 1957.

3. *U.S. News and World Report*, May 26, 1950.

4. *Economic Report of the President*, 1970, Tables C–1 and C–62.

5. Compiled from *Business Conditions Digest*, Dec. 1969, April and July 1970, Series 10 and 625.

6. Marx and Engels, *The Communist Manifesto*, N.Y., 1948, pp. 12–14.

7. Statistical Abstract of the U.S., 1970, Nos. 793, 796.

8. *Business Conditions Digest*, Dec. 1969, Appendix, Series 625, for data on military contracts. Dates of peaks and troughs from Chart A 1.

9. Boeing Corporation, *Annual Report, 1968*, and *Moody's Industrial Manual*, 1970.

10. *New York Times*, Dec. 6, 1970.

11. Lumer, *War Economy and Crisis*, N.Y., 1954, p. 147.

12. Annual growth rate calculated from Business Conditions Digest, various issues. Percent military expenditures of GNP as given in U.S. Arms Control and Disarmament Agency, *World Military Expenditures, 1966–67*, Table 1.

Chapter XI

1. *United Nations Statistical Yearbooks*, 1958 and 1966, Table 248, and *Monthly Bulletin of Statistics*, July 1970, Table 52.

2. *Historical Statistics of the United States*, Series U 47.

3. *Economic Report of the President*, 1970, Table C–90, p. 282.

4. *Treasury Bulletin*, June 1970, p. 30, and *Federal Reserve Bulletin*, Feb. 1972, Tables 6 and 7, pp. A 78 and A 79.

Chapter XII

1. G. Rudenko, "Imperialism's Adaptation to New Historical Conditions," in *World Economics and International Relations*, No.11, 1970.

2. Institut Mirovoy Ekonomiki i Mezhdunarodniye Otnosheniye, *Sovremenniye Tsiklii i Krizisii*, Moscow, 1967, ed. A.M. Rumyantsev, S.M. Menshikov, G.B. Ardaev.

3. Raymond Goldsmith, in Joint Economic Committee, *Employment, Growth and Price Levels, Hearings*, Washington, D.C. 1958, Part 2, pp. 230*ff*.

4. Lenin, *Imperialism*, in *Collected Works*, Moscow, 1964, Vol. 22, pp. 300–01.

5. Jacques H. Dreze, National Planning in "Some Postwar Contributions of French Economists to Theory and Public Policy," supplement to *American Economic Review*, Part 2, June 1964.

6. John and Anne-Marie Hackett, *Economic Planning in France,* Boston, 1963, p. 59.

7. *Economic Report of the President,* 1970, pp. 78–83; and 1971, pp. 94–98.

8. United Nations, *Monthly Bulletin of Statistics,* Nov. 1970.

9. *Ibid.,* Feb. 1972, Special Table A, p. xiv.

10. United Nations, *Statistical Yearbook,* 1958, Table 149, pp. 368–375; and *Monthly Bulletin of Statistics,* Dec. 1971, Special Table B, p. xii.

Chapter XIII

1. 79th Congress, 1st Session, S.380, *Full Employment Act of 1945,* a Bill, by Mr. Murray, Mr. Wagner, Mr. Thomas of Utah, and Mr. Mahoney, Jan. 22, 1945, pp. 2–3.

2. F.D. Roosevelt, Message to Congress, Jan. 11, 1944, in George Seldes' *The Great Quotations,* N.Y., 1960, p. 594.

Drop folios for pages 228-231

Appendices

Appendix Table I

TRENDS IN RATE OF EXPLOITATION OF LABOR
U.S. MANUFACTURING INDUSTRY, 1946–1969
Index Numbers 1957–59 = 100

	Volume of Production	Man-Hours of Production Workers	Productivity per Man-Hour	Real Take-Home Pay per Week	Average Weekly Hours	Real Take-Home Pay per Man-Hour	Exploitation of Labor	Labor's Share in Production
			Col. 1/Col. 2			Col. 4/Col. 5	Col. 3/Col. 6	Col. 6/Col. 3
1946	60.0	98.7	60.8	81.2	101.3	80.2	75.8	131.9
1947	66.4	104.7	63.4	79.5	101.6	78.2	81.1	123.3
1948	68.9	103.2	66.8	81.3	100.6	80.8	82.7	121.0
1949	65.1	92.1	70.7	83.2	98.3	84.6	83.6	119.7
1950	75.8	101.2	74.9	87.7	101.8	86.1	87.0	115.0
1951	81.9	108.5	75.5	86.2	102.1	84.4	89.5	111.8
1952	85.2	108.5	78.5	88.0	102.3	86.0	91.3	109.6
1953	92.7	113.7	81.5	91.1	101.8	89.5	91.1	109.8
1954	86.3	101.4	85.1	91.4	99.6	91.8	92.7	107.9
1955	97.3	108.0	90.1	97.7	102.3	95.5	94.3	106.0
1956	100.2	108.4	92.4	99.8	101.6	98.2	94.1	106.3
1957	100.8	104.8	96.2	99.3	100.1	99.2	97.0	103.1
1958	93.2	93.8	99.4	97.9	98.6	99.3	100.1	99.9
1959	106.0	101.3	104.6	102.7	101.3	101.4	103.2	96.9
1960	108.9	99.7	109.2	102.1	99.8	102.3	106.7	93.7
1961	109.6	96.1	114.0	103.7	100.1	103.6	110.0	90.9
1962	118.7	100.6	118.0	106.9	101.6	105.2	112.2	89.2
1963	124.9	101.4	123.2	108.1	101.8	106.2	116.0	86.2
1964	133.1	103.9	128.1	112.6	102.3	110.1	116.3	85.9
1965	145.0	110.4	131.3	116.6	103.6	112.5	116.7	85.7
1966	158.6	118.0	134.4	116.4	103.9	112.0	120.0	83.3

1967	159.7	115.9	137.8	115.3	102.1	112.9	122.1	81.9
1968	166.8	117.9	141.5	116.3	102.3	113.7	124.5	80.4
1969	173.9	119.5	145.5	115.2	102.1	112.8	129.0	77.5

Sources:

Col. 1. *Business Statistics*, 1969, p. 16. S.C.B., May 1970, p. S-3.

Col. 2. *Business Statistics*, 1969, pp. 72 and 74, S.C.B. May 1970, p. S-14.

Col. 4. *Handbook of Labor Statistics*, 1969, T.88; *Monthly Labor Review*, May 1970, Table 22 (average of no dependent and 3 dependents).

Col. 5. *Business Statistics*, 1969, p. 74. S.C.B., May 1970, p. S-14.

Col. 7. Index of "exploitation of labor" equals index of productivity per man-hour divided by index of real take-home pay per man-hour.

Col. 8. Index of "labor's share" equals index of real take-home pay per man-hour divided by index of labor productivity per man-hour.

Business Statistics and S.C.B. (Survey of Current Business) are publications of the Commerce Department.

Handbook of Labor Statistics and Monthly Labor Review are publications of the Labor Department.

APPENDIX TABLE II

NET GOVERNMENT ADDITIONS TO MASS CONSUMING POWER, 1946–69

(billions of dollars)

	1. Govt. Wages & Salaries	2. Est. Wages, Salaries of Govt. Contractors	3. Govt. Transfer Payments	4. Total Govt. Additions	5. Direct Taxes on Workers	6. Net Addition to Consuming Power	7. Consumer Expenditure	8. Percent Net Addition of Consumer Expenditure
1946	20.7	3.1	10.8	34.6	12.4	22.2	143.3	15.5
1947	17.4	4.2	11.1	32.7	14.3	18.4	160.7	11.4
1948	18.8	7.6	10.5	36.9	14.8	22.1	173.6	12.7
1949	20.6	9.2	11.6	41.4	13.7	27.7	176.8	15.7
1950	22.4	8.5	14.3	45.2	15.9	29.3	191.0	15.3
1951	29.0	15.8	11.5	56.3	21.6	34.7	206.3	16.8
1952	33.1	21.8	12.0	66.9	26.1	40.8	216.7	18.8
1953	34.0	24.8	12.8	71.6	28.5	43.1	230.0	18.7
1954	34.6	21.2	14.9	70.7	27.8	42.9	236.5	18.1
1955	36.2	20.0	16.1	72.3	30.5	41.8	254.4	16.4
1956	38.3	21.0	17.1	76.4	34.5	41.9	266.7	15.7
1957	40.4	23.5	19.9	83.8	37.8	46.0	281.4	16.3
1958	43.5	26.0	24.1	93.6	38.5	55.1	290.1	19.0
1959	45.6	26.4	24.9	96.9	43.0	53.9	311.2	17.3
1960	48.7	26.1	26.6	101.4	47.5	53.9	325.2	16.6
1961	52.2	28.4	30.4	111.0	49.5	61.5	335.2	18.3
1962	55.9	31.2	31.2	118.3	54.0	64.3	355.1	18.1
1963	59.4	32.2	33.0	124.6	59.1	65.5	375.0	17.5
1964	64.3	32.9	34.2	131.4	57.6	73.8	401.2	18.4
1965	69.2	34.6	37.2	141.0	63.0	78.0	432.8	18.0

1966	77.7	40.1	41.1	158.9	74.4	84.5	466.3	18.1
1967	85.7	47.5	48.7	181.9	84.1	97.8	492.1	19.9
1968	95.6	52.6	55.7	203.9	99.0	104.9	535.8	19.6
1969	104.0	54.3	61.6	219.9	117.8	102.1	577.5	17.7

Sources: US Commerce Department, *National Income and Product Accounts of the U.S. 1929–1965; Survey of Current Business,* July 1970:

1. Table 6.2.
2. Federal Expenditures for goods, Table 3.1 (purchases of goods & services less compensation of employees); State and local expenditures for goods, Table 3.3. Col. 2 equals 50% of the sum of these two items.
3. Table 3.9.
4. Sum of Columns 1, 2, and 3.
5. Federal personal taxes, Table 3.1, multiplied by percentage of federal income taxes deducted from payrolls, as determined from Historical Statistics of the U.S. and Budgets of the U.S. Government. State and local direct taxes, Table 3.3; Personal contributions to Social Insurance funds, Table 3.8. Column 5 equals sum of these three items.
6. Column 5 less Column 6.
7. Table 1.1.
8. Column 6 as a percent of Column 7.

231

INDEX